The Myth of Analysis

The Myth of Analysis

Three Essays in Archetypal Psychology

James Hillman

Northwestern University Press
EVANSTON, ILLINOIS

Northwestern University Press
www.nupress.northwestern.edu

Published simultaneously in Canada by Fitzhenry & Whiteside Limited, Toronto. First Northwestern University Press paperback edition published 1998.

Printed in the United States of America

10 9 8 7 6 5 4 3

ISBN-13: 978-0-8101-1651-1
ISBN-10: 0-8101-1651-0

Cataloging-in-publication data are available from the Library of Congres under LCCN 97032837.

∞The paper used in this publication meets the minimum requirements of the American National Standard for Information Sciences—Permanence of Paper for Printed Library Materials, ANSI Z39.48-1992.

CONTENTS

PREFACE

These three essays have gone through several metamorphoses. They were first given as lectures at the Eranos meetings of 1966, 1968, and 1969. They were then enlarged and revised for publication in the corresponding *Eranos Jahrbücher* and were later revised again for publication as a series in *Art International.* Since they were originally lectures, they contain rhetoric which has not been taken out in the revisions. Each was written to stand alone, and no attempt has been made to smelt down and recast them to make them join smoothly into a system. The revision which they have undergone for this book is mainly an expansion, undertaken to point up their internal consistency and to bring about further reflection upon this extraordinary psychological phenomenon of the twentieth century: analysis.

This note gives me the opportunity once more to thank Rudolf Ritsema for the invitation and critical encouragement to lecture at Eranos and to thank Adolf Portmann for repeating the invitation at a time when it was of personal importance. The congeniality and stimulation of the Eranos circle have contributed beyond measure to this work. James Fitzsimmons generously gave room to these papers in *Art International*, thereby drawing me into their revision. Erwin Ackerknecht helped me find my way in the history of psychopathology. I owe a debt to Rafael Lopez-Pedraza for discussing with me many of the ideas and to Eleanor Mattern for her typing and editorial concern. Jeffrey Satinover and Francesca Bush prepared the indexes with the help of Jan Crawford.

J. H.

Zurich
October, 1969

The Myth of Analysis

The definition of man is the definition of his soul.

ARISTOTLE

INTRODUCTION

While working on the problems of method that are raised by archetypal psychology for a book on the *puer aeternus*, I came to realize that a coherent presentation of my viewpoint, and where it differs from a psychology based on analysis (analytical psychology), depended upon ideas discussed in these three essays. Either I should repeat these ideas in that book on the *puer aeternus*, or I should make these essays available as a companion book. I have chosen the latter course because the two books are indeed companions; they have even been written concurrently. The examination of the archetypal structure of eternal youth, which forces out the issue of psychological renewal and the renewal of psychology, was originally part of the same series of Eranos lectures as these three essays. Moreover, there is one central theme running through both books: the transformation of psyche into life.

"Psyche into life" can be put in many ways. Most simply I mean the freeing of psychic phenomena from the curse of the analytical mind. This involves reflection upon the analytical mind, realizing its predilections for psychopathology and the fact that psychology has become a massive yet subtle system for distorting the psyche into a belief that there is something "wrong" with it and, accordingly, for analyzing its imagination into diagnostic categories. Moving the psyche into life means moving it, not from its sickness, but from its sick view of itself as being in need of professional care and knowledge and professional love. By this I do not mean that the psyche does not suffer or fall ill. The helping professions—education, social work, pastoral counseling, psychotherapy—all must envision suffering and illness as something "wrong." They have a vested interest in psychology as it is now conceived. They must see sickness in the soul so that they can get in there and do their job. But suppose the fantasies, feelings, and behavior arising from the imaginal part of ourselves are archetypal in their sickness and thus natural. Suppose they are authentic, belonging to the nature of man; suppose even that their odd irrationalities are required for life, else we wither into rigid stalks of reason. Then what is there to analyze? Surely there are other ways than analysis to discriminate among psychic phenomena. Surely, too, the unconscious and its psychodynamics do not constitute the only model through which our feelings, fantasies, and behavior can be envisioned. Perhaps the "unconscious" and "psychodynamics" are fantasies that could be replaced with better ones. In these essays I offer some archetypal patterns for understanding the psyche's sufferings and syndromes, patterns which I think are as good as those now in use.

An archetypal psychology would also ask the psyche to move *with* its sickness into life. Three generations have passed since Freud, and we have long enough divided ourselves into two souls for two worlds: one normal psyche for life and one peculiar for analysis. The older religious split between weekday and Sunday, between secular and numinous, has become transposed into regular and analytical, where one or the other—psyche or life—becomes "sick." Then we flee the sickness of the contemporary world into analysis, a sanctum for the soul, or we rush into "real" life to avoid at any cost the pathology constellated in analysis.

To leave the sickness behind in exchange for "real life" or "cure" or to put it in the hands of the therapist leaves out too large a portion of the soul. If there is one primary lesson we have learned during seventy years of analysis, it is that we discover a sense of soul in the sufferings of psychopathology. When I am laid low by the misery of depressions, symptoms, and cravings, I meet the irrefutable evidence of the independence of psychic forces. Something lives in me that is not of my own doing. This demon that speaks in dreams and passions and pains will not let go, and I am forced to give recognition to its value for deepening me beyond my usual notion of myself as ego and for bringing to my mind a sense of soul and of death. So to take sickness into life means to take soul with one wherever one goes and to react to life in terms of this soul. As sickness is contagious, so can my concern for soul be infectious, taking soul into the houses of others, taking psyche into life. Then life, too—and not only analysis—becomes a valid place for soul-making. Psyche into life means also taking life as psyche, life as a psychological adventure lived for the sake of soul.

What the psyche has experienced during the past seventy years in analytical therapy should also be possible for it wherever it goes. Symbolic meanings, insight, eros, body, craziness, and the lower aspect of the Gods—the freedom to imagine and to feel psychic reality—may take place in any situation, not only in therapeutic treatment. The psyche can carry its imagination and live from it without professional aid, providing it assumes more confidence in itself. For this, it will first have to dispossess the "inner analyst," who has an armchair in our mind. For he too is but one more fantasy called up by an ego which has needed his support to keep the inherent peculiarities necessary to individuality from threatening the ego's rule. To be individual means to be peculiar, to be peculiarly what one is, with one's own odd patterns of archetypal responses. So we shall not lock the mess away in an inner asylum nor work daily at self-treatment. The peculiarities can be let into life to be enjoyed; and life may even enjoy them. They are, anyway, not mere quirks of the little person trying to hold his life together but are openings downward into collective dimensions of mythical patterns. We are never only persons;

we are always also Mothers and Giants and Victims and Heroes and Sleeping Beauties. Titans and Demons and Magnificent Goddesses have ruled our souls for thousands of years; Aristotle and Descartes did their best, and the analytical minds that followed them are still at it, but the mythic forces have not been slain. As these essays show, the mythic appears within the language, observations, and theories even of science. Analysis itself is one more such fantasy sustained by myth, which, once recognized, would mean the end of analysis as we have known it during this century.

There have been various attempts recently to move out of analysis—group therapy and sensitivity training, to mention only two. But these merely transplant the analytical mind to the group or its leader, shifting the focus and content of what is analyzed. The person still is analyzing himself and expects through this analysis to become more conscious. Love-ins and blowing-the-mind with drugs are also efforts to get rid of the analytical, but conversion of mind into mindlessness is only an enantiodromia. Nothing basically has changed; especially the sense of alienation and the confusions about love remain. Analysis is too potent to be got rid of so easily. It is too much a part of this century's self-conception, too much a requirement of its ego psychology. Analysis will be ended when we discover what myth it is enacting, a discovery which may not come all at once but which occurs as insights reveal the relation of analysis to soul-making. For soul-making is what binds us there, fascinated: not just the diagnosis of what is wrong, not even the cure of our sickness, but the potential in analytical therapy for soul-making.

Part One develops this perspective and gives credit to the creative power of analysis. For we cannot deny how necessary it has been during this century for rediscovering the soul and reawakening its imagination. But the model for the peculiar, intensely personal emotions going on in analysis is neither clinical nor even personal. These emotions arise from an enactment of a myth, which hints that analysis is a myth-making, even a mythical, procedure. Soul-making and myth-making refer to each other. If analysis is an enactment, then a tale about this ritual—a myth—is necessary. The emotions stirred in this ritual are viewed in this first essay as necessary; all of them belong. Authentic to the ritual and necessary for soul-making, they belong to a mythical pattern, needing no treatment other than to be led out (education) and confirmed. They are not revivals or substitutions to be led back (reduced) to primary personal dynamisms. Nor are they transferred from another time and place or from a response belonging to other persons. They are appropriate to the actual ongoing mythical experience of soul-making. Thus, Part One could be subtitled "The End of Transference." Its focus is on the analysand and his emotions; its theme is the psychological relationship.

Consequently, psychological work must be rethought. If soul-making is not treatment, not therapy, not even a process of self-realization but is essentially an imaginative activity or an activity of the imaginal realm as it plays through all of life everywhere and which does not need analyst or an analysis, then the professional is confronted with reflecting upon himself and his work. What is the fantasy he has of what he does? The second paper attempts this reflection. It turns to history first, to the Enlightenment and the nineteenth-century mind, out of which came our ideas of the unconscious, of psychopathology, and of the psyche. But history is only a doorway into further reflection; its value for psychology lies in exposing archetypal patterns. Part Two attempts a reflection from the archetypal point of view upon the language of psychology, the terms with which we conceive psychic phenomena, especially imaginal phenomena, e.g., hallucinations, masochism, etc. Our reflection soon shows that this language is the result of a psychological process, the enlightened egoization of the psyche which learned to cope with its darkness by means of diagnosis and which replaced the imaginal power of the psyche with the concept of the unconscious. Thus Part

Two could be subtitled "The End of the Unconscious." Its focus is on the analyst as professional; its theme, psychological language.

The focus of Part Three is on analytical consciousness; its theme, analysis and its goal. The avenue of approach is the mytheme of female inferiority. We discover that this idea is basic to the structure of the analytical mind, basic to the kind of consciousness which we find in both neurosis and its treatment. Misogyny would seem inseparable from analysis, which in turn is but a late manifestation of the Western, Protestant, scientific, Apollonic ego. This structure of consciousness has never known what to do with the dark, material, and passionate part of itself, except to cast it off and call it Eve. What we have come to mean by the word "conscious" is "light"; this light is inconceivable for this consciousness without a distaff side of something else opposed to it that is inferior and which has been called—in Greek, Jewish, and Christian contexts—female.

Now the theme of ending analysis deepens. Now we find that analysis cannot end unless this kind of consciousness comes to an end, issuing into another archetypal structure with a darker and softer kind of light, based upon other myths, less heroic and less Apollonic, more Dionysian, where female and inferior are inherent in, and not a threat to, consciousness. With this change we would come to the purpose or end of neurosis, which has forced femininity and inferiority upon consciousness. Neurosis compensates the one-sided male and superior structure with which we identify consciousness.

But if consciousness changes, then the neurosis that we have known as its counterpart will also come to an end, and so will analysis, which came into existence as answer to neurosis. If, with insights, we penetrate analysis through to its mythical foundations, it collapses upon its three fallen pillars—transference, the unconscious, and neurosis—which we prefer to call, in accordance with the mythical perspective, the erotic, the imaginal, and the Dionysian.

PART ONE

On Psychological Creativity

Call the world if you please "The vale of Soul-making." Then you will find out the use of the world. . . .

John Keats [1]

. . . and the soul cannot exist without its other side, which is always found in a "You."

C. G. Jung [2]

What Fathers Psyche?

Our field of depth psychology, or the psychology of the unconscious, as it has been called, does not know its father. Our psychology belongs to the tutelage of no God, has no patron saint, is enthralled to no muse. Because modern psychology was born in the consulting rooms of two Viennese physicians and in the locked wards of a Zurich psychiatric asylum, it has been assumed to be an offspring of medicine. Those who work in psychology are considered to belong to the family of the healing arts within

1. From a letter of Keats to his brother George, *The Letters of John Keats*, ed. H. Buxton Forman (London, 1895), p. 326; the passage is quoted in full by A. Ward, *John Keats: The Making of a Poet* (New York, 1963), p. 276.

2. *Collected Works*, Vol. XVI, par. 454.

Note: *The Collected Works of C. G. Jung*, translated by R. F. C. Hull, are published in the Bollingen Series XX by the Bollingen Foundation and Princeton University Press. Hereafter, *The Collected Works* will be referred to as "*CW*."

the specific configuration of Asclepius, son of Apollo, and our work as psychotherapists is considered to be limited to the care and service of the ill psyche. That the psyche at the turn of the century was so ill that it appeared mainly in medical surroundings is no reason for it to remain there. The psyche in the medical consulting room was a necessary fantasy of the nineteenth century; perhaps today, some seventy years later, the psyche and our study of it have radically changed. Perhaps illness as it has been conceived is no longer the immediate issue, because we cannot consider the psyche's illness until we have reflected anew—as we shall throughout these pages—upon "psychopathology." Perhaps we shall miss the need of the psyche and our calling to it altogether if we persist with models of the recent past.

Primary among these models of the nineteenth century which have suffered radical change is the notion "psychology" itself. We can no longer take this word for granted, assuming it to refer to an academic field as presented in a list of courses. In the popular mind "psychology" has come to mean something deeper, referring to the findings of psychotherapy. Psychology now implies something one learns through "analysis"; it refers to processes of the mind, heart, and soul that were not included in the field of psychology in the past century. The field changes as its subject, the psyche, shows different faces at different times. How "psychology" entered consciousness at the beginning of the past century, with what particular bias, and how this bias has affected our souls and our notions of our souls' sicknesses is the concern of Part Two. As we shall use the word, "psychology" must reflect the contemporary soul, the psyche since Freud and Jung, and therefore must be considered in terms of their findings.

We shall consider "psychology" to refer to that psychology which arose within the context of psychotherapy and has been called "depth psychology." Although it first appeared as an empirical field, it ultimately became, through Jung, an ontology of the soul based on archetypes. Because this psychology takes into account the depths of the soul at its most subjective, transcendent, and impersonal level and assumes that personal behavior is derived from something beyond the personal, it attempts a true *logos* of the psyche. Only a psychology which is willing to transcend personal limitations and allow the soul's speculative function to operate as one of the psyche's necessities can attempt to reflect the whole psyche and can earn the name "psychology." Other modifications of the field require qualifying adjectives which point out their specific limits, e.g., academic, social, experimental, clinical, medical, etc. These limitations of the field pursue special ramifications of the soul's activities. But we would put the soul in the center; its archetypal depths are prior to the fields in which they are manifested. Psychology thus becomes *archetypal* psychology in order to be adequate to its subject, the psyche. Therefore, we use the word "psychology" quite differently from the conventional practice, so pejorative to the field and to the soul. For psychologists have regarded the soul's depths and the findings from these depths as derivations of conscious, social, or pathological processes, and the things most important to the soul have become a division of learning theory or information theory, social and economic events, or simply abnormal psychology.

As the care and service of the psyche have become individualized within each therapist, conflicting currents have begun to show themselves which make yet more uncertain the claim for a unified descent from Asclepius. Even if the Apollonic aim of enlightening consciousness remains, questions arise in regard to achieving this aim: through individuals or groups? communication or content? crisis intervention or long-term depth? the client or his social nexus? body or words? The literature is preoccupied with technique (how to enact therapy) and with transference (the felt experience of the relationship). These concerns with technique and transference indicate that the confusions of the encounter have not only forced out the fundamental issue of what analysis truly is today and how to practice it but have also laid bare the deep uncertainty concerning the root metaphor, the true myth of the work.

According to individual art and style—which in turn derive from the individual myth lived into by each analyst —a variety of models of practice are offered: some are high priests of the cult of the soul, or its confessors or directors; others are shepherds of souls, group leaders; some are dialecticians, sophists, educators; some are pragmatists, practical advisers, or biologists minutely examining life-history; some are nursing mothers encouraging growth, inspirers, or confidants; still another may be a *mystēs*, an *epoptēs*, a shaman, an initiator, or a guru of the body, awakening its sensitivity. Medicine is only one variety, and even the models of medical practice vary. So much depends, as Jung said again and again, on the "personal equation," and the personal equation is the individual myth of the therapist himself.

But is it possible to discover the collective pattern, the essential root metaphor, of psychology itself? Can we find the general myth of our field within which our individual, specific varieties fit and function? To discover this *pattern* is to search for our *patron*,[3] the father who creates and is the creative principle in us. This is the first task. We must inquire into how psychology comes into being within the psyche before we can discuss its particular historical deformations. We ought to discover what it is that fathers soul in us before we examine the origins of the neuroses in this soul, the therapy of these supposed neuroses, and the possible purposes of both neuroses and therapy.

Until the confusion in our paternity is cleared up, there will always be justification for statements that our psychology is a bastard, neither art nor science, neither medicine nor religion, neither academic nor free, neither investigative nor healing, but a syncretistic amplification, a potpourri, or a

3. "Pattern" was originally a doublet of "patron," not differentiated from it until about 1700 (*Oxford English Dictionary*).

pot-pour-rire, of anything and everything that has to do with the human soul. Until the father is found, each of us must flounder among the phenomena, inventing languages, diagnosing, devising techniques for separating and tying together the ten thousand things of the soul, uncertain of what we are about, because we are uncertain of our author, from whom would come both our authority and our authenticity. Wavering among shades, shaman and spiritual director, light-bringer and dealer in darkness, worldly counselor and keeper of a mystery, I am a mercurial prostitute earning my money from dreams and passions. I am protean, with all the shiftiness and trickery of the bastard son, of dubious paternity, easily prey to identification with another uncertain son, Lucifer himself.

Psychology suffers in many ways as a result of its complex of the absent father. Not only must we carry the daily anxiety of bastardy and the projections upon us of illegitimacy, but by way of compensation we are too much in the lap of the mother, in those familiar reductive and genetic, those comfortable materialistic accounts of ourselves and our work that prevent clarity of thought and freedom of feeling. The preserves of the mother—childhood and family—have dominated psychology. If we trace things back far enough, we eventually come to her; materialism is but maternalism in acceptable disguise. Not the least of the results of our uncertain paternity is the role forced upon us of the hero (whose birth is peculiar and whose father is ambiguous), that God-Man savior-figure expressed in part through the expectations we have from ourselves and from our field: psychology of the unconscious and analysis as saviors of civilization, or "analysis for everyone." This vision is not restricted to the beginning of the psychoanalytic movement or to the beginning of many analyses. He who has no father is forced to become his own, to create his own pattern, thus becoming the heroic self-created creator. Each analyst creates his own brand of psychology out of his ego, eclectic, neo-, iconoclastic. He is driven into the role of hero. No matter how "related" and "relaxed" he appears, he, too, is fraught with modern man's existential ambiguity that has arisen from the loss of his myth. In his work with his patient he becomes the existential creator; they are two people thrown together in an existential situation where each is in search of a basis for being. The analyst, too, is in search of a father, the spirit that guarantees the existential role, the sustaining myth that tells one "how to be."

Without paternal descent we have no genealogy. Without genealogy, which provides structure and content for mythology, or is a mythology itself,[4] we succumb to the collective matriarchy that aims to hinder the inexplicable movements of the psyche by reduction back into social causes, animal drives, family problems, and all the other aging explanations for the soul's spiritual malaise. We are unable to face a spiritual crisis without at once declaring it social, religious, or something else matriarchally acceptable and resolvable through a collective recipe. Without the paternal principle, analysts build a personal genealogy, tracing lines of descent through other analysts back to the Genius-Fathers Freud and Jung, grouping themselves into families, with patriarchal totems, cross-cousin connections, taboos, and feuds.

But of all such damage, nowhere has the complex of the absent father been more comprehensively disastrous than in the myth of uncertain paternity which Freud, by claiming it to be at the core of personality, placed in the center of our field. In choosing the Oedipus myth, Freud told us less which myth was the psyche's essence than that the *essence of psyche is myth*, that our work is mythic and ritual, that psychology is ultimately mythology, the study of the stories of the soul. And in choosing a Greek example, Freud told us further that the differentiation of psychological consciousness requires a basis in a differentiation of the unconscious as

4. Cf. P. Philippson, *Genealogie als mythische Form* (Zurich, 1944).

expressed more variously and elaborately by Greek mythological culture.[5] But the story he chose to tell us has left behind cursed issues:[6] father-murder, wars of generations, unsolved incest longings and incestuous entanglements in both relationships and ideas, the distortion of the feminine into the Jocasta mold, the anima as an intellectual riddle with a monster's body, and destruction everywhere—suicide, blight and sterility, hanging, blinding—descending to future generations. Is this our myth? If it is, then how can we go from it to "psychological creativity"? Yet depth psychology has proved itself creative. Perhaps the Oedipus myth is relevant only to a certain phase, an early and ill phase in our transforming field of the soul, and, like the medical view itself, perhaps this myth only prolongs the illness of the ill view of the psyche. A wrong myth at the center can distort our psychological perceptions, just as an inadequate cosmological myth can distort astronomical and geographical observations.

Much, then, depends on the recognition of the true father. The discovery of our authenticity could yield acceptance and legitimation within ourselves and society, freeing us from the need to turn to borrowed models. It could liberate us from the mother and from the Oedipal tragedy (not just personally and individually). And it could help to make more human what has hitherto been too heroic and too numinous a field of work. Our search, then, is for our origins, for the loins which engendered us, the seed that

5. "The collective unconscious—so far as we can say anything about it at all—appears to consist of mythological motifs or primordial images, for which reason the myths of all nations are its real exponents. In fact, the whole of mythology could be taken as a sort of projection of the collective unconscious. . . . We can therefore study the collective unconscious in two ways, either in mythology or in the analysis of the individual" (*CW*, VIII, par. 325; cf. *CW*, IX, i, par. 260; *CW*, XI, par. 557).

6. Some negative effects of the Oedipus tragedy for psychology have been shown by R. M. Stein, "The Oedipus Myth and the Incest Archetype," in *Spectrum Psychologiae*, edited by C. T. Frey (Zurich, 1965).

created us. But this is not a historical event, the search through genealogy for the historical father, and so we may not use a historical approach. Rather, the search is for what continues to create in the psyche, for the specific nature of the creative principle within the field of psychology. What spirit creates psyche, and in what way does spirit move the soul? What engenders the psychologist? What calls a person to psyche, to soul, as a vocation?

Could the creativity of psychology—which, after all, was not born before Freud and Jung—have something to do with these Master-Fathers? Could the finding of the fathering principle begin through an examination of these actual fathers and the creative principle in them?

We must first make some differentiations. Which factors in Freud and Jung are specifically "psychologically creative"? Do we refer to the originality of their ideas? Do we mean the discovery of new areas and the extension of order into these areas, as well as the invention of the methodological equipment to deal with these areas and make this order? Or is their "creativity" principally the productivity of their lives, that body of work leading to schools, systems, followers, commentaries? Is it perhaps the aesthetic aspect of Freud's literary style which won him the Goethe Prize? Is it the intuitive grasp of Jung for seizing upon the unique that revolutionizes and reshapes the general pattern, giving, then, coherence to the unique? Is it the vitality, the dynamism of their spirits? For their ideas, as *idées-forces*, are still a scandal today, academically unacceptable, a *bouleversement* of the vested interests of mulish minds, who refuse the reality of the psyche as the primary human fact. Or, to define Freud's and Jung's creativity, must we look rather at the scope of their vision, encompassing history and art, natural science and religion, biology and philosophy, language and ethnology—a synthesis large enough to contain the psyche of the modern human being? Or was it merely that Freud, through the discovery of the "talking cure," as his method was first named, and Jung, through listening and believing in the fantasies of his schizophrenic charges, found again those parts of the soul which had been lost to unconsciousness, and from their own fascination with this discovery engendered in themselves and in others a new sense of soul? If this latter is their special psychological creativity, then we would have to include their exemplary lives, where psychology was embodied in their persons—psychology as lived, themselves as liberators, healers, teachers, fathers, each having lived fully to the limits of his myth, each taming the compulsions and accepting the vicissitudes of his drive to become just what he was. As such, each was true both to himself and to his field of work, psychology, which each created within himself through himself.

However, because their lives are a composite—not the least of which is living from the beginning to the fullest into the archetypal pattern of the wise old man—we must still extract that strand which makes their creativity *psychological.* (That they expressed themselves in psychology rather than in medicine or philosophy or history only begs the question. To say that Freud and Jung were creative psychologists because they lived their creative instinct and were shaped by it, and that they lived this in psychology, is a tautology. It tells us nothing of either the creative or the psychologically creative.) For our statement to make some sense, we must inquire in more detail into how one lives the creative in psychology. Let us give some time to sorting out this issue.

The Opus of Psychology: Creation of Soul

For the painter or the mystic or the physician, living into his myth is prepatterned by tradition. In each of these callings, the individual has, more or less, a way of knowing where he is: there is a collection of paintings; a corpus of mystical ritual, prayer, and instruction; a history of medical science. Moreover, the individual can turn to the study of lives to learn how painters painted, mystics contemplated, physicians practiced. He may also apprentice himself to a teacher, who can demonstrate and advise. He may alter the traditional pattern through his own creativity, but he cannot go beyond the limits which are given immediately, concretely, by the opus. This opus is the objectification of the field within which his life is lived, to which it is dedicated, and with which it is in continuing mutual relation. A field—painting, mysticism, medicine—even when fertilized with *knowledge* from other fields,[7] generally requires a sacrifice of creativity elsewhere. The field objectified in the opus responds and determines the gestalt of the creative force. The creative is shaped by both the general limits of the field and the specific limits of the opus into which it flows. The *oeuvre* shapes the person who is in relation with it: "It is not Goethe that creates *Faust*, but *Faust* that creates Goethe."[8] And we experience our relation to the opus as both fulfillment and suffering: fulfillment because, through the opus, the creative is contained and realized; suffering because the limitation of each opus, each field, tragically limits the creative possibility to the confines of actual realization. So the painter can be only a painter,[9] and his opus must be the canvas and not clay, foolscap, or the human body. From the beginning the opus as problem and fantasy determines my relation to it. It presents me with my sacrifices and constellates the possibilities by means of which I may accomplish a work. Creative people are occupied not so much with creativity as they are fascinated with an opus.

7. Cf. R. E. M. Harding, *An Anatomy of Inspiration* (Cambridge, Eng., 1942), p. 20: "The old-fashioned idea that inborn genius is enough without a solid foundation of knowledge is the reason why Reynolds, Constable and others set themselves against the use of this term and warned their pupils against the state. Without this rock of knowledge genius has no foundation to make it durable." Shakespeare's knowledge is a good example.

8. *CW*, XV, par. 159.

9. There are, of course, the universal geniuses, who in the fashion of the Renaissance or Baroque man can create in several fields, but these exceptions only prove the rule.

Now what is the opus in psychology? If the painter is confronted by his canvas as opus and the tradition of canvases as field, the mystic by God and the tradition of religious disciplines, and the physician by the ailing person and the tradition of the healing arts and sciences, what confronts the psychologist? And if the success or failure of the painter, mystic, and physician is determined by their creative achievement with the opus in their respective fields, what is the goal by which we determine creative *psychological* achievement?

On this analogy, the opus in our field can be nothing else but the psyche itself. It is objectified by the other person, who sets the limits to my work and offers the response to my actions, as does the canvas to the painter, God to the mystic, the ailing body to the physician. The judgment of my accomplishment is determined by what is achieved in, with, and by the other person's psyche. The road of this achievement and the patterns of activity along the way are often so much like what happens between the physician and patient, or between the teacher and pupil, that one sometimes loses oneself in these models.

But these are only partial models, only partly useful. Therefore, our tradition is only partly represented by the medical pattern of our forebears—Galen, Mesmer, Pinel, Charcot, and the many others whose contributions, as well as the peculiar occasion of their origins, we shall discuss in later parts of this book. So, too, the spiritual-director models of guru, of rabbi, of Ignatius or Fénelon, of Zen master, are only substitutions on which we lean for want of surety about the true model for psychology. Because the psyche is hidden in illness or in ignorance, it must be healed or taught. So one is played by these other roles, based on other models. But one is played by the opus itself into these other roles for the purpose of reaching that fundamental aim, which is neither healing nor teaching but the awakening or engendering of soul.

The soul of the other person as opus. Yet, what of one's own psyche? Is not its individuation the aim of psychological life? Moreover, must soul be located so personally, either in me or in you? Surely there is a level of the soul where it is psyche per se, a set of living processes, independent of our notions of personal individuality and redemption. Were the psyche to be conceived in this impersonal manner, the opus would transcend whatever you or I make of our souls during our lives. Then we might speak of psychic development as opus and of psychology as a field quite independent of any particular human personality.

Yet, how else is this opus achieved or soul created except through subjective interrelation with these processes? Soul is not mere nature; our intervention, confused or willful as it may be, seems necessary to its movements. We may very well talk of the objective psyche and may experience psychic movements in fantasy, images, and impulses as necessities that are not personally ours; still the feeling persists that the soul has a personal location. Somehow the notion of soul implies an individual person as its carrier. Hence we inevitably come back to the question of the carrier of the opus: myself or another?

Perhaps the question is put in a false form. For even if a person is necessary to the opus of soul-making, we do not have to distinguish sharply which person. One is incapable of operating in the psychological field of another person unless one works through one's own soul as an instrument. On the other hand, the very word individuation implies a context of others in distinction to whom one differentiates a unique style of fate. The boundaries of the soul are ill-defined, and the locus of psychological work can never be only you or only me; it is both of us.

Here it would be well to define "soul," but I cannot, nor can anyone, define it adequately. Elsewhere I have written an amplification of what I take "soul" to mean, and it may be useful to excerpt some of this:

> Soul is not a scientific term, and it appears rarely in psychology today, and then usually with inverted commas, as if to keep it from infecting its scientifically sterile sur-

> round. . . . There are many words of this sort which carry meaning, yet which find no place in today's science. It does not mean that the references of these words are not real because scientific method leaves them out. . . . Its meaning is best given by its context. . . . The root metaphor of the analyst's point of view is that human behavior is understandable because it has an inside meaning. The inside meaning is suffered and experienced. . . . Other words long associated with "soul" amplify it further: mind, spirit, heart, life, warmth, humanness, personality, essence, innermost, purpose, courage, virtue, morality, wisdom, death, God. . . . "Primitive" languages have often elaborate concepts about animated principles which ethnologists have translated by "soul." For these peoples, soul is a highly differentiated idea referring to a reality of great impact. The soul has been imaged as the inner man, and as the inner sister or spouse, the place or voice of God within, as a cosmic force in which all living things participate, as having been given by God, as conscience, as a multiplicity. . . . One can search one's soul and one's soul can be on trial. There are parables describing possession of the soul by and sale of the soul to the Devil . . . of development of the soul . . . of journeys of the soul . . . while the search for the soul leads always into "depths.". . . This exploration of the word shows that we are dealing not with a concept, but a symbol. Symbols, as we know, are not completely within our control, so that we are not able to use the word in an unambiguous way, even though we take it to refer to that unknown human factor which makes meaning possible, which turns events into experiences, which is communicated in love and which has a religious concern. The soul is a deliberately ambiguous concept . . . in the same manner as all ultimate symbols which provide the root metaphors for the systems of human thought. "Matter" and "nature" and "energy" have ultimately the same ambiguity; so too have "life," "health."[10]

Paradoxically, that interiority which seems most mine, most privately personal, can hardly be said to belong to me.

10. *Suicide and the Soul* (London and New York, 1964), pp. 43–47.

Traditions place soul in every sort of relation with the body and the spirit, and even as substrate of experiencing consciousness, but never is it said to belong to the ego or to be a part of the proprium disposable to the will and understandable by reason. That which is so truly mine and only mine, my soul, cannot be worked upon only by me. Rather, the soul is better imagined, as in earliest Greek times, as a relatively autonomous factor consisting of vaporous substance.[11] Then we may conceive it to be dependent and vulnerably porous. Dependence and need are basic and will appear most strongly in experience whenever we attempt to limit the soul through fixing borders of separated existence. The emotional, imaginal, and interior field of psyche, the analyst's root metaphor, remains fluid and cannot be limited to "me" and "mine." "You will not find the measure of the *psychē* by traveling in any direction, so deep is the *logos* of it," said Heraclitus (Frag. 45, Diels). Not a diamond but a sponge, not a private flame but a flowing participation, a knotted complexity of strands whose entanglements are also "yours" and "theirs." The collective nature of the soul's depths means simply that no man is an island.

Jung recognized the interrelation of souls in therapy very early and led Freud to take the position that the first task for the analyst is that he be analyzed himself.[12] Freud's interest in and observations of his own psyche during his cocaine period[13] and the prolonged analysis of his psyche mark the beginning of depth psychology. Analysis began when Freud turned with fascination to his soul within the relationship to Fliess.[14] "That which is creative must create itself" (said John

11. R. B. Onians, *The Origins of European Thought* (Cambridge, Eng., 1954), pp. 23–44, 93–96; E. Cassirer, "The I and the Soul", in *The Philosophy of Symbolic Forms*, trans. R. Manheim (New Haven, 1955), Vol. II.

12. *CW*, XVI, par. 237.

13. S. Freud, *The Cocaine Papers*, trans. S. A. Edminster *et al.* (Zurich and New York: Spring Publications, 1963).

14. S. Freud, *The Origins of Psycho-Analysis: Letters to Wilhelm Fliess; Drafts and Notes, 1887–1902*, ed. M. Bonaparte, A. Freud, and E. Kris, trans. E. Mosbacher and J. Strachey (London, 1954).

Keats), and our field, psychology, was created in depth when Freud's libido was drawn to his psyche in self-analysis. But it did not happen in isolation. It required Fliess and a friendship that has been called "the closest of his lifetime." [15] It required the interrelation of souls. As Jung said often enough, we can go with another only as far as we have gone with ourselves. This means also that we can go with ourselves *only as far as we have gone with another.* The deeper reasons for this interdependence of psyches for the engendering of soul will become clearer as we proceed. They must become clearer, or we can never grasp what compels us into the intimacy of therapeutic situations and binds us there with transference.

In his essay on transference Jung stresses the importance of the human connection for soul-making, stating that man's "soul . . . can live only in and from human relationships; . . . the conscious achievement of inner unity clings desperately to human relationships as to an indispensable condition, for without the conscious acknowledgement and acceptance of our kinship with those around us there can be no synthesis of personality." [16] Human relationships may be an indispensable condition, but still the opus remains the soul. Neither relationships, nor feeling, nor any of the human context in which the psyche finds itself should be mistaken for the soul-making opus. When we make this mistake, we focus upon the instruments and means and not upon the end. Improving relationships and making connections with feeling is not at all what is meant by psychological creativity. The soul may still lie sterile if it is limited to the human circle, which can never replace the Gods. Yet this human circle is necessary for psychological creativity: there seems to be a necessity for a close and personal world—family, tutelary figures, a friendly society, a beloved, personal enemies. *The world and its humanity is the vale of soul-making.*

15. E. Kris, Introduction, *ibid.*, p. 4.
16. *CW*, XVI, par. 444 (1st ed.).

At this point in our discussion, spirit and soul part company and the paths of spiritual discipline and psychological development diverge. This divergence is usually not understood, since the complexes of the psyche too easily volatilize into the rarefactions of spiritual formulae. Then we seek spiritual guidance for psychological tangles, confusing psychotherapy with yoga and the analyst with the master. Although spiritual disciplines may begin with personifications of the goal and may stress the importance of community and the master, these personifications must later be dissolved in experiences of higher abstraction and objectlessness. Persons and involvements are at best secondary. The psyche, with its emotions, images, and anthropomorphic attachments, is fundamentally a disturbance. Besides, in spiritual disciplines even the community and the master are ultimately transpersonal abstractions. People are never as real as spirit. The vale of the world is transcended through retreat, meditation, and prayer. The spirit calls one up and out; we shall overcome, transcending even the "we."

But psychological development stops in isolation; it seems unable to forego the context of other souls. Thus the psychologist delights in clinical fantasies, his cases, their families; his fascination with social and personal details reflects at the first and personal level his *involvement* with the opus. Why are we so avid for a bit of gossip, and why is scandalmongering so grossly profitable? Gossip is after all a primary activity of the psyche. Something psychological is going on in our craving for tales of souls in a mess. Such tales express the psyche's myth-making function at the personal level of storytelling, tale-tattling. When the psychologist disregards gossip, he may be sailing too high, off into the superiorities of the spirit. Gossip provides the psychic ballast of human dirt that keeps us down to earthly involvement. Soul-making would seem to have a Dionysian hole through which the individual soul is drawn into a communal "madness," misnamed "psychic infection." This leakage, or contamination, between souls dissolves paranoid isolation and seems required by the soul in contradistinction to the spirit, which proceeds, as Plotinus said, from the alone to the alone. Those in spiritual disciplines leave out the personal life, reporting on the objective nature of their experiences: the visions, sensations, texts, diets, and exercises. In alchemy we learn of substances and operations, not of biographical emotions; in mysticism we hear of prayers, rituals, and teachings, not of the relationships with other monks or nuns. But psychology is created within the vale of living intimacy.

Where spirit lifts, aiming for detachment and transcendence, concern with soul immerses us in immanence: God in the soul or the soul in God, the soul in the body, the soul in the world, souls in each other or in the world-soul. Owing to this immanence, dialogue is not a bridge constructed between isolated skin-encased subjects and objects, I's and Thou's, but is intrinsic, an internal relationship, a condition of the soul's immanence. The I-Thou is a necessity, a given a priori with the gift of soul. So soul becomes the operative factor in converting the it into a Thou, making soul of objects, personifying, anthropomorphizing through psychizing, turning into a partner the object with which it is engaged and in which it has implanted soul. Through our souls, as our dreams, projections, and emotions show, we are immanent in one another. That souls are ontologically entailed means that we are existentially involved. Whether we like this or not, whether spirit pulls away and above, we are involved as a psychic necessity. Thus involvement becomes the first condition for admission to the psychic realm, to the field of psychology.

If connection with another soul is specific for psychological creativity, we have discriminated it from other kinds of creativity, and we have qualified an important aspect of it. In a first summary we can say that psychological creativity differs from other sorts in that its opus is the psyche itself, not any one of its specific contents or talents; that is, psychological creativity will not necessarily develop one's thinking, musical faculty, or intelligence. Psychological creativity concerns the soul as opus. It is limited to its effects there: the creating, engendering, awakening, enlightening, and individuating of the soul. How these effects manifest themselves in this content or that attribute is secondary. Even where the opus is another soul, psychological creativity operates through one's own sense of soul as its instrument, like the tuning fork or the lyre which strikes a chord, setting in vibration tones in others, back and forth, reciprocally, mutually in harmony and discord. Training in sensitivity, participation in groups, and emphasis on body experience and imagination have become necessary first-level attempts to awaken psyche by making us aware of soul as it is extended through body, into others, and out to the imaginal realm. These methods want us to notice, attend, and care for soul in many of its manifestations hitherto neglected by psychology. Yet the method again becomes confused with the aim, which is not sensory awareness, visual imagination, or group feeling and involvements but rather psychic consciousness. Psychic consciousness: the experience of life as a mythical enactment and of the soul as the focus of individual destiny. It is a consciousness focused upon the soul and upon the mythical, archetypal forces that are enacted through it. Finally, the creative in psychology does not act solely within one's own precincts, one's private individuation process of symbols and experiences. The opus which challenges the creative, limits its potential, and tests it ultimately is always the other human soul. These limitations set by the opus are felt in any relationship as the fulfillment and the tragedy of the human connection.

Notions of Creativity

Creativity is now voguish in academic psychology, where there is new interest in "individual differences," in education for "excellence," and in the "creative process." How can we develop talent for our national aims? How may we foster creative individuals in our struggle for survival?

Whenever the light and heat of scientific consciousness are turned upon a field, they produce a sudden proliferation, splitting the object under study into ten thousand aspects. With this new interest in the creative and creativity, academic psychology suffers from the same malady of over-differentiation as can be seen in cancer, virus, or nuclear research: the more attention we pay to particulars, the more particulars appear to which we must pay attention. When French psychiatry of the past century focused on madness, it found at least forty kinds of *délires*. When psychology turns to intelligence and learning, more and more factors and variables appear. Once there was sleep, light or deep; now there are many kinds and levels, and some are not truly sleep. So we find that over *one hundred definitions of creativity* have been given by Taylor in his analysis of the creative process;[17] there are bibliographies dealing with only French[18] and Italian contributions to the field;[19] Stein and Heinze have produced a large volume merely by collating the most recent literature on the subject of creativity;[20] and another academic psychologist, Golann, attempts to sort all this material into a study of methodological approaches to creativity.[21] When we study methodology, we have evidence that our theme is overage and uncreative. Creativity is also

17. I. A. Taylor, "The Nature of the Creative Process," in *Creativity*, ed. P. Smith (New York, 1959).
18. R. J. Bédard, *Creativity in the Arts, Literature, Science, and Engineering: A Bibliography of French Contributions* (Princeton: Educational Testing Service, 1959).
19. R. J. Bédard, *Creativity in the Arts, Literature, Science, and Engineering: A Bibliography of Italian Contributions* (Princeton: Educational Testing Service, 1960).
20. M. Stein and S. Heinze, *Creativity and the Individual* (Glencoe, Ill., 1960).
21. S. E. Golann, "Psychological Study of Creativity," *Psychological Bulletin*, LX, No. 6 (1963), 548–65.

the latest subject to draw the attention of the chronicler of our *Zeitgeist*, Arthur Koestler, who has recently published a volume of seven hundred pages upon this theme.[22]

The term creativity is modern. Before the Enlightenment, when we were all God's creatures living in His creation, the word *creative* in the sense of "creativity" was hardly used in English. "Creative" as "productive" entered usage only in 1803 with the new ego of the nineteenth century. Now that "God is dead," and concomitant with his death the threat of the death of every human, creativity is carried more and more by man, so that the word itself has become a conceptual symbol holding projections of hope and free individuality—even, perhaps, of survival itself. An inquiry into the contemporary preoccupation with the creative and what this fascination compensates is beyond our range here.

We can, however, separate the strands of meaning which have gone into this conceptual symbol without attempting the more fundamental analysis of the state of modern consciousness which the projections upon that symbol reflect. This does not quite mean an excursion into the "nature of creativity"—the sort of exercise psychologists have carried out *ad absurdum*. To convert the creative mystery into a problem for solution is not only indecent but impossible. The analysis of creativity would mean laying bare the nature of man and the nature of creation.[23] These are mysteries concerning whence we have come, from what we live, and whither we return. They do not yield to analysis, to an explanatory psychology. We may speculate and fantasy and with our logos tell a tale, that is, confabulate a bit, bringing a mythologem as contribution to "creativity" in celebration of it, communion with it; but we will not attend its sacrifice

22. A. Koestler, *The Act of Creation* (New York, 1964).

23. To "explain" means etymologically to remove the folds, the complications, by laying out smooth and flat. Explanation is therefore served well by two-dimensional models, whereas complex models, such as those of analytical psychology, do not yield satisfactory explanations.

(were this even possible), not its ritual dismemberment by psychological analysis. Therefore, there shall be no definition, which limits and cuts, but rather amplification, which extends and connects.[24]

Creativity as a Human Instinct

We may begin this amplification with some passages from a paper, written by C. G. Jung in English and given at Harvard in 1936, entitled "Psychological Factors Determining Human Behavior."[25] Within a few pages Jung states some basic thoughts concerning the relation of psychology to biology. He sets out "to establish clearly what seems to me to be the relation between instincts and the psyche." He regards the instincts as older than, prior to, and outside the

24. "Definition states what something is and where it is separated from what it is not. Definition excludes by cutting out what does not belong. . . . As much of the soul is ambiguous and as knowledge about it is still incomplete, and may always be, sharp definitions are premature. The major problems which one brings to an analysis are the major problems of every soul: love, family, work, money, emotion, death; and the defining knife may rather maim these issues than free them from their surrounds. Definitions are anyway more appropriate to logic and natural science, where strict conventions about words must be followed and where definitions serve closed systems of operations. The psyche is not a closed system in the same way. Definition settles unease by nailing things down. But the psyche may be better served by amplification, because it pries things loose from their habitual rigid frames in knowledge. Amplification confronts the mind with paradoxes and tensions; it reveals complexities. This gets us closer to psychological truth, which always has a paradoxical aspect called the 'unconscious.' The method of amplification is rather like the methods of the humanities and the arts. By revolving around the matter under surveillance, one amplifies a problem exhaustively. This activity is like a prolonged meditation, or variations on a theme of music, or the patterns of dance or brush-strokes. . . . This permits levels of meaning in any problem to reveal themselves, and it corresponds to the way the soul itself presents its demands by its iterative returning to basic complexes to elaborate a new variation and urge consciousness on" (cf. my *Suicide and the Soul*, pp. 147–48, from which this passage is adapted).

25. *CW*, VIII, pars. 232–62.

psyche (ectopsychic) and characterized mainly by *compulsiveness.* Instinct is subject, however, to "psychization," that is, instinct may be modified through and by various psychic structures. The psychization of an instinct yields the coloring of it that we see. This is the instinct as experienced, felt, and observed in behavior. Because the instinct *an sich* is ectopsychic, it is objectively given by biological nature and may be conceived like the objective wave lengths producing the sensed experience of color.

It would take us too far afield to examine Jung's approach to biology and his use of the concept "instinct." Since even in biology the concept is fraught with complications, it is better to pass over the problems that might enter here and simply follow Jung's usage throughout. Jung presents "instinct" rather classically and straightforwardly in terms of a stably organized pattern of behavior biologically given to organisms in general and characterized by compulsiveness and automatic release toward specific satisfactions.[26] Psyche can tame the compulsions (or intensify them), can postpone release, and can shift the goals of satisfaction. Whatever we know of instinct in ourselves has already been through processes of psychization. We have only those perceptions of in-

26. "Although, in general, instinct is a system of stably organized tracts and consequently tends towards unlimited repetition, man nevertheless has the distinctive power of creating something new in the real sense of the word, just as nature, in the course of long periods of time, succeeds in creating new forms. Though we cannot classify it with a high degree of accuracy, the *creative instinct* is something that deserves special mention. I do not know if 'instinct' is the correct word. We use the term 'creative instinct' because this factor behaves at least dynamically, like an instinct. Like instinct it is compulsive, but it is not common, and it is not a fixed and invariably inherited organization. Therefore I prefer to designate the creative impulse as a psychic factor similar in nature to instinct, having indeed a very close connection with the instincts, but without being identical with any one of them. Its connections with sexuality are a much discussed problem and, furthermore, it has much in common with the drive to activity and the reflective instinct. But it can also suppress them, or make them serve it to the point of the self-destruction of the individual. Creation is as much destruction as construction" (*CW*, VIII, par. 245).

stinct which have been filtered through the prism of our psyche.

In this same paper Jung goes on to describe five basic instinctual groups which he calls, in short: hunger, sexuality, the drive to activity, reflection, and, last of all, a creative instinct. The first four are comparable to Konrad Lorenz' major groups: feeding, reproduction, aggression, and flight.[27] Aggression can be the analogue to Jung's "drive to activity," and flight the analogue to Jung's "reflection," which is, as he describes it, a *reflexio*, a "bending back" away from the stimulus, a "turning inward," away from the world and the object in favor of psychic images and experiences. Lorenz does not mention the fifth instinct, creativity; but then he speaks from observations of animal behavior, while Jung speaks from the study of people.

If we accept the hypothesis of a creative instinct, then this instinct, too, must be subject to psychization. Like other drives, it can be modified by the psyche and be subject to interrelation and contamination with sexuality, say, or activity. (But neither one's sexual drive, nor productive activity in the world, nor reflective consciousness, nor contentious ambition is the ground or manifestation of one's creativity.) Moreover, as an instinct, the creative is able to produce images of its goal and to orient behavior toward its satiation. As an instinct, the creative is a necessity of life, and the satisfaction of its needs a requirement for life. In the human being, creativity, like the other instincts, requires fulfillment. According to Jung's view of man, activity and reflection are not enough; there is a fifth component, as basic in man as hunger and sexuality, the *quintessentia* of creativity. What grand possibilities are opened here! Although I know of no other psychologist who has so boldly and bluntly declared for the creative as the essence of man, I have not found in any other part of Jung's work a development of this posi-

27. K. Lorenz, *Das sogennannte Böse* (Vienna: Borotha-Schoeler Verlag, 1963), pp. 128–33.

tion. However, his major concern in both his therapy and his writing was with the manifestations and vicissitudes of the creative instinct and with disentangling it from the other four. Consequently, we are led to state that Jungian psychology is based primarily upon the creative instinct and in turn to infer that Jungian psychology is primarily a creative psychology.

Jung did not explicitly work out his view because of a muddle we all tend to make: that frequent confusion of the creative with the artistic. Jung generally writes about creativity in connection with the artistic personality and artistic work, thus limiting the creative instinct to special cases and finding it "not common." [28] But if it is a basic human instinct, then its "uncommonness" is not a logically tenable consequent. Where he does turn to the creative instinct as such, his descriptions are given under other conceptions of it: the urge to wholeness, the urge toward individuation or personality development, the spiritual drive, the symbol-making transcendent function, the natural religious function, or, in short, the drive of the self to be realized.[29] He strongly affirms that this urge to self-realization works with the compulsiveness of an instinct.[30] We are driven to be ourselves.

28. E.g., *Psychological Types* (*CW*, VI) and "On the Relation of Analytical Psychology to Poetry," "Ulysses," "Picasso," and "Psychology and Literature" (all in *CW*, XV).

29. Throughout Jung's works we can find passages which state or imply that the development of personality, individuation, or self-realization is *the* creative human task, both as an ectopsychic urge which cannot be denied without neurosis or worse and as the ultimate aim of psychotherapy as he conceives and practices it in contradistinction to Freudian or Adlerian therapy, which has the elaboration of other instincts in main view. For a brief and excellent collection of such statements from Jung see the section entitled "The Development of Personality" in *Psychological Reflections*, ed. J. Jacobi (New York: Harper Torchbooks, 1961), pp. 265–83.

30. *CW*, IX, i, par. 634: "As I have said, mandala means 'circle.' There are innumerable variants of the motif shown here, but they are all based on the squaring of a circle. Their basic motif is the premonition of a centre of personality, a kind of central point within the psyche, to which everything is related, by which everything is

The individuation process is a *dynamis,* not a matter of choice or for a few. And in therapy it was evidently the creative instinct and its vicissitudes that were uppermost in his mind.[31] As he himself says, often his cases had already been through long periods of analysis (presumably where the problems arising from the psychic modifications of the other instincts were the major concern) and were "not suffering from any clinically definable neurosis, but from the senselessness and aimlessness of their lives . . . the general neurosis of our age." [32] We might say that they suffered, as we are suffering, disturbances in the psychization of the creative drive. Thus Jung characterizes therapy, in the same passage, as the process in which "we must follow nature as a guide, and what the doctor then does is less a question of treatment than of developing the creative possibilities latent in the patient himself."

Jung affirmed often enough that the creative instinct is *sui generis* and independent of neurotic psychodynamics.[33] It is not a gift or special grace, an ability, talent, or trick. Rather it is that immense energy coming from beyond man's psyche which pushes one to self-dedication via one or another specific medium. Creativity impels devotion to one's person in its becoming through that medium, and it brings with it a sense of helplessness and increasing awareness of its

---

arranged, and which is itself a source of energy. The energy of the central point is manifested in the almost irresistible compulsion and urge to *become what one is,* just as every organism is driven to assume the form that is characteristic of its nature, no matter what the circumstances. This centre is not felt or thought of as the ego but, if one may so express it, as the *self.*" *Ibid.*, par. 289: ". . . the strongest, the most ineluctable urge in every being, namely, the urge to realize itself. . . . The urge and compulsion to self-realization is a law of nature and thus of invincible power, even though its effect, at the start, is insignificant and improbable."

31. His insistence upon finality in regard to the libido, upon the final point of view toward all psychic phenomena and upon the prospective interpretation of the dream—all have as basis a creative psychology.

32. *CW*, XVI, par. 83.

33. *CW*, XVII, par. 206.

numinous power. Hence our relation to creativity fosters the religious attitude, and our description of it often uses religious language. Our experiences of the force of individuality and its relentless pressure upon each soul to realize its potential are difficult to distinguish from experiences of the immanent Gods in their creator roles. For the Gods, too, are ectopsychic, "beyond" the soul, neither wholly in it nor of it.

The creating Gods are the destroying Gods. As Jung said, "Creation is as much destruction as construction."[34] The ectopsychic instinctual force, because it comes from beyond the psyche, is more than human and mightier than its possessor. Its possessor is, in fact, always in danger of possession. Working as a compulsion, the force is always "too much." One spends one's life trying to slow it, tame it, give it enough time and space, because its haste is the destructive devil within the creative impulse itself. Suicide always remains the fundamental possibility of psychological creativity, as its reversal, since the destruction of soul is the counterpart of the creation of soul.

The opus is forever in danger of destruction, of which overt suicide is but one form. Again, we can understand the extreme emphasis that must be placed upon involvements whose claims help to keep soul-making from being soul-destroying. Studies of suicide speak of the increased possibility of suicide when there is a loss of the "significant other." The loss of a partner, a child, a parent, the end of the affair may cut loose the soul to create itself or destroy itself. The opus can be destroyed by the creative instinct when it loses the touchstone of others, the human context of psychic reactions. Sometimes we find a delusion of soul-making, replete with all the grand words: "dedication," "integration," "realization," and a "Self" discovered through "introversion"—all of which may well be masking a destructive process of gradual isolation in subjectivity. Introversion never meant

34. *CW*, VIII, par. 245.

isolation from the human community. Introversion is an attitude, a description of energy flow, and not the precondition for soul-making; it must be carefully distinguished in theory and in actuality from the opus.

Since psychological creativity will occupy the same destructive/constructive poles that describe the instinct in general, we are left with the realization that *soul-making entails soul-destroying*. An analysis for the sake of soul-making cannot help but be a venture into destructiveness. In another context I expanded upon analysis from the perspective of suicide and described the therapeutic process as a "prolonged breakdown" where "analysis means dying."[35] Alchemy gives a series of images for the soul-destroying parts of the opus: mortification, sacrifice, putrefaction, fermentation, torture, and dismemberment. In addition, there are delusions that spring forth to batten upon any relationship, delusions technically referred to as the "neurosis" of transference. The therapeutic delusion that is most soul-destroying is the one which refuses to see what is actually happening, contending, for example, that whatever takes place within the context of analysis is soul-making, while all soul-destroying activities are outside (in the parents or the marriage, in enemies, institutions, society, etc.). Here analysis serves to split apart the destructive and constructive aspects, and creativity divides against itself; but the essence of creativity is that these aspects exist within each other *in every act:* that which builds at the same time tears down, and that which breaks up at the same time restructures. When the analyst (or anyone in the close situations of loving, healing, counseling, teaching, ministering) will not see that his constructive work with the soul is also destructive, the destruction takes place out of sight, unconsciously, and is assigned outside and elsewhere. This is one of the ways in which we have become victims of therapy and its good intentions—and the analyst can get off scot-free by again ascribing the destruction of the involve-

35. *Suicide and the Soul*, pp. 56–94.

ment to that magic word "transference," negative, unresolved, or severed.

Since destruction endangers the opus in any creative venture, the question of management becomes paramount. We study with fascination the lives of the "great" to see how they succeeded. In regard to psychological creativity, two means of management suggest themselves: first, the discipline imposed by the opus (in psychology, discovering and meeting the peculiar needs of the soul); second, the limits placed upon the creative impulse by the psyche (through the context of relationships). The first means finding out how to culture the soul, to give it scope, exercise, and enjoyment and to meet its ever-returning interest in death. The second means observing relationships as rituals that provide channels for creative pressures. Relationships offer containers for the craziness. The deeper they go, the more they can hold. They provide places for sacrifice and for protection against the destructive aspect of the creative. When these channels are neglected, when the instinct cannot be shaped through adequate psychic modifications, and especially when there is no containing opus for creativity, we have the archetypes bursting straight onto the stage: the creative-destructive primordial urge; man driven, desperate, dismembered; the self in its psychotic process.

We may also conclude that the creative as instinct cannot be limited to the few, to geniuses and artists. This would be again to confuse the artistic with the creative. If it is a basic instinct along with hunger and sexuality, activity and reflection, then, like these, it is given to all. We need no longer divide mankind into two groups, holding with Jung, and then with Neumann, that creativity and the creative person are different, special, and outside the laws of nature as they affect and control us common men.[36] (This view of

36. Cf. the section in *Psychological Reflections* (pp. 163–87) entitled "Awareness and Creative Living"; E. Neumann, "Der schöpferische Mensch und die grosse Erfahrung," *Eranos Jahrbuch*, XXV (Zurich, 1957).

das Schöpferische and of the creative man is itself archetypally determined—as we shall soon see—by one of the ways we regard and experience creativity.) The so-called creative genius may have a more direct and uncomplicated relation to his instinct; he may have special constitutional talents (e.g., artistic, mathematical, contemplative) which facilitate psychization. Many factors, including personal and historical ones, here play their role. Nevertheless, any notion of two kinds of psychology—one for you and me and one for the creative person—cuts off the creative from common humanity and you and me from creativity. So many of the great—Eliot, Mann, Freud, Matisse, as notable recent examples—have insisted upon their unexceptionable regularity and their bourgeois dullness as persons that we ought to listen to them. If the creative instinct is given to each of us, and its modification through psyche is given to each, then we can no longer maintain a rift and split between human and genius.[37]

Why must the person who lives largely in terms of the creative instinct be damned out of common humanity? And the reverse: why can't the common man change his heroically romantic nineteenth-century concept of genius, so charged with ambition and envy, and be done with this fantasy of the extraordinary personality? Has not each of us a genius; has not each genius a human soul? Could we not find a similar extraordinariness within ourselves in our relation to the creative instinct as we experience it? Even without artistic talent, even without the ego strength of great will, even without good fortune, at least one form of the creative is continuously open for each of us: psychological

37. This view would alter Yeats's verse: "The intellect of man is forced to choose / Perfection of the life, or of the work" ("The Choice," in *The Collected Poems of W. B. Yeats*, 2d ed. [London: Macmillan, 1950]). The *soul* of man does not force a choice. As long as the soul is the opus, life and work are not alternatives. For the psychologist both life and work are areas of soul-making; life is the work and the work is life, but both from the point of view of the soul.

creativity. Soul-making: we can engender soul. Or, as Jung puts it: "But what can a man 'create' if he doesn't happen to be a poet? . . . If you have nothing at all to create, then perhaps you create yourself." [38]

An Archetypal Basis for the Notions of Creativity

We need yet to explore the notions of creativity. We have grounded the principle of creativity outside the psychic realm, and because it is a mysterious unknown we have called it variously and vaguely "instinct," "spirit," or "divine." However, what relation do our *notions*—those one hundred conceptual connotations of the term—have to the creative instinct? Where do they come from? Can we bend backwards and reflect, not upon creativity, but upon the *notions*, so that when we use the word "creative" we may better understand what is going on in us? Can these notions tell us something phenomenological about creativity itself? In other words, can we use our psychology, not to analyze the creative principle, but to analyze our ideas of it?

Our study of creativity aims less at understanding the "instinct" and its "process," or the "nature of genius," than it seeks to discover what the psyche says about the instinct when it speaks of creativity. The ectopsychic urge belongs beyond the human and to the Gods; but the psychic is for us to ponder upon and differentiate. By applying psychology to psychology—the major intention and method of this book—we may learn something psychological, finding another use for all the research that has been done about creativity. We examine this research, not for its positivistic, objective, scientific "facts," but for the fantasies expressed in it. We turn to academic psychology for its *psychic content* (as we shall turn in later parts to psychiatry and embryology) in order to see what the psyche is saying about itself through

38. *CW*, XI, par. 906.

the language of research. We will not take this language at its face value, because we can approach it through its fantasy, much as we look at dreams, alchemy, or religious statements as psychic expressions. The statements about creativity can also be examined for their root metaphors. The many notions of creativity are comparable to the many notions of any basic symbol (matter, nature, God, soul, instinct). The very existence of so many notions is evidence for the variety of root metaphors by means of which the psyche perceives and forms its notions. The perceptions are filtered through the prism of the psyche. We stand inescapably in the light of one or another color band, giving us a definite perspective and bias. By applying psychology to psychology, by analyzing our views, we may become aware of our perspectives and their inevitable bias. Our method then becomes part of the opus of soul-making: it leads the soul to awareness of its relation to fundamental symbols, one of which is creativity. Perhaps this clarification may also lead psychology to a less cumbersome connection to the creative possibility in its own field.

The notions of creativity are gathered mainly from the self-perceptions of those who have been particularly dominated by this instinct. They have described the creative process in diaries, notebooks, letters, memoirs. The study of their lives (as well as the compulsive-destructive distortions of it in psychotic lives) has given us, despite the hundred varieties, a rather uniform set of ideas of the creative. These notions form a phenomenology of ways in which the creative is perceived. They arise empirically from felt experience, lived events in actual lives, as psychic perceptions of instinctual processes. Jung has called "the instinct's perception of itself" the archetype or primordial image.[39] We may therefore

39. ". . . the way in which man inwardly pictures the world is still, despite all differences of detail, as uniform and as regular as his instinctive actions . . . ; in order to account for the uniformity and regularity of our perceptions, we must have recourse to the correlated concept of a factor determining the mode of apprehension. It is

expect that the uniformity of our notions of any instinct are archetypally based, that is, there are definite archetypal patterns in the descriptions of creativity which shape both our experience of creativity and our notions of it. Even the ideas that the "artist" or "genius" has about what is happening to him and what he is doing are archetypally conditioned by these perceptional substructures. Let us turn to these typical notions of creativity and their archetypal background.

1. "In the beginning God created Heaven and Earth." The myth of Genesis shows the creation as the handwork of the paternal power, that immense He who separates, differentiates, and forms—and declares the goodness of his work. Differentiation, order, and goodness proceed together. Order is good; order is God; God is good. And there is only one God, only one right way, one truth. He is supreme and alone. The notion of creativity filtered through the father archetype shows method and hierarchy, a structured kingdom. The deed or word must be brought into being; some area of existence must be ordered by formula, charted by map, built of stone. Without production, active or reflective, nothing is created at all. A monument must be left behind, a seed sown to continue in perpetuity to beget generations after its own kind. Carriers of this seed may be the pupil, son, heir, or simply an impersonal organization—but never the friend or the beloved. So Kant, methodically proceeding through the realms of reason; so Bach, fathering twenty children and leaving no musical form as he found it but recreating all music; so Hobbes, at forty, coming upon his calling through geometry and analyzing the principles of civil power and mathematical order into his nineties. So, too, the individual who identifies the creative process with differentiation (for example, Linnaeus) and who attempts with his work to produce the finally authoritative, the unquestionable, classical, and permanent, by means of systematic co-

this factor which I call the archetype or primordial image. The primordial image might suitably be described as the *instinct's perception of itself*" (*CW*, VIII, par. 277).

herence and axiomatic law. *Creativity, then, is defined as an ordering process,* integrating toward unity, mandala as goal. Moreover, the moral and aesthetic orders are joined: justice, proportion, fittingness, system; everything in its own place. The *nous* soon becomes a pleroma with no irrational or moving parts, and as creativity fits more and more the archetypal notion, shaping into stable perfection, it passes into the sterility of the *senex.*[40] Darkness of matter, temporal evil, and chaos reemerge in the form of the despised feminine (we shall study this misogyny in Part Three). Thus does the primordial father-image shape a notion of the creative instinct.

2. Different is the notion that creation is novelty and that the creative is true to its name only as *creatio ex nihilo,* that it must bring something altogether new. The creative reaches into the future, and the creative person has an aura of futurity. This notion is bound to time, as time's enemy or as time's child, breaking through time's limits to eternity. Or, as a carrier of time, it is the advancing *Zeitgeist* that creates, perhaps in the manner of Bergson, by evolving the future out of itself, perhaps through the dynamics of Marxian history, perhaps as a Chardinesque teleological ascent. Always it is in movement, and the movement is from the known toward the unknown, from the old to the new. The notion is suffused with hope and optimism, growth and joy. A green age to be, new lands and prospects. Emphasis is upon the unique, the one and only. *Creativity will be defined principally by the word originality, and its negative expression will be narcissistic irresponsibility.* Because nothing lasts, and one can make nothing endure without killing the spark that is not meant to last, there must be continual flux and flexibility, advance, spontaneity, *inspiration from the divine*—unconditioned, uncaused, unprecedented. Consolidation and maturity prevent the break-through flashes of mercurial novelty; thus play, luck, tricks, humorous juxtaposition—not

40. A further elaboration of the primordial father as *senex* can be found in my "Senex and Puer," *Eranos Jahrbuch,* XXXVI (Zurich, 1968).

work—is the method, and youth is the time. "Toujours ouvert, toujours disponible," as Gide has phrased it. Free, open, awake to everything. Already we can see that this notion of the creative is the self-perception of the instinct through the image of the *puer aeternus* [41] and the archetype of the divine child.

3. If the new must sever with the old, and if *ex nihilo* implies annihilation of what is, creativity will be colored by another factor: it will be marked by ferment; the onrush of sap bark-bursting dry wood; *turba*, Wotan, Shiva, Rudra the howler. Emotionality rides the night's tiger, and we rage with iconoclasm, rebellion in the name of liberation, the creative process as protest. Under the aegis of the shadow, the creative becomes contaminated with activity (primitive levels of aggression), with hunger (greed for more, and the cult of experience), and with sexuality (phallus becomes the potent penis). Moreover, this contamination seems to be the very aim of the shadow's influence, as if to reinforce the creative instinct through appropriation of other instinctual energy. This misappropriation of energy is then justified by the so-called darkness of the creative urge, which according to the dogma of the shadow is supposed to be kept in the irrational dark so that its primal power will not be inhibited.[42] *Creativity becomes primal power* itself, reflected in the abnormal, the extraordinary, the capacity for extremes of intensity. The libido becomes unchained, desublimated in liberation, reflecting the God, Liber; freedom expresses its verbal roots in Frey and Frigg—archetypal patterns behind the release of the inferior and raw man. In place of intellect and reason, creativity means the primitive, the naked, the ignorant, the black, the deprived and depraved. Raw power becomes creativity, and its reverse, too: raw dismemberment, torn and tearing to pieces in the creative drama of the

41. Cf. "Senex and Puer."
42. Cf. K. Schmid, "Aspects of Evil in the Creative," *Evil*, Studies in Jungian Thought (Evanston: Northwestern University Press, 1967).

shadow. This view of creativity insists that it must conflict with whatever yokes its power—cultural canons, standards of taste, bourgeois morality. As the source of this dynamic vitality is in the dark, it is an invocation of the occult, and it demands a descent to the abyss of disorder, even through derangement of the senses (drugs, drink, magic, perversions). It feeds on excess and conflict, linking *Genie und Irrsinn,* "the lunatic, the lover, and the poet," and giving us the corollary notion that the creative lives best at the destructive frontier, close to evil, close to death.

4. The association of creativity with evil and with darkness through the shadow is not to be confused with the trickery and thieving which also belong to a notion of creativity but which fall within another constellation. The Promethean theft of fire was neither out of the shadow nor for the shadow. It was rather an announcement to the Gods that the human ego had come upon the scene. All peoples have fire; no animals have fire. Through fire, nature's substances can be altered and nature's processes hastened. Through fire man can invent and discover; he can convert nature's mystery into a problem to solve, thereby extending the realm of conscious control. *The creative as perceived by the ego is inventive problem-solving, anything instrumental to the extension or enhancement of consciousness.* This notion of creativity is not worshipful, not romantic; it sees the profane utilitarian fire, not the *feu sacré;* and it is this functional view that is common in our culture today, with its emphasis upon ego psychology.

The ego originates against the Gods. The ego steals its light from the *lumen naturae,* and the ego expands, not at the expense of primordial darkness, where there is no light to be had, but at the cost of childhood's godlike, dimmer light of wonder, of imagination, and the symbolic, natural mind. Creativity through the ego is necessary and yet is a theft,[43] a sin,

43. Carl Kerényi calls the Promethean deed "the inevitable theft" (*Prometheus: Archetypal Image of Human Existence,* trans. Ralph Manheim, Vol. I of Bollingen Series LXV [New York, 1963], p. 79).

a Luciferian fall. When the larger awareness is robbed of its light, the primordial world is plunged into darkness, splitting human and divine, and pain is the ego's reward. The ego's light must be maintained, the fire kept alive through the sweat of the smith, through concentrated, patient attention and *hard human work*. This notion says that creative activities are "nine-tenths perspiration": John Wesley, itinerant preacher of fifteen sermons a week, reading as he rode horseback 5,000 miles a year; Anthony Trollope, clocking in 250 words every quarter-hour; and the prodigious physical drudgery of Lope de Vega, Michelangelo, Voltaire, Scott, Balzac, Edison.

5. Another notion, usually given little respect, deserves our attention because it is a psychological fact. In the popular mind and in dreams creativity is identified with eminence, the top of the ladder in any field, where the road of ambition is crowned with the success of fame. Here the creative is perceived through the persona. Outer and public invade and consume inner and private; one becomes one's image. And this image, as part of collective consciousness, both leads the culture as a *représentation collective* and is victim to its projections. Then the individual who wears the mask can no longer put it down because the mask itself has become the psychic carrier of the creative instinct, sometimes sacrificing the person in suicide and personal tragedy for the sake of the personality image which the public requires someone to carry for it. He cannot yield his role, partly because of power motives, but largely because the role carries his creative effectiveness. His mask represents a collective force, transpersonal, archetypal, so that he must wear it in order to be in relation with the Gods. Persona here no longer means outward show, a staged performance that hides a true self; it now is the true self in its archetypal enactment. What could be more "real" than this performance? In this way "persona" recovers its original meaning, which is necessary for the reality of theater and tragedy, where all the world's a stage. When the persona absorbs the creative instinct, all the quirks and facets of a life

become symbolic. The kaiser's tastes, the dictator's habits, the stars' and sports-heroes' diets and opinions take on an ultimate, mythical importance. And when these figures appear in dreams, they point to visitation in the soul by a numen of an era, through which figure the dreamer may be acknowledging his need to express creativity effectively in the world, merging individuality with society, realizing himself as shaper of collective consciousness, as an actor in a historical drama.

6. One more major idea of creativity appears in the writings of psychologists and historians of religion and culture, as well as in accounts of the great. Creativity has been given the meaning of *renewal*, and the path to it is *cyclical regression.* The creative is then presented as the indestructible timeless ground of nature: earth, home, root, womb, or the transforming seas engirdling the world. We are its servants, waiting, passive. The creative is an external source, a mothering unconsciousness, nourishing and regenerating, at the ground of each human being, and naturally subject to periodic barrenness, like the seasons. Creativity may fall like a mantle upon some favorite son, the creative hero, who must fight this ground and even slay it. But for all its earnestness, this fight is only a mock struggle, since the primordial source can never be overcome and there is no real death, only rebirth. We need not go on to complete this notion of creativity derived from the archetype of the Great Mother.

A life may be affected by several of these notions as archetypal stages in experiencing the creative. We may proceed from child to ego to father, or from ego to shadow to mother, and so forth. Creative *crises* can often be attributed to difficulties in transitions, as, for instance, the critical period of middle life, when a new psychization of the instinct is called for, bringing with it a new self-perception in style and content.[44] The brilliance of earlier work (*puer*) may have

44. Examples are given by E. Jaques, "Death and the Mid-Life Crisis," *International Journal of Psychoanalysis*, XLVI (1965), 502–14. He investigates the pattern of transition of child to ego to father,

to yield to a major, serious, ordered tome (father); or success (persona) may be forsaken for a destructive attack (shadow) on the society that gave the success; or steady work (father) may be abandoned during years of barrenness and gestation (mother). Creative *possessions* may be attributed to identifications with one or another of these archetypal modalities that make one cling to only one pattern, while creative *tensions* would refer to contestations between these modalities. Each of these perceptions of the instinct not only gives a different notion of what creativity is but provides its own sense of meaning and its own position of truth. Thus we find seriously upheld and diametrically opposed views of the nature of creative art or the creative person, each of which, if we penetrate deeply enough, will reveal an archetypal basis given by the self-perception of the creative instinct through one of the primordial constellations.[45]

Furthermore, there may also be *contaminations*, unholy conjunctions, of these archetypal experiences of the creative:

---

where divesting oneself of a puerile attitude is experienced as a "death." Other patterns are not mentioned in his paper, for instance, the problem of *destructivity* as psychization through the shadow, or that of *sterility* as psychization through the father.

45. Thus it is not surprising to find, in Jung's observations on the creative, passages of apparent contradiction, which in fact are all notions arising through different archetypal modes of perception, e.g.: (the Shadow) "Creative life always stands outside convention. That is why, when the mere routine of life predominates in the form of convention and tradition, there is bound to be a destructive outbreak of creative energy" (*CW*, XVII, par. 305); (the Child) "The creation of something new is not accomplished by the intellect, but by the play-instinct acting from inner necessity. The creative mind plays with the objects it loves" (*CW*, VI, par. 197); ". . . we know that every good idea and all creative work are the offspring of the imagination, and have their source in what one is pleased to call infantile fantasy. Not the artist alone, but every creative individual whatsoever owes all that is greatest in his life to fantasy. The dynamic principle of fantasy is *play*, a characteristic also of the child" (*ibid.*, par. 93); (the Mother) "The psychology of the creative is really feminine psychology, a fact which proves that creative work grows out of unsconsious depths, indeed, out of the region of the mothers" ("Psychology and Poetry," in *Transition* [Paris, 1930]). For creativity and the persona see *CW*, VII, pars. 237 f.

child and shadow may not be separated enough, giving us the *enfant terrible;* child and father together present the old fool, dabbler in magic, an ineffective Falstaff or a charlatan of wisdom; or worse, the mother and shadow, who, together, merge all clarity and differentiations and bring forth the blood-earth cult and regressive savagery in the name of strength-through-joy and vital renewal.

So far so good. Yet these archetypal notions have not answered our original questions: What is the creative paternal principle in our psychology? What is psychological genius, the genius of psychology which engenders the sense of soul and generates psychological reality? What myth are we enacting in the ritual of analysis today if not Freud's Oedipal tragedy or Jung's myth of the hero? If the soul is the opus of psychology, what engenders it? And why does this engendering of soul, or psychological creativity, depend so upon the human connection?

Anima and Psyche

One pattern of creativity giving us yet another notion is feminine—but not feminine like the mother. In the academic literature this aspect of the creative *personality* is described as "psychosexual ambivalence" or as "sensuality, sentience, aesthetic interest, and femininity." [46] This aspect of the creative *activity* is called incubation—even pregnancy and birth; and this aspect of the creative *product* is called its imagination and beauty. Then we find: passivity, receptivity to what comes, ingestion, following images of fantasy as they flow feelingly through or floating upon them, the thin-skinned sensitivity that absorbs the world through the pores into one's own blood stream, the pout and sulk at the bid of fancy's whim, the moods, the loves, the vagaries—and, below it all, the humiliating service to a mistress, the opposite feminine principle, in whose hands lie both the fluency of images and the lines of beauty.

46. Golann, "Psychological Study of Creativity," p. 557.

Jung has made it possible for us to know this notion of the creative better. His elaboration of the *anima* as a function of every man's personality moves the discussion of creative experience from the special case of the artist to the case of each of us. Each of us has an anima and through our experience of "her" we can approach what goes on in others.

Although Jung has given us this concept of the anima, he has limited it by definition to the psychology of men. Empirically, the anima shows first where a man's consciousness is weak and vulnerable, reflecting his interior contrasexuality as a feminine inferiority—he whines and bitches. However, the *archetype* of the anima cannot be limited to the special psychology of men, since the archetypes transcend both men and women and their biological differences and social roles. The representations of the anima in Greek mythology, where the archetype appears in the configurations of nymphs, maenads, amazons, nereids, and so on, or in the more numinous and articulated divine forms of Persephone-Kore, Aphrodite, Artemis, Hebe, Athena, refer to a *structure of consciousness* relevant to the lives of both men and women. Therefore, psychological creativity is not limited to men only, nor is the anima archetype a masculine prerogative.

If we have found the opus in psychology to be the soul, and if anima is *âme, alma, Seele*, "soul," will not psychological creativity have something to do with engendering soul or psyche through anima? Both anima and psyche are traditionally feminine. Are they identical? How do they relate to "soul"? The modern use of the term "anima," following Jung, takes it to be a personification of the soul, and anima figures are supposed to be soul images that reveal the soul's character and predilections. In a late discussion of the anima, Jung makes it clear that for him it is an "empirical concept, whose sole purpose is to give a name to a group of related or analogous psychic phenomena." [47] He warns that it "should not be confused with any dogmatic Christian idea of the soul

47. *CW*, IX, i, par. 114.

or with any previous philosophical conceptions of it." [48] Instead he refers to classical ideas—even to Chinese—in order to prevent an assimilation of his empirical concept, derived from the phenomena of analysis and life, into the usual religious ideas of the soul. Jung therefore generally steers clear of the term "soul," using, instead, "anima," "psyche," and "self."

Psyche and soul may be differentiated according to a variety of fantasies or schemata. Jung defines psyche as a totality of all psychic processes, the intentional subjectivity of this totality being the "self." "Soul" is a functional complex of the psyche, acting as a mediating personality between the whole psyche, which is mainly unconscious, and the usual ego. The image of the soul-personality as an opposite to the usual ego is contrasexual; therefore, empirically, in a man this "soul" is feminine, i.e., the anima.

However, the soul presents aspects that extend beyond a man's unconscious femininity—his dream figures of favorite women and his inner personality. These wider aspects touch questions of loss of soul, immortality and redemption, human vitality, sacredness and relatedness, and they also evoke the cosmic *anima mundi*, intimating a world-soul, or the psyche at common levels of subjectivity. Soul, psyche, anima, and animus (unlike "self," which is a more abstract and reflective symbol) have etymological associations with body experiences and are concrete, sensuous, and emotional, like life itself.

We have difficulty with these terms because they are not true concepts; rather they are symbols which evoke meanings beyond any significations we give them through definitions. Anima will always evoke its Latin and Greek influences,[49] which blend it with *psychē*, and the experiences of it as an emotional, amorphous, living presence of great value to the individual human. In this sense, "soul-making," which evokes the sense of this presence, implies the stirring of an

48. *Ibid.*, par. 119.
49. Onians, *The Origins of European Thought*, pp. 93–122, 168–73.

emotional and living factor of overwhelming importance for my well-being now and for my death. A psychology whose aim is soul-making strikes wholly different chords—in the soul itself—than does ego psychology. "Depth psychology," as it was originally named in German, leads eventually to the recognition of soul as the inward, downward factor in personality, the factor which gives depth.

We may also conceive of the relation between anima and psyche as an example of the potential and actual. The soul as anima, as interior personality, will carry all aspects that have been neglected by the exterior persona. At first level, these aspects are necessarily unconscious, sensitive and effeminate and typical of all the anima traits Jung has described. But once they are contained, lived with, and fantasied, they take on more and more psychological character, providing insights, symbols, and connections. In fact, we are forced to develop these psychological differentiations in order to keep our balance in the midst of anima obsessions. Through interest in these feminine aspects and through dialogue and intercourse with them, something psychological emerges from an anima state. In other words, anima becomes psyche, giving us an increasing sense of soul as the anima awakens into psyche. Therefore, latent within all the anima confusions is the psyche, straining to awaken; and this psyche, as the old tale tells us, was a beautiful, moody, suicidal, rather inexperienced girl, in naïve relation with her sisters and the Goddesses.

If anima is the way to psyche, then anima experiences will be an initiatory way for psychological creativity. Thus Jung speaks of the anima as the way to psychic wholeness and of the repeated *coniunctio* with the feminine through its different stages of development. This cannot mean just that the anima brings "the other side," just that the anima has a special relation to the "wise old man" as his daughter—that the path to the wisdom and folly of full masculine humanity is through the cultivation of the anima. It must mean that, at the beginning of the process, the anima is psyche itself, still symptomatic, still labile and unknown. And at the core of every anima fascination is the irresistible beauty of that most beautiful of all created forms, Psyche. Erotic desire, as the Platonic Socrates makes clear, is always toward the beautiful: "To love is to bring forth upon the beautiful, both in body and in soul" (*Symposium* 206B). That which attracts us most of all, more even than the Goddess of Beauty, Aphrodite, is the mortal, Psyche, the mortal human psyche.

In a man's dreams the anima is often the image for neurovegetative symptoms and emotional lability; that is, she represents the semisomatic events which are not yet psychic experiences, which have not yet undergone enough psychization. In these dreams she is closed off, under water, "unable to come out"; or she is as magical and incomprehensible as the symptoms themselves; or she may still be a child at the threshold of puberty; sometimes she is drowned, burned, frozen, idiotic, dwarfed, syphilitic—in need of care; sometimes she is part of a mythical inscape where fairies and animals move through the vegetation not yet cut into by human perceptions.[50]

In these dreams a man may attempt to bore through a wall to reach "the girl in the next room," or he may find the line cut on the telephone so that he "can't get through." Sometimes the attractive girl speaks only a foreign tongue, comes

50. For further examples of anima-images and emotions and their psychological meanings as experiences see Jung, *CW*, VII ("Anima and Animus"); *CW*, IX, i ("Concerning the Archetypes, with Special Reference to the Anima Concept" and "The Psychological Aspects of the Kore"); *CW*, IX, ii ("The Syzygy: Anima and Animus"); *CW*, XIV (*Mysterium Coniunctionis*). See also E. Jung, *Animus and Anima*, trans. C. F. Baynes and H. Nagel (New York: Spring Publications, 1969); H. G. Baynes, *The Mythology of the Soul* (London, 1940); C. Brunner, *Die Anima als Schicksalsproblem des Mannes* (Zurich, 1963); J. Hillman, "Inner Femininity: Anima Reality and Religion," in *Insearch* (New York: Scribner's, 1967); E. C. Whitmont, "The Anima," in *The Symbolic Quest* (New York: Putnam's, 1969); Ann Belford Ulanov, *The Feminine in Jungian Psychology and in Christian Theology* (Evanston: Northwestern University Press, 1971). See also the writings of Linda Fierz-David, Frances Wickes, and Esther Harding.

from some heathen culture, and draws him back into the historical past; such figures enter, excite the dreamer erotically, and disappear. Or an insect or mouse that he tries to crush reveals itself as a beautiful but tiny girl. Nothing makes sense; seductions abound. Day after day a man is victim to feelings and fantasies that turn his head on every street corner. Just when the sails of fantasy swell and the voyage of imagination is about to get under way, his symptoms lay him low. The classical approaches that he can use for dealing with other archetypal assaults, such as refusing the mother or confronting the shadow, fail utterly. In response to questioning she smiles and fades. He falls asleep or wastes the day in a bad mood. She resists all analytical approaches that would reduce her, interpret her, or explain her. Only one way seems open, a hint of which is given by her easy seductiveness—the erotic way. A man is asked to love his soul.[51]

The conclusions to which we are forced by the empirical data in analytical work are that *anima becomes psyche through love* and that *it is eros which engenders psyche.* Thus we come to one more notion of the creative, this time as perceived through the archetype of the anima. *The creative is an achievement of love.* It is marked by *imagination* and *beauty,* and by connection to *tradition* as a living force and to *nature* as a living body.[52] This perception of the in-

51. Parallels for feminine psychology are evident. The animus is often a wanderer, soldier, prisoner, someone lamed or weak or too young, or a drunkard or a poor driver, remaining either ineffectual or "overeffectual" as a primitive sexualized threat or a collective hero-figure until he is given the woman's love.

52. The Romantics—particularly in England and particularly John Keats—provide a good example of the creative perceived through the anima, which led them to describe the creative as Eros; in consequence there was an extraordinary development of psychological insight during the Romantic period, especially in Keats himself, who lived only twenty-five years. (See A. Ward, *John Keats: The Making of a Poet.*) Keats shows the signs of anima involvement: preoccupation with beauty, imagination, ancient tradition, and nature. He was rightly accused by a critic of his day for holding "to that abominable principle of Shelley's—that sensual love is the principle

stinct will insist on the importance of love: that nothing can create without love and that love shows itself as the origin and principle of all things, as in the Orphic cosmogony. Since this perspective seems the one most in keeping with the intentions of the psyche in its configuration as anima, it is this view of creativity which we shall expand upon in regard to the opus of analytical work.

The awakening of the sleeping soul through love is such a recurrent theme in myth, folk tales, and art forms, as well as in subjective experiences, that we may be justified in designating it archetypal. Because the process of psychic development, of soul-awakening and engendering, is a self-description or self-perception of the creation of psyche, we may now be in a position to offer a fundamental myth of psychological creativity and, therefore, of our work and our field as well. The myth which presents this pattern has already been psychologically interpreted by Erich Neumann

---

of things" (Ward, p. 141). Through his own creative imagination he felt he could "enter into the identities of other beings" and find the beauty that was truth. The "essential beauty" of the soul of all things (the *anima mundi*) was revealed through love, through participation or "fellowship with essence" (p. 160). His comparatively late poem, *Ode to Psyche*, came after he had read the Apuleius tale. His worship of the feminine (in the person of Fanny) placed him in danger of identification with Eros (Endymion, Hyperion, or, as Shelly called him, Adonais), but at the same time he was the first to perceive the importance of the tale of Psyche for modern consciousness: "As Keats mused over her story, she became the figure 'of all Olympus' faded hierarchy' who held most meaning for the modern world, in which nature was no longer god-haunted. The sacred region was now . . . the mind of man. . . . Psyche, as woman who had to submit to the trials of 'a world of Circumstances' before her own soul was formed, was its tutelary goddess" (pp. 279–80). Blake provides a second example. As Kathleen Raine puts it, "Eros" is "occasionally spoken of in higher terms as the 'creator' and 'maker' of the soul" (*Blake and Tradition* [Princeton, 1968], I, 204; see also *ibid.*, "Blake's Cupid and Psyche"). Cf. G. Enscoe, *Eros and the Romantics* (The Hague and Paris, 1967), and N. A. Robb, *Neoplatonism of the Italian Renaissance* (London, 1935), last section, on comparison of Romantic and Neoplatonist views of Eros. See, further, D. Bush, *Mythology and the Romantic Tradition in English Poetry* (Cambridge, Mass., 1937).

in his work on Apuleius' tale of Amor and Psyche.[53] His illuminating discussion is one in a long series that extends back to Fulgentius and continues to the present. Scholars of the classics, of literature, of *Märchen,* as well as psychologists, have not been able to leave it alone. Merkelbach has brought together more than a dozen papers written on the tale during the past century,[54] but one could add to his collection of material with discussions of the importance of the theme in the Renaissance and among the Romantics. Scholars of course place emphasis upon historical antecedents and literary parallels. But they tend to neglect the *psychological* context of the tale as originally told in Apuleius' *Golden Ass,* which is a mystery text of personality transformation.[55]

Although Neumann (in his Postscript) notes the Egyptian and Oriental background to the tale of Amor and Psyche, thereby paying his respects to the concerns of classical scholars, he lays his stress rightly upon the unique meaning of this tale for psychology. Merkelbach, on the other hand, seems to miss the fact that his emphasis upon the initiatory aspect of the tale supports rather than detracts from Neumann's psychological view. It is precisely the initiation role of the tale that makes it so revelatory and valuable for the transformation of consciousness in any epoch (as with Keats in the Romantic period, Robert Bridges in the 1890's, or, in our day, as retold by C. S. Lewis in *Till We Have Faces*). In

53. E. Neumann, *Amor and Psyche,* trans. R. Manheim (New York, 1956). The ensuing discussion of this tale is based on his account. References to other interpretations of the tale are given by Neumann in his Postscript. R. Merkelbach (*Roman und Mysterium in der Antike* [Munich and Berlin, 1962], pp. 6–7) adds further references; his thesis, developed in detail and with authority, is that the tale is a mystery text, that Psyche is Isis, and that the whole account belongs within the ritual context of initiation, that is, the tale refers to realities of the soul.

54. G. Binder and R. Merkelbach, *Amor und Psyche* (Darmstadt, 1968).

55. Cf. the interpretation by M.-L. von Franz, *A Psychological Interpretation of "The Golden Ass" of Apuleius* (New York: Spring Publications, Seminar Series 3, 1970).

all discussions about historical origins we must remember that a living mythologem cannot be understood simply through its antecedents and parallels; we need also to take into account its specific relevance and its effects, i.e., we must discover how the human psyche received the tale. We need to remember also that this tale, regardless of its antecedents and parallels, is the only one we have about psyche as such and that it will therefore always be particularly relevant for psychology. However, in distinction to Neumann, who takes the tale as an archetypal expression for the development of the feminine, this myth, which recounts the processes that go on between eros and psyche, may become the centerpiece for a creative psychology as it confronts us today.

For today, the myths which we have inherited, although necessary, are no longer adequate. Today the "unconscious" is no longer a monster but a house pet, taken for granted, or a house god, worshiped with little rites of dream journals, symptom interpretation, and guilt-stimulating and guilt-allaying techniques. Oedipus in 1900 (Freud) and the heroic night-sea-journey in 1912 (Jung) concern the struggles of consciousness with the incestuous family problem and with the unconsciousness of the negative Mother. As these mythemes represent the beginnings of depth psychology, so they represent the opening of human consciousness toward an individual destiny. They give it separateness and personal responsibility. But are we not beyond this phase in ourselves and in our field? In general, our practices confirm that the family problem is old hat [56] and that the relation to the un-

56. To the alarm of moralists and sociologists, the nineteenth-century model of the family is disintegrating. When this problem of the family is conceived only through the Oedipus myth, not only is it old hat, but the family complex becomes insoluble and family life insupportable, necessitating the myth of the hero whose journey toward consciousness leads away from home. But we cannot go home again, not even as repentant prodigals. Nor can we moderns, whose consciousness is characterized by uprootedness, exile, and an "anti-family" bias, attempt to restore a model of the nineteenth-century family by repeating it in our own lives. The reconstitution of family can be based on neither the former metaphor of parent and child nor

conscious in psychology is no longer negative in the way that it was. Separation from it and rebirth through it no longer constitute the heroic task. The heroic age in psychology is past. The hero of consciousness is now further along. Like Hercules, he must serve that Lydian queen, must spin and find his female soul, or like Ulysses must find his way home

---

the new one of a democratic "functional" family. To recreate family in our generation, eros and psyche must have the possibility of meeting in the home; this would favor soul-making and give an altogether different perspective to family relationships. This perspective looks less to the hierarchical connections of parent-child and the issues of early childhood, authority, and rebellion and more to the soul connection, as between brother and sister. Mother-son (Oedipus) and father-daughter (Electra) expose only half of the dual conjunction; where concern for soul is paramount, a relationship takes on more the nature of the brother-sister pair. Compare the *soror* in alchemy and the appellations of "Brother" and "Sister" in religious societies. Compare also the symbolic interrelations in the *I Ching,* where six of the eight hexagrams are "sons" and "daughters," which, to one another, are brothers and sisters. Kinship libido, which, as Jung points out, is behind incest phenomena, would flow on the brother-sister model into the mutuality of soul-making rather than regressively toward parents. As J. E. Harrison says (*Prolegomena to the Study of Greek Religion* [Cambridge, Eng., 1922], p. 655), Eros is also the dance, and the dance is not a hierarchical phenomenon. It takes place between partners. The implications for psychotherapy of the family problem are obvious: if soul-making is the aim, then the equality of the brother-sister relation must be paramount, else eros and psyche cannot constellate. Paternalism and maternalism become clinically unsound if soul-making is the aim. Clinics themselves still retain an unconscious predilection for the old model of family, but the obituary of this family form was written early in the century by Galsworthy and Proust, and by Mann in *Buddenbrooks.* An indication of the new model of family is presented in J. D. Salinger's work. In his Glass family, the brother-sister relations are primary, and the passionate interest and devotion to each other's psychic life provide an example—even a therapeutic example in *Franny and Zooey*—of soul-making through the constellation of eros and psyche in the home. Furthermore, a model of family where eros can meet psyche gives new opportunity to that woman who can no longer fill the nineteenth-century model of motherhood, that breasted, nourishing comforter. The woman of today who is sometimes called the anima, *puella,* or *hetaira* type finds that her natural interest is in the relationships with her family as individual people, her interest constellating eros and psyche.

to Penelope by lingering awhile with Circe. The problems we meet today have brought a "new morality" to theological thinking, and these same problems also require a "new mythology" in psychological thinking. At the first level these problems are ones of love, marriage, and divorce; couples in confusion; homosexuality; erotic promiscuity—the desperate compulsive search for *psychic relatedness* and *erotic identity*, a search which can best be understood in terms of an ectopsychic force, an instinct which has lost its mode of psychization. To look for the problem's source within vicissitudes of the sexual instinct alone is no longer effective in practice or sound in theory. The search for illness makes for illness. We must turn rather to the creative instinct as it appears to the psyche, that is, to the phenomena of love, to find out what has gone so wrong. To meet the new problems in the analysis of today we need a new myth. The tale of Eros and Psyche has advantages over its predecessors; for, although the other myths are not wrong, they are but predecessors. We must see the succession of central myths in psychology as portraying a movement of consciousness. The shift in great classical themes from Oedipus and the hero to Eros and Psyche provides a description by means of metaphor for the archetypal change taking place in the psyche and its field, psychology.

It has been said that myth arises only from ritual, as an account, a tale told after the events, revealing the mystery of what is being enacted. However, a new life-form often comes before it can be understood. The ritual, the new life-form, which gives rise to this new mythical interpretation is—as we mentioned at the outset—the *transference*, those peculiar phenomena of the analytical relationship. No approach to the transference mysteries has as yet been adequate. The Oedipal account is particularly unfortunate. Jung has given us a comprehensive mythical basis for these so frequently erotic phenomena in his rich work on alchemy, especially in regard to the conjunctions of male and female, of which transference is one instance. But our tale of Eros and Psyche, as Neumann was quick to perceive, presents the mythical background in less abstract form.[57] It is explicit, emotional, human; it gives the feeling of how it is enacted in *any* life. Our myth portrays the interplay of eros and psyche as a ritual today taking place between people and *within each person,* i.e., not only in analysis but in life. The main advantage of this myth is that it speaks to all times, and so to our times too, when the need of the soul is for love and the need of eros is for psyche. Today we suffer and are ill from their separation. This myth has also the advantage of validity for man and woman equally. It is a tale of relationship between the sexes, between the component opposites within each sex, and between the sexes and the Gods. Furthermore, it is a tale of redemption, yet it does not leave out torture, suicide, and Hades. An Oedipus complex, like the Oedipus tragedy, has no apparent redemption, nor does the hero of the night-sea-journey, who, becoming *senex*-king, must in the end himself be overthrown. The curse on the hero-king must pass to the next generations, and a psyche mimetic of these archetypal models will be locked in the blind and dark heroic struggle of the family problem.

These predecessors can no longer wholly apply because the heroic age in our field is past. *Psychological consciousness is changing.* Its concern now, when a series of computer accidents could destroy us all, is with the fate of the soul, its sacredness, the possibility of its immortality, the fertility of its imagination (is that the meaning of the flowering field where the figure of Eros is so often found?), and, above all, with erotic identity within psychic relatedness, with the binding connection of love between humans and between

57. Before Neumann, Beatrice Hinkle, an early pupil of Jung's, in her work *The Re-Creating of the Individual* (New York: Harcourt, Brace, 1923), pp. 344–46, already hinted in this direction. She identified the creative *daimon* with the God-like self-figure of the *puer aeternus* in both man and woman who must unite with the feminine soul in "psychic coitus" for psychological creativity.

the human and the divine. Yet this identity and relatedness are altogether beyond the human, depending partly, as do the Gods themselves, upon an inhuman factor, Eros.

Eros

Before redemption, before King can consort with Queen in a *hieros gamos*, each was once a child. We all are children, more often than we like to be. Psychological childhood has been examined enough through the sexual and nutritive instincts. But the creative, too, must have a genetic aspect. Does not creativity also have a childhood? To this theme those children-lovers, Eros and Psyche (and all their mythologemic variants),[58] can speak. By transposing the emphasis from oral and genital to the creative, we do not mean to neglect the role of the child in practical therapy. Instead we return to the childish, less for fulfilling or transforming oral gratifications and polymorphous perversity than for the sake of regaining the childlike. We regard childhood wounds less as the result of nutritive and sexual traumata than as wounds of love. We feel the wounds as abandonment: one's inmost person (soul) bereft of love, oneself abandoned to desire's clutch, one's swollen reservoir of love unwanted, without adequate or permitted recipients. The wounds of love stunt psyche, because the natural weakness and simplicity of its juvenile stage turn into a protective infantilism. These wounds may be redeemed through the childlikeness of loving. Early appearances of the psychization of the creative instinct occurs by means of a child-image, whose essential meaning is self-transformation through its own *vis naturalis*.

But the child's simplicity has two sides: pleasure and joy, and the wound that is unaware of its own pain. The approach

58. Cf. Daphnis and Chloe in the tale of Longus, and the tales collected by H. von Beit, *Symbolik des Märchens*, Vol. II, "Die gegenseitige Erlösung der Geschwister" (Bern: Francke Verlag, 1956).

through eros lets us return to that same innocence, which heals by awakening the child to itself, but now with retrospective distance. How to care for the childishness of psyche (that natural resistance to self-reflection) and how to meet the influences of childish eros (the only natural desires still dominated by the mother complex)[59] can also be evolved from our tale. However, the wound of the child, its not-yetness, is not healed through "bringing it up" with parental attitudes. Rather, this healing, which is the same as growing, takes place through the effect of eros upon psyche and psyche upon eros. They prompt each other. And the healing of the wounds, psychological and erotic, is reflected in the dream motif of the children, yours and mine, who meet and grow up together.

Let us say it: Freud is mistaken in taking childhood primarily sexually. The lovers Eros and Psyche are so often depicted in statuary and gems (from Hellenistic and Etruscan periods consistently into modern times) *as children* that we are obliged to read their love *not* in a sexual sense. To find in childhood's eros and the childish psyche a predominating sexuality is to read backwards—the adult into the child; this transplants or transfers the adult's longings for polymorphous freedom back into the imaginal childhood of Eden. The

59. The "mother-complex of Eros" is represented by the mother-figures in the variations of the Eros myths. In the Apuleius version, Aphrodite is jealous of Psyche and attempts to keep Eros from her. For Eros to be committed to Psyche means the end of "that darling naughty boy" who ranges the world, his mother's playful messenger. The mother of Eros in the *Symposium* myth is Penia, or "need." When negative, this need is the voracious, selfish demand for love; it is never satiated, always "empty." Positively, this same need is the potent motive force within all psychological development, the Faustian drive. Jung writes: "Without necessity nothing budges, the human personality least of all. It is tremendously conservative, not to say torpid. Only acute necessity is able to rouse it. The developing personality obeys no caprice, no command, no insight, only brute necessity; it needs the motivating force of inner or outer fatalities" (*CW*, XVII, par. 293). The individuation impulse that rouses the personality out of its inertia and toward its development would then be Eros who is born of Penia, need, acute necessity.

eros-psyche relation characterized as a union of children gives another meaning to "polymorphous" and the "conjunction." It points to an original polymorphous hermaphroditism that is pregenital and prior to opposites of a bodiless soul and a soulless body, to experiences where opposites are not riven to be rejoined through sexual desire and where play, fantasy, and sexuality, too, are modes of eros and psyche. If they are depicted as children, then eros and psyche meet each other in our childishness and in the kind of imaginal consciousness that belongs with the child.

Besides reconfirming the creative significance of the child,[60] we must consider another image of eros which offers misleading ambiguities. I refer to the early stone representations of the ithyphallic, priapic Eros. Do these images not affirm that love is a derivative of the sexual instinct, that the creative is ultimately sexual?

The Freudian view—for which Lucretius (*De rerum natura* IV) is a precursor—derives love from sexuality.[61] Eros and phallus are reducible to penis. The Freudian error lies not so much in the importance given to sexuality; more grave is the delusion that sexuality is actual sexuality only, that phallus is always only penis. The phallus-penis riddle has long troubled psychology, and this trouble will continue because this riddle is an essential mystery of the psyche and not merely a difficult psychological problem. A revelation of this riddle is at the core of initiation and of the mysteries for men and for women—not only in antiquity. *Initiation as a transformation of consciousness about life involves necessarily*

60. Cf. Jung and Kerényi, "The Myth of the Divine Child," in *Introduction to a Science of Mythology*, trans. R. F. C. Hull (New York and London, 1951).

61. For a comparison of the Freudian and Platonic Eros see T. Gould, *Platonic Love* (London: Routledge & Kegan Paul, 1963). F. M. Cornford ("The Doctrine of Eros in Plato's *Symposium*," in *The Unwritten Philosophy* [Cambridge, Eng., 1950]) finds the "ultimate standpoints of Plato and of Freud seem to be diametrically opposed." In Plato, Eros is a spiritual energy from the outset and only "falls" downward, while with Freud it is sublimated upward.

a transformation of consciousness about sexuality. The absence of initiation and of mysteries in our culture is largely responsible for our preoccupation with sexuality, for our misapprehension and faulty psychization of its manifold nature, and thus for our immense difficulty with erotic identity. The manifold nature of sexuality, the oft-noted plasticity of the instinct and its facile contamination with orality, aggression, and creativity, mean that sexuality is never "always" or "only," never one and the same. It not only changes through the developmental stages shown by Freud, but as an instinct it can be psychized through the shadow, the mother, the child, the anima/animus, etc., offering a variety of perceptions about its nature. The Freudian notion of full genitality is, at best, an account of the sexual instinct perceived through the father archetype. Similarly, the politics of violence and freedom are perceptions of the sexual ideas of Reich and Marcuse through the shadow. Sexuality changes as the Gods who carry its token—the phallus-penis—change through life's phases. Pan, Priapus, Hermes, Dionysus, Zeus, Apollo, Eros, the Kouroi, Kabeiroi, Sileni, Satyrs, Centaurs—each represents a way of initiation into sexual being, each represents a fantasy pattern through which the instinct can be experienced. The figure of Jesus, both textually and iconographically (with rare exceptions or in disguised form), omits this token altogether. As a result, the individual in our culture is given no God-image as example for the initiation into sexual being. One of the many unfortunate consequences of this omission is our continuing Western concern about the nature of eros. Initiation would provide us with mythic patterns for the psychization of this instinct; without this ritual we misapprehend and rationalize our sexual fantasies and become the victim of our complexes.

If we are here confronting a mystery, then those who know these secrets do not speak and those who speak do not know. So we can proceed only from the hints given by similar initiatory mysteries as they unfold in our analytical work, where at one point the development of the psyche calls for discrimination between penis and phallus and between sexuality and eros, while at another moment it becomes equally essential that they merge into a numinous unity. Oedipus and the thousand-faced hero choose only one side of the phallus-penis riddle. The former acts out incest with the mother in the flesh; the latter frequently denies the flesh, and his battle with the mother becomes symbolized by the chastity of sexual denial. We know from practice that love and sexuality are not identical. There is an eros, wrongly called Platonic, that omits the sexual, just as there is a sexuality without eros. They can go their separate ways, usually to the detriment of both. Perhaps we should turn to the anima, as Socrates turned to Diotima, for another approach. Diotima leaves the matter ambiguous in her definition of love: engendering by beauty in both body and soul, or in body, or in soul. This higher feminine wisdom does not attempt an intellectual or moral separation of penis and phallus even on the upward path. (From what we know of Socrates, he never abandoned the level of the alchemical "dog and bitch," even if he seems to have refused Alcibiades its concrete enactment.) The Kundalini yoga, which is a major representation of the upward path, insists upon the circulation downward, continually returning to the anal-genital root of *muladhara;* it is not left behind. Beauty would unite both in yet a further mystery—for what is beauty? The archetypal anima expressed through the voice of Diotima would seem to want to shift the phallus-penis mystery from the level of insoluble problem to that of symbol—an object for and source of continuing fantasy. In this way it becomes a creative symbol and a symbol of the creative, since it unceasingly gives rise to psychic fantasy and reflection.

The phallic aspect of eros points to its male essence. This quality has sometimes been forgotten by analytical psychology, especially when eros is contrasted with logos and is then associated with the lunar and feminine side. Kerényi assures me, however, that the usage of the word in the classical corpus shows a preponderantly masculine context. In addition, the avatars and forms of Eros are masculine; as satyr, boy, arrow or torch, as Kama, Frey, Tammuz—or incarnated into enlightened love as Krishna, Buddha, Jesus—the principle of active love, the function of relationship, of intercourse, of the *metaxy* ("the place between") is masculine. Whether as grace of spirit descending, as Platonic yearning upward, or as Aristotelian principle of universal motion, love summons, starts, quickens, creates into life. Eros has particular mythical connections with Phanes, the light-bringer; with Hermes, the male communicator; with Priapus, the phallic incarnation; with Pan, the male force of nature; with Dionysus, indestructible living energy.

Moreover, his wings, which still remain attached to Eros in the baroque cherubic imagery of our times,[62] represent what the early Greek philosophers formulated as the concept of "self-movement," a primary characteristic of the masculine principle.

We cannot place all love at Aphrodite's altar. Love wears many guises, only some of which are governed by the Goddess; and the Goddess too has many faces, giving different archetypal perspectives to our loving. Nor may we avoid the masculinity of Eros by taking him as bisexual, as union of Hermes and Aphrodite, the original brother-sister hermaphrodite. Although the feminine form of love may be primary and masculine eros may develop out of it, as from an egg, we need to keep some distinction between the masculine Eros of the creative principle and the love represented by the Great Goddess and all her configurations. In the first place, Aphrodite is born of the waters, while the imagery of Eros does not present him associated with the moist element but rather with fire and air.[63] Eros as "son" embodies and

62. J. Kunstmann, *The Transformation of Eros* (Edinburgh and London: Oliver & Boyd, 1964).

63. Psyche's attempt at suicide by drowning may be understood also in terms of the elements associated with the two kinds of love: to plunge into water would mean returning to Aphrodite, who was born of the sea and was worshiped with Poseidon; whereas Eros ignites. "It is death to souls to become water," Heraclitus said (Frag.

brings into action the feminine receptive need, lovingness, and beauty of the mother and is in a sense forever her son. But another quality is shown by the Goddess herself, whether Aphrodite, Cybele, Ishtar, Freya, Kuan-Yin, or Maria: the essence is more passively serving, more accepting, less differentiated. Expressed negatively, this essence is her demanding emotionality and notorious promiscuity; expressed positively, it is her endless fecundity and all-embracing mercy and compassion. To the loss of distinction between the Gods, and between the masculine and feminine, we can attribute our loss of erotic identity. Masculinity has come to mean the rejection of the erotic as effeminate, leading to a compensatory coarsening of eros or to substituting sexuality for it. Women must carry it all: feeling, fantasy, loving, relating, inspiration, and initiative.

The faculty of relationship is emasculated, resulting in a mixture of passivity and promiscuity, without the personal directedness of the Eros arrow, the light of the Eros torch, and the male courage to trust and to follow love as a reality of the masculine, and without the recognition by women that their archetypal femininity is not enough for women. Eros

---

68, Burnet), and in Neoplatonic thought this meant that moist souls descended deeper and deeper into the merely generative principle, a dissolution into primordial nature, over which the Goddess of love, sexuality, and fertility ruled. If salvation depends on the soul's ascent, then the upward idealizing impulse of masculine Eros is also required; its elements are air and fire. Metaphors of fire are frequently used to describe eros (see G. Bachelard, *The Psychoanalysis of Fire,* trans. A. C. M. Ross [London: Routledge & Kegan Paul, 1964]). A psychological account of the eros-fire analogy, their common destructive-creative potential, would be a valuable undertaking, which can obviously only be hinted about here. The alchemical fire which is the basis of the entire transformative process, its stages and management, takes on additional meanings when understood on the analogy with Eros, stated most barely by the apocryphal statement that Jesus as Love is also Fire. In regard to our main theme, the eros-psyche union, the "wetness" of the soul becomes an important consideration for their union. It must be neither too wet, as Heraclitus pointed out, nor too dry and thirsty with longing, else there shall be that passionate conflagration—"for I was flax, and he was flames of fire."

as son—another kind of loving—needs to be born. The development of psyche in man and woman begins—according to our tale—only when one ceases to serve only the principle of feminine love and instead becomes joined with masculine eros.

The familiar question, "Why are men more 'creative' than women?" can be given a psychological answer as well as the usual biological and sociological ones. If eros is the transcending creative principle needed for heightened psychological capacity and if eros is masculine, then it is less difficult (more natural) for a man to gain direct access to this aspect. For a woman it requires an addition to her female identity; she has to bring it out of herself, give birth to it. But first comes impregnation, and so women quest for and cling to relationships in order to become fertilized and to generate. "Castration" for woman then means an identification with Aphrodite and with that single form of feminine loving; for, no matter how fecund and promiscuous, she remains "castrated"—that is, uncreative—without the masculine attributes of Eros. In this way we may understand penis-envy as eros-envy. The Freudian equation penis = child is correct when "child" means eros, the lover-son-child, the creative new masculinity necessary to feminine creativity.

Crucial to any comparison of masculine and feminine loving in regard to its effects upon the psyche will always be the specific role that Venus-Aphrodite plays in the myth of Eros and Psyche. Psyche is the servant of the Goddess, that is, a priestess or one consecrated to that form of love. Some have taken her to be a junior representation of Aphrodite, as Hebe is Hera in youthful aspect, implying that the relationship between the two harbors a Mother-Daughter mystery. However, in this relationship, *Aphrodite is manifestly against the eros-psyche union.* The opposition of Aphrodite is not merely a folk-tale motif of the bad mother who is an obstacle to love. Aphrodite rather expresses the fundamental *antipsychic* component of one sort of loving. Our tale tells of a difference between Aphroditic loving and psychic loving. Aphrodite can of course govern the loving of men or women; that is, she does not govern only some component of human femininity or of the female sex. The tale presents three different constituents of love—Aphrodite, Eros, and Psyche—and their relations. Psyche may well be a devotee of Aphrodite, but she must nevertheless find her own style of love, which is not Aphroditic. Aphrodite would keep both Psyche and Eros for herself—by keeping them from each other. She seems not to want love to find soul or soul to find eros. She not only represents the archetypally antipsychic component in loving, but also she would block the transformation of eros by preventing it from connecting with soul. Because the love of Eros is aimed at Psyche, it becomes the task of psyche in each individual, when under the fiery compulsion, to discriminate, where possible, between those movements of eros which are soul-making and another kind of feminine love which insists that all psychic events are merely servants of Aphrodite's needs. Psyche does indeed insist that love comes first; she lays her life on the line for love—but this love is Eros and not Aphrodite.

Despite this emphasis upon love, we would be mistaken to "locate" the creative spirit of psychology only within the erotic as it is conventionally conceived. By love we do not mean "simply a state observed in souls," [64] the affects and enthusiasms of a psychic function. Eros is not a function of Psyche, any more than the eros we experience is a component of our human individuality, something "inside" our "unconscious" that is subject to development, to analysis, to adaptation. Eros is never something we have; it has us. "What is Love?" Plotinus asks. "A God, a celestial Spirit, a state of mind?" [65] If the last, then we have psychologized the God.

Kerényi has written that Eros "embraces in his essence the phallic, the psychic and the spiritual, and even points

64. Plotinus *Enneads* III. 5. 1.
65. *Ibid.*

beyond the life of the individual being." [66] More than child, more than phallus-penis, more than the moving masculinity of love, Eros stands in the context of Greek consciousness as we reconstruct it as a figure of the *metaxy*, the intermediate region, neither divine nor human, but the principle of intercourse between them. As Robin has put it, Eros in Plato acts as synthesizer and intermediary.[67] Kerényi points out the connections with Hermes which emphasize Eros as communicator and psychopompos.[68] The paucity of early representations of Eros in comparison with other mythological figures places him in another, perhaps less representable world, neither wholly archetypal and divine nor wholly personal and physically human. Eros does not appear as one God among others; he is not a lover, like Zeus. "It is remarkable that in traditional mythology there is no tale ascribing a love-adventure to Eros." [69] The fact that he is not represented like the others indicates that he is less a gestalt than a divine function, less a specific pattern than a means of entering into any pattern and coloring it with eros. We may imagine this function as operating between and among the Gods, and we may conceptualize it by the consubstantiation and unity of the Gods and by their participation with the human. Eros connects the personal to something beyond and brings the beyond into personal experience.[70] It leads (psychopompos) the soul to the Gods and brings some glimmer and sublime horror of the divine into the soul—for we are at our best and worst in love. This *metaxy*, this intermediary region, would best be described today as the *realm of psychic reality* (not

66. C. Kerényi, *Hermes der Seelenführer* (Zurich: Rhein Verlag, 1944), p. 70.

67. L. Robin, *La Théorie platonicienne de l'amour* (thesis, Paris, 1908), Chap. III.

68. Kerényi, *Hermes*.

69. P. Grimal, "Die Bedeutung der Erzählung von Amor und Psyche," in Binder and Merkelbach, *Amor und Psyche*, p. 10.

70. See D. de Rougemont, *Love Declared*, trans. R. Howard (New York: Random House, 1963), on the "Tristan" phenomenon in our loving, which insists that Eros aims always at the beyond and thus cannot be realized here and now.

personal in the usual sense of love), extending at the one end to the cosmogonic spiritual eros and at the other to the physical and phallic.[71]

By erotic experience we mean not merely the seizures of love, the burn or arrow's stab, the *mania*, nor even the yearning upward of unfulfilled life for an erotic ascent by the mystical ladder. These accounts tell only part of the tale, and mainly the part where love is passion. These attempts to describe Eros by the conventionally erotic fail to recognize the *metaxy*, the mediate nature of erotic experience. The compulsive urge of the behavior pattern is self-inhibited by the other end of the same eros spectrum. Eros, as intermediary, creates his own psychic space, his own world between, by a peculiar sort of psychic interference or intervention—"the inexplicable" [72]—which interrupts, redirects, symbolizes behavior, sometimes in the midst of its sequence or even before the pattern is released. Time intervenes between impulse and action. Direct action is impeded, becoming indirect and imaginative. Through this development of inner space, time, and imagination, the psychic world comes into actuality. Light is born. The coming-into-being of the psychic realm or a new aspect of it frequently appears in dreams as the twin motif, the doubling of imagery, the number two in all its ambivalent variety (instead of the singleness of compulsion), the devilish duplicity of consciousness. Once it was called a daimon.

According to Dodds, "psychic intervention" in the Homer epics was attributed to an occult soul, a daimon.[73] The

71. W. Reich's orgone theory is the latest recapitulation of the archetypal idea which attempts by means of Eros to unite cosmic energy with human sexuality.

72. C. Kerényi, *Der grosse Daimon des Symposion* (Amsterdam and Leipzig: Pantheon, 1942), p. 18.

73. E. R. Dodds, *The Greeks and the Irrational* (Boston: Beacon Paperbacks, 1957), pp. 2–18. Plutarch's *De genio Socrates* ("On the Sign or Daimon or Genius of Socrates") is the main post-Platonic text that presents a psychological phenomenology of "psychic intervention."

daimon both instigates an abrupt change of behavior pattern and at the same time gives a conscious reason or verbal account. The daimon was located in or worked through the *thymos* (felt to be in the chest or midriff), which was the seat of emotional consciousness.[74] One could converse with it. The double aspect of the demon/daimon—instigating a pattern of action and inhibiting it—begins with Homer at the origins of Western psychological reflection, where the immortal protective carrier of individual fate, the tutelary spirit or daimon, seems to be inextricably connected with the bestial soul, and continues throughout the Platonic account, even in its end development (*Timaeus*). According to Dodds, separation of these aspects (irrational beast and controlling daimon) yields only fission and rupture and no longer accurately describes empirical man, in whom they are two aspects of one natural force.[75] Demonic impulse and daimon, the spectrum's red end and blue, belong together, as much as do the constructive/destructive poles of creativity, and we can never be sure which end or aspect is the demonic and which the constructive; we know only that *both* belong, that one alone means something is missing, and that inhibition and indirection belong as much to eros as does destruction to creativity. Consciousness cannot escape its origins in ambivalence.

Socratic Eros

For Plato, Eros was a daimon, as were psyche and other vaguely conceived "functions" (*Symposium* 202E). But was the individual experience of the personal daimon, as it appears in its most articulated form in the psychologically creative person of Socrates, itself Eros? If Socrates' daimon—his inner cautionary spirit, the "nay" which "never counsels positive action,"[76] the inexplicable moment of intervening inhibition

74. R. B. Onians, *The Origins of European Thought*, pp. 44–65.

75. Dodds, *The Greeks and the Irrational*, pp. 213–14.

76. P. Friedländer, *Plato*, trans. H. Meyerhoff, Bollingen Series LIX (New York, 1958), Vol. I, *Demon and Eros*, p. 34.

and prescience that engenders psychic reality and also connects with the archetypal powers—is the eros principle, then Eros is the God of psychic reality, the true lord of the psyche, and we have found our paternity, the creative principle which engenders soul and is the patron of the field of psychology.

But what of logos? Is not psychology the *study* of the soul, as indicated by the very words *psychē-logos?* If it should appear that the logos (*pneuma, nous*) component is neglected in our account of psychological creativity, it is not only because today's generation is particularly caught by the problems of the Psyche-Eros myth. Logos appears within eros itself as the inhibiting daimon with which one can speak, which acts as spiritus rector, and which has an upward, pneumatic tendency. But primarily the logos in the paradox of creativity is expressed in the mythic substratum in which Psyche and Eros are themselves immersed. Logos creates the world as tale and as such is a priori to all its contents and happenings. "For myth is the first emanation of the Logos in the human mind, in the human language; and never could the human mind or its language have conceived the Logos, had not the conception been already formed in the myth. Myth is the archetype of every phenomenal cognition of which the human mind is capable." [77]

The best example for our point that it is eros rather than logos which creates psyche is the figure of the Platonic Socrates. The Platonic and Neoplatonic writings bear witness to the assertion that in Socrates the voice which spoke through his personal daimon was that of eros. Socrates: that model of psychologist, whose first concern was with the health of the soul, who had the gifts of clairvoyance, prophecy, and other psychic powers, which he attributed to the effect of the daimon, whose psychological anima showed in his susceptibility to and concern with beauty and in his mythopsycho-

77. H. Broch, "Introduction" to R. Bespaloff's *On the Iliad,* trans. M. McCarthy, Bollingen Series IX (New York, 1947), p. 15.

logical imagination, and who, by teaching creatively through dialectic and his own example, was a psychopompos. Robin, Cornford, Gould, Dugas, and especially Friedländer have done the scholarly work in support of this view.[78]

Friedländer refers to Proclus' statements: "Socrates is at once an erotic and a demonic person. . . . The demon is to him altogether responsible for love." [79] Gould says that the subject of the *Symposium* is "the identity of desire and learning, of love and philosophy, Eros and Socrates." [80] In the dialogues, Socrates repeats, in various ways: "I say of myself that I am ignorant about all things except the nature of love." [81] Does this not imply that the ignorance or evil which he would purge from the soul through his conversations is not ignorance of truth or of the right definition or of what is fitting? It is an ignorance of Eros—the only thing which he himself knows anything about. Eros is the very means of true cognition, binding together in synthesis all psychic faculties of cognition, conation, and affectivity.

Friedländer notices that Eros has a double aspect. "The Socratic 'daimonion' must have been for Plato a part of the demonic, as the name indicates . . . ; daimonion and *Eros*, the inhibiting and driving force, cannot but appear as fundamentally akin." [82]

Those twins, compulsion and inhibition, are familiar enough in all creative efforts where one is both driven and blocked, enthusiastic and critical, on fire and fearful. In the language of the *Symposium*, one is both "full" and "empty," descriptions directly referring to Eros. Our tradition's earliest

78. Cornford, *The Unwritten Philosophy;* Gould, *Platonic Love;* L. Dugas, *L'Amitié antique* (Paris, 1894); Friedländer, *Plato,* Vol. I.

79. Friedländer, *Plato,* I, 44.

80. Gould, *Platonic Love,* p. 23. In this Gould follows M. Ficino, who writes (*Commentaire sur le "Banquet" de Platon, VII,* 2, ed. R. Marcel (Paris, 1956): ". . . when Plato portrays Eros, it is the portrait of Socrates that he paints, and it is by means of the person of Socrates that he describes the figure of the God, as if love and Socrates were absolutely similar" (my translation).

81. *Symposium* 177D; cf. *Theages* 128B; *Lysis* 204B.

82. Friedländer, *Plato,* I, 44.

conceptual division of the inner promptings of human beings appears in Homer's language as *thymos* and *psyche;* the first is passionate and related etymologically to "smoke"; the second is cognate with "breath" and implies "cold." The creative may be a single urge, yet we are always "of two minds." [83] Eros is both direct, like fire and arrow, and indirect, like the wreathed garland, also its symbol.

The compulsion-inhibition ambivalence shows in ritual, in play, and in mating, eating, and fighting patterns, where for each step forward under the urge of compulsion there is a lateral elaboration of dance, of play, of ornamentation—a "breather," which delays, heightens tension, and expands imaginative possibility and aesthetic form, making patterns, delightful and devious, cooling the compulsion of inborn release mechanisms for direct fulfillment in relation to the stimulus object—whether it is to be copulated with, eaten, or killed. The opus is elaborated into a gestalt even while the gestalt is being closed by the elaboration. The indirect movement is not a pattern of flight, though it may be intertwined with the reflective. It is not, essentially, a bending-back or a turning-away from the object; it is rather a continued ad-

83. The hypothesis that compulsion and inhibition are polar components of the same functional complex I have elaborated in specific regard to masturbation and its natural inhibition through fantasy and conscience ("Towards the Archetypal Model for the Masturbation Inhibition," *Journal of Analytical Psychology,* XI [1966]). This model may also be fruitful for regarding the phenomenon of ambivalence. Compulsions, as they are called in psychopathology, often show similar patterns of driving urge and inhibition wound round each other. In these conditions the inhibition—rather than performing as a ritualistic fulfillment through the lateral and slowed elaboration of the compulsive end of instinct and a transmutation of its energy—becomes mere blockage, an unimaginative prohibition. Instead of reflecting the compulsion, the inhibition appears as obsessive thoughts, at the root of which are often "death" fantasies. We may suppose that the difficulty of compulsion and inhibition may be at core an erotic one. The pairs full-empty (Plato), *accessum-recessum* (Stoics and Scholastics), diastole-systole (Romantics), like the all-or-nothing reaction, express the fundamental dynamics of the archetypes. As they are structured with two sides, so their dynamics are ambivalent.

vance upon it, but indirectly and *with a different timing,* and it overcomes compulsion, yet fulfills its need in another way. (We may speculate that this phenomenon, occurring even in higher animals—which Lorenz suggests makes aggressive behavior patterns susceptible to transformation through love,[84] and which Portmann, in his masterly work, refers to as the creative spirit—may be none other than Eros, opening the middle region, the *metaxy,* wherever there is life, creating psychic reality with endless imaginative and aesthetic complexities to which the human being responds through the sensual delight of his own erotic nature.)

What in Homer Dodds calls "psychic intervention," what in Plato Friedländer calls Socrates' "inner voice of warning," [85] and what is associated by Onians with the individual *genius*[86] appears in Christian contexts as the still, small voice of the immanent God—conscience.[87] Curiously, the phenomenology of conscience, as well as the history of the conscience concept, shows that it, too, is an inhibiting function. Conscience does not tell us what to do; it tells us what not to do. It says "no." From this inner voice, variously named but similarly experienced, originates guilt. As Dodds says, the daimon is the true carrier of guilt in the deepest sense of self-injury, which is at the same time an injustice to one's *moira,* one's individual portion of fate. So Socrates can say, concerning his coming death: "Since the prophetic voice, the sign of the god, did not once oppose me during my defense, it follows that what happened to me must be something good" (*Apol.* 40A–C). He is guiltless because the inhibiting voice did not impede his actions. His death was not opposed by his daimon. Death was rather the final expression of his

84. K. Lorenz, *Das sogenannte Böse.*

85. Friedländer, *Plato,* II, 152.

86. Onians, *The Origins of European Thought,* pp. 162 ff. (However, by Roman times the *genius* seems to have ascended from the midriff to the head.)

87. Cf. *Conscience,* edited by the Curatorium of the C. G. Jung Institute, Zurich; Studies in Jungian Thought (Evanston: Northwestern University Press, 1970).

union of eros and psyche, his final constructive-destructive act, his evidence of soul-making, witnessed by his faith in the immortality of the psyche and by the exemplary effect on those around him.

By not inhibiting the death, Socrates' daimon acted in accordance with eros psychopompos, the "Eros with crossed legs and torch reversed . . . the commonest of all symbols for death" in later antiquity and in Orphic thought.[88] Eros leads the soul, not only as the Freudian life-instinct separated from and contrary to Thanatos; Eros is also a face of Thanatos, has death within it (the inhibiting component that holds back life), and leads life into the invisible psychic realm "below" and "beyond" mere life, endowing it with the meanings of the soul given by death.

The ancient locus of this inhibition within the emotional charges of the *thymos* compares with the proximity of *manipura* and *anahata* in Kundalini yoga, where the daimon would be experienced as the fleeting signals of feeling that inhibit the compulsive simplicities of dense and smoky *manipura*. The daimon would be the detached aspect of the emotional charge, aerated and of the heart, as the light plays through the fire. So Phanes is both bull-headed and enlightener.

Finally, it is the daimon which works the effects in the other, not only by awakening his psyche but by igniting the other's daimon as well. Malraux describes the creative impulse in the arts: it leaps like a spark from one artist to another through the work of art. It is the creative, and this alone, that kindles the creative in the other through the opus. Applied to our theme of the psychologically creative, we are obliged to conclude: eros alone calls out love. It is as if love had in its nature a mission to ignite, educate, and convert, spreading its mercurial fire in the soul, transferring itself

88. A. B. Cook, "Orphic Theogonies and the Cosmogonic Eros," in *Zeus* (Cambridge, Eng., 1914–40), II, ii, 1045. Cf. E. Wind, "Amor as a God of Death," in *Pagan Mysteries in the Renaissance* (Harmondsworth: Peregrine, 1967), pp. 152–70.

from person to person. It is as if eros thrives in transference, demanding it for its creative work, both as fuel to fire and as *complicatio* for its devious indirection.

Art, mission, and transference make eros manifest; so does education. For Socrates, all true teaching—teaching that was not sophistical and bought and sold—was possible only through the daimon of eros. The daimon alone determines whether the educative association between two people is possible or not.[89] If true education comes through love, there is implied a reverse proposition: love proves its true nature when it educates. Friedländer says, "For him true love is love that educates."[90] We know that, for Socrates, love and teaching go together, that love is teaching itself, and that "there was no philosophy without friendship or love."[91] The awakening of the psyche depends altogether upon the eros daimon. The psyche is educated, led out of its chrysalis, through recollecting its preexistent wings, that is, its a priori relationships with the divine archetypal nature of all things. We experience these through the anima's cosmic overtones and associations with nature and with the past. The educative process of love through which anima becomes psyche begins when the soul senses its modern isolation, starts to long for the archetypal connections and cultural roots of tradition, and needs to be in touch again with the unity of all things, which is psychic wholeness or the health of the soul, "our first concern." This yearning is suffering; it is experienced as transference and is a sign of soul sickness and also of movement. Eros gives the psyche this yearning, which is its educative impetus. Eros both teaches and heals.

Eros has a mission with the soul. Socrates' stress upon "care of the soul" is, according to Jaeger, nothing less than *psychēs therapeia.* "Socrates always uses the word *soul* with exceptional emphasis, a passionate, a beseeching urgency. No

89. Friedländer, *Plato* ("Theages"), II, 148; see also Plato *Theataetus* 151A.
90. Friedländer, *Plato,* I, 196.
91. *Ibid.* ("Lysis"), p. 104.

Greek before him ever said it in that tone. We can feel this is the first appearance in the Western world of what we now, in certain connexions, call the soul." [92] His philosophizing is not abstract thought, definitions, and eristics but a driven mission to move the soul toward awareness of its archetypal background.

The teaching-healing effect of Socrates is described in detail by Theages in the apocryphal Platonic dialogue of that name. Does it not echo our contemporary experiences of transference in therapy or in any intense involvement:

> One thing, Socrates, I must say which you will find unbelievable, but which is nevertheless true. I never learned anything from you, as you well know. However, I profited when I was with you; even when I was only in the same house, without being in the same room; and when I was in the same room, I would have my eyes fixed upon you while you talked, and I felt that I profited more than when I looked elsewhere. But most of all I profited when I was seated next to you and when I touched you.[93]

Psyche-Eros in Felt Experience

Let us return now to ourselves. We can draw some inferences from our individually felt experiences, which are always the final touchstone in psychological discussion. We recognize psychologically creative eros in the moments of fullness in the opening flow of the erotic and in the movements toward the soul, phallic even in their sudden leaping, the intercourse that overcomes distance, the penetration toward engendering. But we also recognize the creative in the daimon when we feel the emptiness of need, the poverty of having nothing to give, of closing, of the cautionary daimon's "no." Demon and daimon are one; if we suppress the com-

92. W. Jaeger, *Paideia,* trans. G. Highet (Oxford, 1944), II, 40. Cf. Plato *Protagoras* 313A, *Apology* 29D–30B, *Gorgias* 464B, *Laches* 185E.

93. My rendering of Dugas's version in *L'Amitié antique,* p. 58.

pulsion, we lose touch with the guiding voice of the daimon. Socrates had his creative daimon all his life, perhaps because, as he says at the conclusion of his speech in the *Symposium* (212B), he has worshiped *all* the elements of love and will go on paying homage to the power of love all his life. *By accepting the demonic, he kept contact with the daimon.* We can hear the inhibiting "no" only when we are open to the compulsion, which leaves us with the paradox that love and fear go together, forming a kind of awe, transforming the psyche's awareness, giving it a religious sense that it must tread with care, fearfully, joyfully.

Fear also belongs to eros and speaks through the *thymos*, inhibiting by means of psychic intervention. This fear keeps us close to humble reality; it is the cautionary cramp inhibiting the *superbia*, the *Hochgefühl*, of the ascending, winged Eros.[94] "Take care," "go slow," "do nothing" are also words of eros. Such denial (i.e., denial by the same voice which affirms) arouses the anima to differentiate its psychological needs. The anima becomes aware of its intentions, thereby building distance in time and space and expanding the realm of psychic reality, which it does, for instance, by observing its erotic fantasies, bodily feelings, moods, and flights. The psyche, by containing this increased tension, can transform eros and teach it to differentiate the aims of its drive. The psyche may also mirror, take the lead with its lamp, or lay the thread through the labyrinth, finding the way through the outer relationship or inner puzzle. Fear, as the daimon's inhibition of the demonic, is the beginning of psychology. Rejection, impotence, and frigidity may also be eros ex-

94. F. Lasserre, in *La Figure d'éros dans la poésie grecque* (thesis; Lausanne, 1946), pp. 220 ff., examines the tradition of winged figures in Greek myth and relates the wings of Eros to velocity (Homer), to night, to the harpies, and especially to the winds (Eos, Boreas, Zephyr). Where wing = wind, the exhilaration of the eros experience takes on a dangerous quality: the rush of being swept away by an overpowering demon. Thus, Lasserre speaks of love's wings, not in the modern sense of an angelic uplifting by an impotent spirit, but as a "monstrous" and "tempestuous" energy.

pressions, part of the daimon's "nay." This fear is as much the spontaneous gift of eros as is the erotic impulse itself. Trusting and doubting, yielding and denying, opening and closing, back and forth, are part of the interplay of eros and psyche, each bringing the other into being, from the coyest flirtation of children to the rhythm of opposites in the *mysterium coniunctionis.*

The importance of fear has been given too little true psychological attention. We have had either physiological investigations, initiated mainly by Cannon; sexualized interpretations, in accordance with Freudian anxiety theory; or philosophical descriptions, such as existential dread. The biblical statement that fear is the beginning of wisdom is a significant psychological statement. Fear is not merely something wrong, to be overcome with courage, or, at best, an instinctual protective device, but is rather something right, a form of wise counsel. Jung, in his unpublished "Seminar Notes," speaks of fear *(phobos)* rather than power as the true opposite of eros. We are familiar with this idea from I John 4, where fear is related to love as its enemy. Love stirs fear. We are afraid to love and afraid in love, magically propitiating, looking for signs, and asking for protection and guidance. Even if all the world loves a lover, the world also fears the lovers for the destruction which accompanies their joy. When Psyche panics in our tale and would throw herself into the river, she is saved by Pan, who is both the panic and the goaty erotic compulsion. Thanatos and Eros are not so far apart as Freud would have us believe. At the deepest level of fear an eros appears, like the frenzied copulations in times of terror and war or like the nightmares brought on by Pan, which are also erotic. Fear seems an inherent necessity to the eros experience; where it is absent, one might well doubt the full validity of the loving.

A consequent of this fear is that we can trust eros. Instinct contains its own self-regulator, eros its own daimon. The compulsion is checked by the counsel of wise fear—elaborating, ritualizing; if the daimon is unheeded, the compulsion is checked by the counsel of neurosis and symptom. Even if we could, we do not need to control the creative in psychology with prohibitive ego strictures and technical rules, because the daimon, when given trust, can steer by means of the natural inhibitions. We need, however, to heed them: to receive, listen, and contain; we need to hold and hang onto the cautionary cramps, the coolness. Then eros need not be fought, controlled, or transformed into something nobler. *Its goal is always, in any case, psyche.* We are obliged to trust eros and its goal. Can anyone live with authenticity unless he believes and trusts in the basic meaningfulness and rightness of the movements of his love? We can be transformed by eros, but we cannot directly transform it, no matter how hard we will, since it is the upward impulse or, in Aristotelian language, the actualizing, self-realizing motion which performs the transformations in the psyche. The same ascension and collapsing dejection occur in the individual's eros experience of glorious inflation each time he "falls" in love.

As reflection is inward, or leaning back and away, and as activity is directed outward and toward, so the creative—conceived as eros in Orphic, Platonic, and Neoplatonic thought—is an *upward* motion.[95] The axis is vertical: *Omnis amor aut ascendit aut descendit* (Augustine). Classical writers never fail to note this in their warnings against the descent toward the pole of *physis* and flesh. Therefore we find in the eros literature the recurrent symbols of the fallen sparks, the ladder, the ascending fire, the wings, the Olympian goal of immortality. The transcendent function as that aspect of the individuation process which surmounts incommensurable opposites by creating symbols is also to be attributed to eros as the upward impulse. Eros as synthesizer, binder, and intermediary brings two realms together; he forms symbols. Eros is more than *dynamis* of symbol-making and of the transcendent function; to eros must be attributed

95. See A. Nygren, *Agape and Eros,* trans. P. S. Watson (London: S.P.C.K, 1953), for a lengthy treatment of the ascending Eros.

the urge of the process itself, which Jung describes in the traditional language of the upward spiral. The emphasis upon the upward movement places Jung's description of individuation (as a process of Socratic dialectical activity with visions of immortality) close to the pre-Christian tradition of eros. This contrasts with typical Christian thought, which indicates that redemption through the descent of grace depends more on *caritas* and *agape* and less upon eros.

The question of trust and betrayal in the eros-psyche relation is better asked of psyche than of eros, although in antiquity storm warnings against Eros were raised, and he was called in the tragedies "a hostile god" and in the lyric poets "a madman, liar, bringer of woe, tyrant, deceiver" [96] or "a god to be dreaded for the havoc he makes of human life . . . a tiger, not a kitten to sport with." [97] This description of eros fits when it is still not contained by psyche, still fickle and possessed by the mother complex, owing mainly to an anima not yet emerged from false values, vain notions of beauty, and psychological uncertainty about itself as soul and therefore not yet a vessel which can adequately contain the creative force of eros.

Because destructiveness composes one pole of the creative instinct, psychic development proceeds through prolonged experiences of erotic destruction. The anima is taught by the openings of love and by the sudden shifts, frustrations, and deceptions of the erotic impulse that it is both overwhelming and unreliable, wholly engaged and then gone. The movement from anima to psyche means discovery of the psychic aspect in erotic perversions and in love's vicious hatreds and cruelties, and not mere reaction to them with innocence, resentment, and anima tears.

Unless there is an interplay with erotic destruction, psyche remains virgin. We have discussed this virginal psyche in the hysterical symptoma, the overeffeminacy of a psyche still

96. Gould, *Platonic Love*, p. 24.
97. A. E. Taylor, *Plato*, 5th ed. (London: Methuen, 1948), p. 65.

struggling to emerge from its anima chrysalis. But the virgin psyche is not merely anima-like. It is marked mainly by a displacement of instinctual libido, so that the role of the creative is depotentiated and usurped by other drives,[98] principally by reflection. One commits the sin of mistaking reflection for creativity and thus inadequately defines the aim of psychotherapy as "becoming conscious." [99] Nietzsche has warned that insight for its own sake is wrong: "One day we shall be completely entangled in it." And which of us by taking thought can add one cubit to his stature?

Psyche joined with reflection is a union of sames without the tension of opposites; psyche is itself the feminine reflector, the mirror of the moon-mind. A union of sames brings two together that should not have been divided. It knits and heals; but it does not create, because the radical perplexity of oppositions and their destructive uneasy effects on each other

98. *CW*, V, par. 199: "Experience shows that instinctual processes of whatever kind are often intensified to an extraordinary degree by an afflux of energy, no matter where it comes from. This is true not only of sexuality, but of hunger and thirst too. One instinct can temporarily be depotentiated in favour of another instinct, and this is true of psychic activities in general." Cf. *Psychological Types* (*CW*, VI, par. 690), Definition 8: "Every instinct, every function, can be subordinated to another. The ego instinct or power instinct can make sexuality its servant, or sexuality can exploit the ego."

99. " 'Reflection' should be understood not simply as an act of thought, but rather as an attitude. . . . As the word itself testifies ('reflection' means literally 'bending back'), reflection is a spiritual act that runs counter to the natural process; an act whereby we stop, call something to mind, form a picture, and take up relation to and come to terms with what we have seen. It should, therefore, be understood as an act of *becoming conscious*" (*CW*, XI, p. 158, n. 9). Even if Jung here points to the importance of reflection for consciousness, he does *not* identify the two. Reflection is *one* of the ways, "an act" of the process of becoming conscious which surely requires acts (doing, feeling, sensing) other than reflection. Furthermore, the fear and inhibition of the daimon present a reflective moment within eros itself, so that both creativity and even "becoming conscious" may result from the eros impulse alone, without benefit of psychic reflection. We see this in the highly conscious products of art, politics, or science, which may have in them no reflection of a psychological nature and are yet creative (even if not *psychologically* creative).

are never constellated. Psyche joined with reflection produces the *unio mentalis*, or mental health. However, the soul not connected to body through eros is still out of it—aware, yes, but unawakened; mental, yes, but with a consciousness not of the heart and *thymos*. Hence the importance of the phallic aspect of eros, the foolish downward movement which brings psyche down to body and burns the wings of the soul in the fires of living and which, at the same time, curiously uplifts and idealizes.[100]

Fascination with dreams and visions shows the virgin psyche at the brim of discovery but still reflecting. We should not confuse psychological creativity with beautiful interior imagery. Hallucinogenic drugs can turn inscapes on at will, giving us the "hip-gnosis" of today's counterparts of antiquity's long-haired *puer*-priests of the great mother. The illusions and visions indicate less a fertile psyche than the fertility of the great mother's teeming natural richness and her alluring way of satisfying her children's oral needs with visual feedings. Dreams, inscapes, and visions are not creative; they are but aspects of reflection until they cross the threshold of erotic involvement.

Creative imagination that bespeaks the imaginal realm—upon which we shall have more opportunity to expand in Part Two—results from vitality and passion. It is born in blood from the awakened, not the dreaming, psyche. True imagining is neither an introverted retreat to fantasy nor a manic extraverted notion of creativity as physical productivity. True imagination may use the mirrors of reflection, but its emotional impulse is the creative instinct. It is implied in *Symposium* 202E that Eros is needed for participation in the imaginal world through which man has intercourse with the Gods—whether awake, asleep, or in a trance, whether in

100. C. Kerényi, *Hermes der Seelenführer*, pp. 69–70: "Vorausbestimmung, Gerichtetsein durch Urbilder, Idealismus gehört zum Eros. . . . Von der Welt der hermetischen Möglichkeiten aus gesehen, erscheint Eros trotz seines umfassenden Wesens beschränkt: ein etwas idealistischer und dümmer geratener Sohn des Hermes."

visions, in prophecy, or in the mysteries. From analytical experience we know that mere imagery or even the active observation of fantasy without vivid libidinal participation has little effect.

The imaginal is entered primarily through interested love; it is a creation of faith, need, and desire. We must want it passionately even if we cannot will it. From alchemy, from Avicenna, from Taoist yoga, from Paracelsus and Albertus Magnus we have been given distinctions between false and true imagining, which, so it was said, goes from the heart (place of *thymos* and daimon) to the heart of the universe, the sun, and thence to the macrocosm. True imagining goes beyond the *unio mentalis* of our microcosmic fantasy life, the reflective broodings of the mind developing its "consciousness."

This imaginal consciousness is hermaphroditic, uniting masculine and feminine polarities, however they may be constellated at that moment. (We shall return to hermaphroditic consciousness in more detail in Part Three.) Such consciousness differs from the usual ego-consciousness of reflection. Because the latter discriminates, it tends to be divisive, making heirarchies of better and worse; and its continuity depends much upon the will. On the other hand, imaginal consciousness, by bringing together incommensurables, is symbolic. The hermaphrodite shows the unifying and thus healing eros aspect of this sort of consciousness. Moreover, since any union of opposites is paradoxical, it cannot be willed. This consciousness simply happens—as moments of synchronicity happen, as symbols happen.

Comparable to the painter who puts his life into paint, sacrificing to the limiting demands of the opus, is the psychologist dedicated to soul-making. But when this marriage to the work means "seeing the world psychologically," it is based on reflection, which means depotentiating the erotic affects of love, taking only a part of it and turning it into the mental instrument of analysis. This is a false marriage, and the psyche of analysis remains a virgin bride, looking out the window at life in the street, interpreting, understanding, compassionately empathizing. The soul is analytically reflected upon, not lived, not loved.

The specific technique by which the creative can be depotentiated in favor of the reflective is called, in analytical psychology, "withdrawing projections." This process is, of course, essential if ego-consciousness is to work through its transferences; but it is also the virtue that becomes a vice when the image is preferred to the person or the meaning is favored over the experience. Then reflection becomes entangled in the paranoid misapprehensions of the ego, which seeks to control the natural involvement in the world by an ambitious ideal of becoming "objectively conscious" about it. Only if carried through radically can the reflective withdrawal or projections prove its true value. First one must withdraw the primary projection upon the ego itself as the sole carrier of consciousness achieved through reflection. This leads to immersion in the projected field, surrendering to it in love, entering into it to such an extent that one becomes oneself a projection of the imaginal realm and one's ego becomes a fragment of a myth. Reflections may then occur just as spontaneously as projections, but they will no longer be an achievement of the will and the ego, which seek to *make* consciousness by withdrawing projection.

These observations upon reflection lead us to consider "therapeutic eros," the name often given to compassionate empathy. Is there a special sort of eros which belongs to the therapeutic profession, an eros which is "good for you"? Socrates said that the human psyche has something divine about it (Xenophon *Memorabilia* IV. 3. 14) and that one's first interest is to look after its health (Plato *Apologia* 30A–B). We know from both Plato and Jung that its health is its psychological integrity and that eros is the integrating factor which binds, holds together, and *conjoins opposites.*[101]

101. Love is a unity that makes for unity. Cf. Freud's definition of Eros: ". . . sexual or life instincts, which are best comprised under the name *Eros;* their purpose would be to form living substance into

This eros is neither kindness nor compassion nor therapeutic concern; it is love as a whole which makes for wholeness. And whole love includes hatred as creativity includes destructiveness. So-called therapeutic eros has always something about it of condescending *agape*, of mothering and fathering; it is only good. How can it close a wound from below and within? Eros itself departs from so-called therapeutic responsibility because it is always curiously weaker than the problem it must deal with. It has something in it of the child—foolish, spontaneous, ruthless in its directness, but playful. So it can recreate from within the wounds. It does not desire the other person's welfare or health; it desires the other person. What heals is our needs for each other, including mutually destructive components, not your need to be healed, which calls forth my compassion. Therapy is love itself, the whole of it, not a special part of it. Again we can refer to "Socrates":

> For Love, that renowned and all-beguiling power, *includes every kind of longing* for happiness and for the good [*Symposium* 205D].
>
> . . . and this is why I cultivate and worship *all the elements of Love* myself, and bid others do the same [*Symposium* 212B].
>
> Perhaps I can assist you in your pursuit of the beautiful and the good because I am a lover myself. For when I desire someone, I give the *whole strength of my being* to be loved by him in return for my love, to arouse longing in

ever greater unities, so that life may be prolonged and brought to higher development" ("The Libido Theory" [1922], in *Collected Papers*, ed. J. Strachey [London: Hogarth Press, 1950], V, 135). Also Tillich: "Love is the drive towards the unity of the separated. . . . Love manifests its greatest power there where it overcomes the greatest separation." "The ontology of love leads to the basic assertion that love is one." The *eros* quality of love, he says, "strives for a union with that which is a bearer of values because of the values it embodies" (*Love, Power, and Justice* [New York: Oxford Paperbacks, 1960], pp. 25–30). See also *Aurora Consurgens* (attributed to Thomas Aquinas), ed. M.-L. von Franz (New York and London, 1966), for similar passages from Thomas Aquinas on "union is the work of love."

> return for my longing, and to see my desire for companionship reciprocated by his desire [*Memorabilia* II. 6. 28; all italics added].

The whole of it includes my *himeros*, my desire toward you, my wanting something with you, and my foolish idealizations that you get better, grow, transform, and find your wings; it includes also my *pothos*, that yearning, needing, longing on your account, and my need for your *anteros*,[102] your answering love in return—all these things that embarrass me to admit that I am so involved with you, the other person, or with myself and my own soul. This love is always there, as the creative instinct is always there potentially in all of us, so that "in reality, we are all lovers all of the time." [103] Or, in the words of Socrates: "I could not name a time when I was not in love with someone." [104] Being in love reveals, as Gould says, "what we are really after"; for being in love is, following the *Phaedrus* (250D–252C), "really growing one's spiritual wings again," since "l'âme, dans son

102. The importance of the answering response for the development of love is a favorite theme in the pictorial representations of Eros and Anteros (contesting for a palm, wrestling with a cord, etc.). Themistius (fourth century A.D.) repeats an older legend that "Venus was troubled because Love, her son, was not growing, to which reply was made that only a brother could cure him. This was Anteros, who is placed opposite Love, his peer." See Guy de Tervarent, "Eros and Anteros or Reciprocal Love in Ancient and Renaissance Art," *Journal of the Warburg and Courtauld Institutes*, XXVIII (1965). Pausanias reports that in a temple to Aphrodite in Megara there were statues to Eros, Himeros, and Pothos. According to Harrison, *Prolegomena*, p. 638, the trinity does not really obtain, even though she discusses another example of it in a vase painting. It evidently was, as it is now, difficult to differentiate Eros into aspects, as if it by nature works toward wholes, is whole-making. The differentiation of love into kinds and "faces" is an exercise, even if indulged in by most writers on the subject, that leads away from the fundamental *unity* of eros which Socrates so stresses. Plato (*Cratylus* 420) distinguishes the faces of love, but ironically and by means of an etymological game, which eventually ends up showing that truth does not reside in these sorts of distinctions. The mighty demon Eros does not present the soul in one face only but as a complex unity which itself makes for unity.

103. Gould, *Platonic Love*, p. 47.

104. Cf. Friedländer, *Plato*, I, 46 (Xenophon *Symposium* IV. 27 f.).

acte essentiel, est donc amour," and "soul is wholly soul when it is a loving one." [105]

Therefore, therapy is love of soul. The teaching and healing therapist—if we use the Socratic-Platonic model of philosopher who teaches and heals—is on the same plane of being as the lover; both take their origins from the same primordial impulse behind their seeking (*Phaedrus* 248D).[106] Therapy as love of soul is a continual possibility for anyone, waiting upon neither the therapeutic situation nor a special "therapeutic eros," a misnomer which is a construct of reflection. This love would show in therapy through the spirit with which we approach the phenomena of the psyche. No matter how desperate the phenomena, eros would keep connected to the soul and seek a way through. This spirit of resourceful inventiveness and creative intelligence, our tales of Eros tell us, he has inherited from his father, either Poros or Hermes. Love not only finds a way, it also leads the way as psychopompos and is, inherently, the "way" itself.[107] Seeking psychological connections by means of eros is the way of therapy as soul-making. Today this is a way, a *via regia*, to the unconscious psyche as royal as the way through the dream or through the complex.

Creative insights are thus not only the reflective ones; they are those *vivencias*, those exciting perceptions arising from involvement. Psychological perceptions informed by eros are life-giving, vivifying. Something new comes into being in oneself or the other. Love blinds only the usual outlook; it

105. The quotes are from Gould, *Platonic Love*, p. 48; A. E. Taylor, *Plato*, p. 309; Robin, *La Théorie platonicienne de l'amour*, p. 167 (cf. Augustine: "No one is who does not love" [*Sermo* 34]); and Friedländer, *Plato*, I, 194.

106. In the light of the *Phaedrus* equation, philosopher = lover, we can understand from another perspective an apocryphal statement of Jung's that was reported by Lewis Mumford (*The New Yorker*, May 23, 1964, p. 162): " 'When I die,' Jung smilingly told a friend of mine, 'probably no one will realize that the old man in the coffin was once a great lover.' "

107. Kerényi, *Hermes der Seelenführer*, p. 66: "Metis' Sohn Poros (übersetzt etwa: der Klugheit Sohn namens 'Weg')."

opens a new way of perceiving, because one can be fully revealed only to the sight of love. Reflective insights may arise like the lotus from the still center of the lake of meditation, while creative insights come at the raw and tender edge of confrontation, at the borderlines where we are most sensitive and exposed—and, curiously, most alone. To meet you, I must risk myself as I am. The naked human is challenged. It would be safer reflecting alone than confronting you. And even the favorite dictum of reflective psychology—a psychology which has consciousness rather than love as its main goal—"Know thyself," will be insufficient for a creative psychology. Not "Know thyself" through reflection, but "Reveal thyself," which is the same as the commandment to love, since nowhere are we more revealed than in our loving.[108]

Nowhere, too, are we more blind.[109] Is love blindfolded, in statuary and painting, only to show us its compulsion, ignorance, and sensuous unconsciousness? Love blinds in order to extinguish the wrong and daily vision so that another eye may be opened that perceives from soul to soul. The habitual perspective cannot see through the dense skin of appearances; how you look, what you wear, how you are. The blind eye of love sees through into the invisible, making the opaque mistake of my loving transparent. I see the symbol you are and what you mean to my death. I can see through the blind and foolish visibility that everyone else sees and into the psychic necessity of my erotic desire. I discover that *wherever* eros goes, something psychological is happening, and that wherever psyche lives, eros will inevitably constellate. Like the early Eros figures, I am naked: visible, transparent, a child. Like the later Amor figures, I am blind: seeing none of

108. Cf. Ortega y Gasset, *On Love,* trans. T. Talbot (New York: World, Meridian Books, 1957), pp. 82 f., for the theme that love is revelation of self. "In their choice of lovers both the male and female reveal their essential nature."

109. E. Panofsky, "Blind Cupid," in *Studies in Iconology* (Oxford, 1939; New York, 1962); E. Wind, "Orpheus in Praise of Blind Love," *Pagan Mysteries in the Renaissance,* pp. 53–80.

the evident, obvious values of the normal world, open only to the invisible and daimonic.

Now our image of the goal changes: not Enlightened Man, who sees, the seer, but Transparent Man, who is seen and seen through, foolish, who has nothing left to hide, who has become transparent through self-acceptance; his soul is loved, wholly revealed, wholly existential; he is just what he is, freed from paranoid concealment, from the knowledge of his secrets and his secret knowledge; his transparency serves as a prism for the world and the not-world. For it is impossible reflectively to know thyself; only the last reflection of an obituary may tell the truth, and only God knows our real names. We are always behind with our reflections—too late, after the event; or we are in the midst, where we see through a glass darkly.

How can we know ourselves by ourselves? We can be known to ourselves through another, but we cannot go it alone. That is the hero's way, perhaps appropriate during a heroic phase. But if we have learned anything from the rituals of the new life-form of the past seventy years, it is just this: we cannot go it alone. The opus of the soul needs intimate connection, not only to individuate but simply to live. For this we need relationships of the profoundest kind through which we can realize ourselves, where self-revelation is possible, where interest in and love for soul is paramount, and where eros may move freely—whether it be in analysis, in marriage and famliy, or between lovers or friends.

The Suffering of Impossible Love

We can recognize another consequent of a psyche without eros from felt experience. We suffer. This torment of the soul in its relationship to eros is a major theme in the tale of Eros and Psyche.[110]

110. As R. Reitzenstein pointed out in 1911, the suffering is mutual: if the soul is tormented by eros, eros, too, suffers. See his discussion of this imagery in *Das Märchen von Amor und Psyche bei Apuleius* (Leipzig, 1912), pp. 9 ff.

From the mid-fourth century before our era until the sixth century, when it was absorbed by Christian allegory, the collective witness of terra cotta, sculpture, engraved gems, and bas reliefs attests to the popularity of this tale, in its *fabula* form as *Märchen* or folk tale. These figurative works, examined first by Otto Jahn (1851); collected and published by Collignon,[111] and discussed by Reitzenstein especially, state better than any texts, better than the literary style of Apuleius (written hundreds of years after the sculpted witness), that the psyche is tortured by love.[112] We find Psyche sad, kneeling, weeping; Psyche, the begging suppliant, prostrate at the feet of Eros; Psyche chained or bound to the chariot of love; Eros shooting and wounding Psyche; Psyche's wings burnt, or the burnt moth or butterfly, whose name in Greek gives them symbolic identity. (The same motifs occur in dreams today. A woman dreams that she tries to burn a wormlike insect in a bonfire; but it proves indestructible, and out comes a winged butterfly. A young man dreams of crushing green winged creatures on his ceiling and whitewashing over the spot, or of ridding himself of a caterpillar by setting fire to it; but in a later dream a crowned and winged frog-insect appears.) The insistence upon this aspect of the Psyche-Eros tale became redoubled in the Renaissance representations, where Psyche is tied in cruel knots, crushed in the press, burnt at the stake—in an extraordinary mixture of Christian metaphors with the pagan tale of love and torture.[113]

The torture of the soul seems unavoidable in every close involvement, of which the transference of an analysis is one example. Despite all one does to avoid and to alleviate suffering, it would seem that the process in which the people find

111. M. Collignon, *Essai sur les monuments grecs et romains relatifs au mythe de Psyche* (thesis; Paris, 1877).

112. The Apuleius version omits these torture aspects of the earlier tale, and so Neumann mentions them only in his Postscript.

113. M. Praz, "Profane and Sacred Love," in *Studies in Seventeenth-Century Imagery*, 2d ed. (Rome, 1964), esp. pp. 151 f.

themselves arranges it, as if we were driven by a mythical necessity to enact Psyche and Eros. Jung has discussed the motif of torture, raising the questions: What is tortured? What does the torturing?[114] Our myth tells us that psyche suffers from love; a girl is tortured into womanhood, as a man's anima is awakened through torment into psyche, a torment which, as Neumann observes, transforms eros as well.[115] Eros is tortured by its own principle, fire. It burns others; and it burns alone when cut off from psyche, that is, when it is without psychological insight and reflection. Psyche pursues its tasks, without hope or energy, loveless, inconsolable. Their separation is the split we experience: while eros burns, psyche figures out, does its duties, depressed.

Before connection is possible, psyche goes through the dark night of the soul (the burnt wings of the night moth), that *mortificatio* in which it feels the paradoxical agony of a pregnant potential within itself and a sense of guilty, cut-off separateness. The torment continues until the soul-work (Psyche's tasks) is completed and the psyche is reunited with a transformed eros. Eros needs to regress, it would seem, into a state of burning unrest and agitation, dominated by the mother, by Penia or deprivation, in order to realize that he has himself been felled by his arrow and has found his mate, Psyche. He gains psychic consciousness. Only then does the union take place, and for it the sanctification of the Gods is required.

Their long separation, Psyche's tasks, and their mutual torments—being burnt, chained, dragged—present the images of erotic obsession complete even to its sadomasochistic aspects. Without wings the soul cannot soar above its immediate

114. "The Philosophical Tree," *CW*, XIII, pars. 439 ff.

115. Cf. the transformation of eros in alchemy, in particular the taming of *cupido*, the compulsive aspect, through union with the "salt" of suffering; see Jung's writings on the "reddening" and on "sulphur" in "The Philosophical Tree" and in *Mysterium Coniunctionis* (*CW*, XIV).

compulsions, can gain no perspective. For our psyche to unite legitimately with the creative and bring to sanctified birth what it carries, we evidently need to realize both our loss of primordial love through betrayal and separation and also our wrong relation to eros—the enthrallment, servility, pain, sadness, longing: all aspects of erotic *mania*. As Jung says, ". . . for always the ardour of love transmutes fear and compulsion into a higher free type of feeling." Seen against the Oedipal background, these torments cannot redeem, since in that myth compulsion overcomes love; in our tale, despite the same phenomena of torment, love—because it finds soul —overcomes compulsion.[116]

The myth of the process "arranges" suffering; yet this suffering is neither blind and tragic, as with Oedipus, nor is it the endurance of the hero in the belly of the whale. The suffering in our tale has something to do with initiation, with changing the structure of consciousness. The tale itself has deep roots in ancient Isis mysteries; as Merkelbach says, "Initiation rites are a symbol of a whole life." [117] As such, the ordeals of Psyche and Eros are initiatory; they are symbolic of the psychological and erotic ordeals to which we are put. This gives us a wholly different view, not only of transference and analytical suffering, but of the ground of neurosis in our time. Neurosis becomes initiation, analysis the ritual, and our developmental process in psyche and in eros, leading to their union, becomes the mystery.

We must have a new way of grasping what goes on in our lives and in our practices, another view of the women who leave their children for a lover; the women who fall in love with youth, as the men do with beauty; the insupportable triangles and jealousies we suffer; the repetitive erotic entanglements which, because they are soulless and without psychological reflection, lead only to more despair; the divorces that become the necessary path for psychic develop-

116. On the taming of love through chastity and its imagery see E. Panofsky, "Der gefesselte Eros," *OUD-Holland*, L (1933), 193–217.

117. R. Merkelbach, *Roman und Mysterium*, p. 50.

ment when there is no possibility for eros in a marriage; the marriages that need to be held together if only for the sake of the psychic suffering, which then may constellate eros in a new way; the analyses that are haunted by images of former loves, going back sometimes fifty years, and how these become the redeemed and redeeming figures; or the fact that failed love often means failure as a person and leads to suicide, and why the worst of all betrayals are those of love. These situations, and the intense emotions flowing from them, feel central to a person's being and may mean more to working out his fate than the family problem and his conscious development as a heroic course. These events create consciousness in men and women, initiating us into life as a personal-impersonal mystery beyond problems that can be analyzed.

When these events are told through this tale, portraying "an Odyssey of the human soul" [118]—a tale of union, separation, and suffering and an eventual reunion of love and soul blessed by the archetypal powers—they can be handled in another spirit: one of confirmation and encouragement. *For whatever the disguise, what is taking place is the creative eros connecting with an awakening psyche.* All the turns and torments are part of—shall we say Bhakti yoga?—a psychological discipline of eros development, or an erotic discipline of psychological development, aiming toward psychic integration and erotic identity. Without this devotional discipline we have the easy playboy's pairings of Alcibiades, anima and sex, ending in power, not love. Thus we can understand why we meet so much "impossible love": [119] the

118. P. Grimal, "Die Bedeutung der Erzählung von Amor und Psyche" (n. 69, above), p. 12.

119. The term is from Neumann, *Amor and Psyche*, p. 138, but our view of "impossible love" should be distinguished from two particular distortions of it, the first being the Freudian interpretation that such torment has its origins in the fundamental masochism of the feminine, and the second being the Romantic notion that subjective states of intensified passion are preferable to love's fulfillment. Cf. M. Praz, *The Romantic Agony*, trans. A. Davidson (London: Fon-

dead lover or bride, unrequited and humiliating love, the love choice of the "wrong" person (who is married, or cannot divorce, or is the analyst, or is homosexual, or is in a distant land or ill). The arrow falls where it will; we can only follow.

Of all forms of impossibility, the arrow strikes us into triangles to such an extraordinary extent that this phenomenon must be examined for its creative role in soul-making. The sudden dynamic effect on the psyche of jealousy and other triangular fears and fantasies hint that this constellation of "impossibility" bears as much significance as does the conjunction. To explain it Oedipally or through the anima/animus, to see it morally and negatively, does not allow it objective necessity. So necessary is the triangular pattern that, even where two exist only for each other, a third will be imagined. In the fantasies of analysis, when there is no third, the two collude for one; or the analyst is the third in the patient's life, while the patient is the third in the analyst's; or the previous patient is the third. The constructive-destructive aspect of eros creativity intervenes like a daimon to prevent the *hieros gamos* by insisting upon "the other," who becomes the catalyst of impossibility. We witness the same Eros which joins two now breaking the reciprocity of the couple by striking his arrow into a third. The stage is set for tragedy and for every extreme sort of psychic and erotic aberration. Perhaps this is its necessity: the triangles of eros educate the psyche out of its girlish goodness, showing it the extent of its fantasies and testing its capacity. The triangle presents eros as the transcendent function creating out of two a third, which, like all impossible love, cannot be lived fully in actuality, so that the third comes as imaginal reality. But it comes not as imagery in meditation but through violence and pain and in the shape of actual persons, teaching the psyche by means of the triangle that the imaginal is most actual and

---

tana, 1960), and D. de Rougemont, *Passion and Society*, trans. M. Belgion (London: Faber & Faber, 1956).

the actual symbolic. We say, at one and the same time: "It's nonsense, a projection, all in my imagination" and "I can't go on without the actual you."

All impossible love forces upon us a discipline of interiorizing. Anima becomes psyche as the image of the impossibly loved person who tends to represent the daimon that, by inhibiting compulsion, fosters new dimensions of psychic awareness. These experiences show most transparently eros actually making soul. They also show the countereffects of the soul upon eros. The psyche acts as a *causa formalis*, making qualitative changes possible in eros. This maturing process provides the basic pattern described in so many fictional "love stories." The effect of psyche upon eros is primarily one of a process character, a change in timing, yielding qualities of subtlety, awareness, and indirection within involvement. These qualitative changes come about when one accepts as *necessary for the soul* all the desires, impulses, attachments, and needs of eros; these form the primary material for the transformation. Similarly, the effect of eros on psyche is characterized by what we have already described as an awakening and engendering. And this too has a prerequisite: bringing eros to *all psychic contents whatsoever*—symptoms, moods, images, habits—and finding them fundamentally lovable and desirable.

The idealizations which eros tends always to constellate can be counterbalanced: creativity expresses itself also as destruction. Love's torture may not always lead to the happy ending of our tale. The idealizations may be further weighted by recalling the connections in Hesiod, the Orphics, and Renaissance Neoplatonism between Eros and Chaos.[120]

Eros is born of Chaos, implying that out of every chaotic moment the creativity of which we have been speaking can be born. Furthermore, eros will always hearken back to its origins in chaos and will seek it for its revivification. Aris-

120. Cf. M. Ficino, *Banquet de Platon*, I, iii. For a thorough examination of Chaos in its early Greek mythic context see J. Fontenrose, *Python* (Berkeley: University of California Press, 1959), pp. 217–73.

tophanes writes even of their mating. Eros will attempt again and again to create those dark nights and confusions which are its nest. It renews itself in affective attacks, jealousies, fulminations, and turmoils. It thrives close to the dragon.

The voice of order in us will have none of this. Eros, yes; but chaos, never. In a passage from the taxonomist Simpson, quoted by Lévi-Strauss, we hear this voice of Apollonic reason and its enmity to chaos: "Scientists do tolerate uncertainty and frustration, because they must. The one thing that they do not and must not tolerate is disorder. The whole aim of theoretical science is to carry to the highest possible and conscious degree the perceptual reduction of chaos." [121] By refusing chaos, its consequent, eros, may also be lost to science, which may or may not damage science in its quest for order. But it will damage the scientist's soul-making and creativity. The mythic relation of Eros and Chaos states what academic studies of creativity have long said, that chaos and creativeness are inseparable.

Since chaos is also a gap, an emptiness or lacuna, eros has a predeliction for the psychopathic holes in the psyche, for its formlessness, its not-yetness and hopelessness. (Psyche is always depicted as a young girl, which has less to do with youth than with the lacunae of the anima, its emptiness, which we feel as despair, a wound, and as an aesthetic vagueness, especially when touched by eros.) To call this unformed void of psychopathic darkness in one's nature the shadow does it only partial justice, because shadow tends to mean moral evil as seen from ego. But chaos refers to a *prima materia*, indicating a peculiar inherent connection between the worst inert sludge of human nature, its inchoate *increatum*, and the attractions of eros. This alone gives some account of the peculiar and "impossible" fixations in our lives between the erotic and the psychopathic, between the idealizations of eros and its affinity for chaos. Thus, behind the idealizations of Othello's eros for

121. Quoted by C. Lévi-Strauss, *The Savage Mind* (London, 1966), from G. G. Simpson, *Principles of Animal Taxonomy* (New York, 1961).

Desdemona lies the lacuna of his psychopathy, so that he is compelled to say: ". . . and when I love thee not, Chaos is come again" (*Othello* III. iii).

The eros arrow points to these wounds, making us aware of these gaps in personality, these unhealed aspects, these places of chaos. Out of these wounds flows love, for it flows more readily from weaknesses and psychopathologies than from strength. To have invulnerability as goal or cure means to be safe from the arrows of eros and his torch and nevermore to feel the erotic point and flame. In weakness, too, eros makes soul, because it reveals to the psyche the wounds of its inability. The imagery of wounding in dreams and fantasies should not always be interpreted in terms of the medical pattern, of binding up and healing, since these same wounds may be the lacunae that give rise to eros and provide a target for his arrows.

The idealizations of eros are not new, belonging only to the romantic love of modern times and its inflations. The Renaissance knew of this *acclivitas* from the Schoolmen; so did the Troubadours, Lucretius, and the Platonic Socrates. These idealizations are an inherent aspect of the upward impulse. To refuse them in the name of taming eros and of making love less a romantic inflation also removes the possibility for change through eros. The pangs of eros belong to its romance and to the *pothos* for the unattainable.[122] However, these pangs also pertain to our victimized psychopathic woundedness, when we cry, "I can't do anything about it!" To change truly means to change even on that psychopathic level which is

122. Denis de Rougement (*Passion and Society* and *Love Declared*) calls the *pothos* component the "Tristan" complex, finding it to be forever opposed to "Don Juan," or the actual realization of physical desire (*himeros*). In antiquity, before either Tristan or Don Juan had appeared, *pothos* and *himeros* were not so divided from each other, even if the tendency to polarize Aphrodite into heavenly and earthly aspects seems a recurring archetypal necessity for some. The Renaissance Neoplatonists tried to restore the original interrelation between *pothos* and *himeros* and not to fall prey to the Tristan complex of medieval man.

clinically defined as an inability to change; to change truly means also to change on the psychotic level which is clinically defined partly in terms of irreversible psychic processes. Because eros touches even these levels of our eternal hells, it affects the psyche at the crucial levels of its craziness. Eros is always somewhat psychotic and psychopathic; in love we must be mad.

While the erotic can be a form of *mania*, as Plato said, it also beautifies. Moreover, beauty is the first attribute which draws Eros to Psyche. "To love," says Diotima, "is to bring forth upon the beautiful." We have had to neglect beauty in our work because, on the Oedipal model, it was regressive, seductively sexual, the attraction of Jocasta. On the heroic model, beauty too often represented the merely aesthetic approach, producing an embellishment rather than a meaning, a *puer* avoidance of the battles of purposeful achievement, and a neglect of the ugly bitterness of the shadow. Perhaps now we may realize that the development of the feminine, of anima into psyche, and of the soul's awakening is a process in beauty.[123] This implies that the criteria of aesthetics—unity, line, rhythm, tension, elegance—may be transposed to the psyche, giving us a new set of qualities for appreciating what is going on in a psychological process. The beauty of soul which alone surpasses the allure of Aphrodite will show in the aesthetic imagination of the psyche and the attractive power of its images. It will show in the ways in which the psyche gives form to its contents—for instance, the manner in which the anima contains the erotic. But mainly the beauty of psyche refers to a sense of the beautiful in connection with psychological events. By being touched, moved, and opened by

123. Cf. Plotinus *Enneads* I. 6. 9 for the classical passage describing the soul's awakening and development as a process in beauty. However, our tale reminds us that Psyche's natural beauty is not enough, for as such it is only nature, only in the service of Aphrodite. Psyche's tasks represent the transformation of the beauty of the natural soul into the beauty of a loving conscious soul. The tale reveals the fate that every beautiful aspect of the psyche must go through in its process of initiation and redemption.

the experiences of the soul, one discovers that what goes on in the soul is not only interesting and meaningful, necessary and acceptable, but that it is attractive, lovable, and beautiful.

The ultimate beauty of psyche is that which even Aphrodite does not have and which must come from Persephone, who is Queen over the dead souls and whose name means "bringer of destruction." The Box of Beauty which Psyche must fetch as her last task refers to an underworld beauty that can never be seen with the senses. It is the beauty of the knowledge of death and of the effects of death upon all other beauty that does not contain this knowledge. Psyche must "die" herself in order to experience the reality of this beauty, a death different from her suicidal attempts. This would be the ultimate task of soul-making and its beauty: the incorporation of destruction into the flesh and skin, embalmed in life, the visible transfigured by the invisibility of Hades' kingdom, anointing the psyche by the killing experience of its personal mortality. The Platonic upward movement toward aestheticism is tempered by the beauty of Persephone. Destruction, death, and Hades are not left out. Moreover, Aphrodite does not have access to this kind of beauty. She can acquire it only through Psyche, for the soul mediates the beauty of the invisible inner world to the world of outer forms.

We recognize the first fruit of a psychologically creative union by experiences of *pleasure*—for such is their first child's name. Pleasure, delight, joy, *voluptas*, *Wonne*, *ananda*, laughter, bliss—by any name as sweet. The rose within the thorns—the red, red rose; the sweetness within the suffering and the salt and the heroic death on the tall cross; for the sweet *voluptas* of the soul, the mystics' *sabrosa*, that taste of the soul's sweet joy, has been the concealed and pregnant goal throughout the entire opus. For pleasure is not merely that infantile beginning in the *jardin des délices* which must be left heroically behind or sacrificed to a Freudian reality principle. In our tale, the fulfillment of Psyche is Pleasure, the pleasure born of the soul.

Merkelbach, in his authoritative interpretation of the tale, omits discussion of this final act, the birth of Voluptas. He finds the conclusion a "riddle" and can give "no Greek-Egyptian equivalent." [124] His failure is final evidence for the inadequacy of the historical and literary method in providing sufficient amplification for psychology. Although there may be no earlier parallels to this event, the birth of Voluptas from Psyche can be amplified through *later* initiatory and mystery experiences, e.g., those presented by saints and mystics, by poets, by the dream symbols of moderns, and through felt experiences.[125]

If the tale ends with the birth of this child, then it is no mere incident. The goal of *voluptas* affirms that the process of development modeled upon the union of eros and psyche is not Stoic, not a way of denial and control, of work and will. It is not at all a way of ego development in the usual sense of ego as reality opposed to pleasure. In Epicureanism, in Neoplatonic thought, in the Renaissance philosophy of Ficino and Pico, and still in the Romantics, there is no real enmity between higher and lower pleasures or between one's work and one's delights, since the creative eros propels both. On the authority of Plotinus, *voluptas* of the senses is the model for the soul's joy, and divine ecstasy is comparable to the passions of lovers.[126]

124. Merkelbach, *Roman und Mysterium*, p. 53, n. 2.

125. Cf. Neumann's discussion of Voluptas in *Amor and Psyche*, pp. 140 and 144; see also E. Wind, *Pagan Mysteries*, pp. 50 ff., 55, and 66 ff. For a different view of the box of beauty, Voluptas, and Olympus at the end of the Psyche-Eros tale see M.-L. von Franz (*A Psychological Interpretation of "The Golden Ass,"* Chaps. VII and VIII), who attributes negative psychological values to these three motives, interpreting *voluptas* as "sensuous lust," the box of beauty as an unpsychological anima-aestheticism, and the sanctified marriage on Olympus as an ascension out of the life of mortal reality. She relates the tale to the imagined personal psychology of the hero-author (Lucius/Apuleius) and his individuation process, which, because of these final motives and her interpretation of them, must be considered to have failed; this failure then gives rise to further efforts in the remainder of *The Golden Ass*, where the Psyche-Eros tale forms but one sequence.

126. Plotinus *Enneads* VI. 9. 9; VI. 7. 33–36. On the Neoplatonic view of *voluptas* see E. Wind, *Pagan Mysteries*, pp. 50 f., 68 f., 273 f.

Ficino and the Neoplatonic Academy insisted that *voluptas* and joy were more important than cognition and were even a manner of insighting; in this they are rather like Shelley, who proclaimed the sensuous as the essence of living things. For the Neoplatonists *voluptas* was generally both sensual voluptuousness and a transcendent bliss beyond the senses. We might call it *psychic sensuality*, the physical delight in the opus of soul-making, the psyche so infused with eros that its movements—from rarefied insight to clinical aberration—yield a voluptuous enjoyment.

A final consequent in felt experience is demonstrated in the story by Eros and Psyche's arrival on Olympus and their celebration by the Gods. We need not imagine that this refers to the goal of individuation and immortality for those who accomplish the process. Such a reading is not psychological even if presented in the language of current psychology; it does not refer to felt experience but reflects a wish and a hope of theological eschatology. Psychology has put the wish for redemption in the frame of an individuation process, complete with a pilgrim's progress toward a lofty goal. Such a reading suits neither Jung's meaning of individuation (becoming all that one is) nor the structural implication of our tale.

The end of a tale reveals its a priori structure, what it was from the beginning. The end of this tale states again, and with crescendo, that eros and psyche are ruled by archetypal powers, which have been mythically presented by the figures of the Gods. Moreover, the processes—today called psychodynamic—which we are forced to go through are mythically governed. What transpires *in* our psyche is not *of* our psyche; both love and soul finally and from the beginning belong to the realm of archetypal reality. This psychological lesson gives an impersonal quality to the entire creative opus of soul-making within each individual's subjectivity. No matter how personally we feel them as our "own," eros and psyche are archetypal powers that find their final and their original "home" when placed where they belong, as transpersonal events which paradoxically form the ground of personality.

Precisely this insight—that neither psyche nor eros can be identified with our souls and our loving—is the upshot of the long discussion. This insight is also the upshot of the Platonic description of love. Love starts in the personal and means me; then it means my soul and my whole being. Then it moves me, my soul, and my being into archetypal being, into a sense of interiority: an interior process contained within me, and myself contained within the interiority of a chaotic universe transformed by love into a cosmos. I feel myself held within something larger and feel in myself a larger dimension directed by powers, the voices of which I try to differentiate and to follow. Thus does Eros lead to the Gods or lead the psyche to an awareness that helps penetrate the dragon of psychic opacity. The meanings begin in the burn of desire and are refuted by the frozen panic of withdrawal; but, though tormenting, these movements pass through one as objective givens which simply must take place as part of the eros-psyche game, which creates personality but is not personal. As myth is something that never happened but always is, so the Eros-Psyche story is always going on in us.

At first the entanglements which Eros constellates seem personal, as if all of love hung on the right word or move at the magical right time, as if it were a matter of effort and doing. But then the entanglements become reflections of archetypal patterns, patterns that appear in everyone's life. The images (*eidola*) are what everyone has experienced in his psyche through loving. In this way Eros leads to the archetypes behind the patterns, and we are played into myth after myth: now a hero, now a virgin running, now a satyr who must clutch, now blind, now soaring. Precisely this mythical awareness and enactment result from psychological creativity.

Thus we begin to recognize in ourselves that eros and psyche are not mere figures in a tale, not merely configurations of archetypal components, but are two ends of every psychic process. They always imply and require each other. We cannot view anything psychologically without an involvement with it: we cannot be involved with anything without its entering our soul. By experiencing an event psychologically, we tend to feel a connection with it; in feeling and desire we tend to realize the importance of something for the soul. Desire is holy, as D. H. Lawrence, the Romantics, and the Neoplatonists insisted, because it touches and moves the soul. Reflection is never enough.

Reflection may make consciousness, but love makes soul. This is implied by the motto from Jung placed at the beginning of this essay. It is implied in Jung's acknowledgment of Eros in a last passage of his biography at the end of his life:

> At this point the fact forces itself on my attention that beside the field of reflection there is another equally broad if not broader area. . . . This is the realm of Eros. In classical times, when such things were properly understood, Eros was considered a god whose divinity transcended our human limits, and who therefore could neither be comprehended nor represented in any way. I might, as many before me have attempted to do, venture an approach to this daimon, whose range of activity extends from the endless spaces of the heavens to the dark abysses of hell; but I falter before the task of finding the language which might adequately express the incalculable paradoxes of love. Eros is a *kosmogonos*, a creator and father-mother of all higher consciousness . . . ; [it] might well be the first condition of all cognition and the quintessence of divinity itself. Whatever the learned interpretation may be of the sentence "God is love," the words affirm the *complexio oppositorum* of the Godhead. In my medical experience as well as in my own life I have again and again been faced with the mystery of love, and have never been able to explain what it is. . . . For we are in the deepest sense the victims and instruments of cosmogonic "love.". . . A man is at its mercy. He may assent to it, or rebel againt it; but he is always caught up by it and enclosed within it. He is

dependent upon it and is sustained by it. Love is his light and his darkness, whose end he cannot see. "Love ceases not.". . . Man can try to name love, showering upon it all the names at his command, and still he will involve himself in endless self-deceptions. If he possesses a grain of wisdom, he will lay down his arms and name the unknown by the more unknown, *ignotum per ignotius*—that is, by the name of God.[127]

Transference

Now we are in a new position to look at transference, the main theme of this whole part. First, we see it no longer within its psychotherapeutic context, but rather as the paradigm of relationships in general. It occurs wherever there is close involvement as a factor of soul-making; as such, it is necessitated by psychic life. Jung recognized this, saying: "Indeed, in any human relationship that is at all intimate, certain transference phenomena will almost always operate as helpful or disturbing factors."[128] Already in 1907, when Freud and Jung had their first meeting, Jung, in response to Freud's question about transference, replied that it was "the alpha and omega of the analytical method."[129] He departed from this emphasis upon transference as *method* but never from its significance as *substance*. In his major work on the theme, Jung repeatedly says that transference phenomena are immensely complicated, involving every sort of emotion and fantasy and offering no simple solution. Transference is an intensified replica, or archetypal paradigm, of every human connection. We are in transference wherever we go,

127. C. G. Jung with A. Jaffé, *Memories, Dreams, Reflections*, trans. R. and C. Winston (London: Collins and Routledge & Kegan Paul, 1963), pp. 325–26. This acknowledgement to Eros in that almost penultimate passage of his autobiography compares, in its placement, to the reference in the *Enneads* to Eros and the Psyche-Eros mythologem (VI. 9. 9, i.e., the last section but two), where Plotinus affirms that "the soul . . . needs love."
128. *CW*, XVI, par. 357, n. 14.
129. *Ibid.*, par. 358.

wherever a connection means something to the soul. Jung presents this archetypal paradigm by means of alchemical imagery in order to gain a historical and symbolic perspective on what is usually experienced as hot and close. This imagery refers to the union of male and female, spirit and body, and other pairs usually conceived as opposites.

Behind the pairs is the phenomenon of the union itself, the third thing. Is it the psyche in which they are joined, or eros by which they are joined? Jung implies both: "If no bond of love exists, they have no soul." [130] The *coniunctio* requires both love and soul, which in their union are themselves one. He suggests further that the anima develops toward this capacity for union through four stages of erotic phenomenology: Eve, Helen [of Troy], the Virgin Mary, and Sophia. He considers them to be "four stages of the Eros cult." [131] He makes further allusions in this work on transference to phenomena familiar to us from the Eros-Psyche myth. For example, he writes of "psychic pregnancy" and of the "soul's child" in regard to the opus.[132]

If transference is the alpha and omega of the analytical scheme of things, it becomes that with which analysis began and with which it ends. Transference becomes both the conclusion to analysis, in the sense that analysis ends when the transference has been resolved or severed, and also the purpose of analysis, that for the sake of which analysis exists. If transference is modeled upon soul-making as presented in the Eros-Psyche mythologem, then it is for the sake of realizing this mythologem that analysis comes into being in an individual's life, i.e., he goes into analysis. It means also that analysis goes out of an individual's life when he realizes that this is what he has come for: to find soul for his eros and love for his psyche. To call this myth, as enacted in analysis, "transference" grossly deceives both the soul in its needs and eros in its desires. This deformation of the soul's experiences through

130. *Ibid.*, par. 454.
131. *Ibid.*, par. 361.
132. *Ibid.*, par. 465.

the language of professional psychology will be examined with care in Part Two of this book.

Before we have done with transference, we may still draw new meaning from it if we ask what exactly is transferred by whom, from what, and to whom. Originally transference meant only "new editions of early conflicts, in which the patient strives to behave as he originally behaved" but now within the precincts of, and in regard to the person of, the physician treating him.[133]

However, if the analyst works from the model that we have been amplifying—the engendering of soul through love—then we must admit that what he brings to the encounter, the so-called countertransference, is actually prior to transference. The analyst starts from a well-conceived position given to him by the daimon of his desire both to bring the health of awareness, imagination, and beauty to life in the soul and to constellate with his psyche the eros of the other. It is no longer the analyst upon whom projections are transferred; rather, through the analyst the intentions of the *coniunctio* myth are transferred upon the analysand, who counters these effects of the analyst from the start. He counters, opposes, and resists the mission of the psyche and eros of the analyst. These form the so-called "transference reactions" and "transference neurosis" of resistance, which, when they are not clearly familial but are mainly similar to our myth, are indeed the alpha and omega of the creative work. (Splendid examples of such resistance patterns can be found in the moods and arguments brought against Socrates by his pupils and fellow conversationalists.)

Transference has long been recognized as a demand for love; but this demand has usually been placed by analysis against too personal a background: the family problem and personal needs. Hence, the demand for love is never wholly acceptable. It is too much because its "impossibility" is at

133. S. Freud, *New Introductory Lectures on Psycho-Analysis*, trans. W. J. H. Sprott (London: Hogarth Press, 1933), p. 380.

root the incest desire. But, within the metaphor we are using, until my daimon has caught fire, I remain stuck in my transference and have legitimate need for the spark of another's eros for my self-development. The less the other can reveal his eros, the more I will demand it; for how else will my process be kindled? My own individuation impulse, my desire for psyche, must be ignited. This love for psyche—and not the analysis of "transference reactions"—alone resolves the stuck transference.

By giving precedence to the analyst's own eros and psyche, we seem to have come a long way from Freud's notion of the analyst as reflector. Rather than being in danger of becoming a cold mirror, we are in the new danger of becoming image-maker, a sculptor who fashions figures and warms them into life only to be unable to separate from them. A new analysis, then, will have its new shadow, no longer the omniscient wise old man of reflection, but the loving fool, whose knowing is only loving, identified with his creations, perhaps like Pygmalion. Fortunately, as in any creative work, the opus has its effects on the operator, so that the analyst is transformed by the countereffects of his work upon himself, by the ways in which he is encountered. He finds himself its servant, played by the imaginings in the opus, fascinated by its beauty, a symbol in the other's soul history as his own ego is a symbol in his own, and moved by the other's daimon.

We must still consider the objective level of what is transferred, whose source has only indirectly to do with the persons involved, with their psychic needs and erotic desires as each personally feels them. This objective level refers mainly to the anima and its connection with tradition. Eros has no past; he is of the Gods, is conceived to be ever young, ever renewed, a youth, a flame, a quickening arrow. Eros is the original revolutionary, always outside history. The anima, on the contrary, has levels of culture going back through history and down into nature. The myth of Apuleius presents these aspects of Psyche in terms of her family and her human history. These complications and entanglements which the anima brings to union are transferred to it as part of her dowry. There is a *historical level to transference;* there are social and cultural aspects that influence the soul's needs and reactions beyond the behavior transferred to it from childhood and parents. History begins further back, and so does transference. One does not come into an involvement as a clean babe with a soft, waxen mind. Love may melt one down, but it must burn deep and very long to transform and educate the historical level of one's unconscious soul patterns. The weight of this unconsciousness provides both an anchor for love's ascension, a container to keep it entangled, and a substance for reflection. Transference drags on so long for the very reason that it slows down the work; the anima provides the resistance of conservative nature and traditional culture. This huge burden transferred to the opus by the anima is the historical precondition of the work.

We have spoken of the psyche as reflector, the anima as the feminine moon mind, a reflection which differs from the cautionary daimon within the eros impulse. This voice cannot claim to be psychological, for it still performs with the spontaneity of nature. The daimon inhibits compulsion but does not reflect it. The preferred instinct of the anima—if we may speculate about ectopsychic powers—seems to be what Jung has called the reflective instinct. The bending-backward and turning-away of *reflexio* appear as the shy, virginal, and retreating heroine of fairy tale and myth and as Venus with a mirror. In the Apuleius tale the tasks of Psyche better enable her to represent the reflective instinct. "The richness of the human psyche and its essential character are probably determined by this reflective instinct. . . . Through the reflective instinct, the stimulus is more or less wholly transformed into a psychic content, that is, it becomes an experience. . . . Reflection is the cultural instinct *par excellence,* and its strength is shown in the power of culture to maintain itself." [134]

134. *CW,* VIII, pars. 242 and 243.

Through reflection psyche brings culture to eros, because psyche is already embedded in a historical context. The process that goes on in analysis transfers culture to drive and sometimes vice versa. This cultural process is mistakenly called "sublimation" (another of those words like "transference," "psychodynamics," "therapeutic eros" that disturb our perception of psychological events). Sublimation implies the transformation of the lower into something higher or finer, a metaphor which here does not apply at all. We are merely recognizing the objectively historical and cultural background of psyche as the reflector of the creative impulse, through which this impulse must filter, by which it will always be complicated, and in which the opus is formed. Transference represents the *experience* of the effects of history upon desire, of culture upon creativity, of soul upon impulse.

Since transference occurs in any close involvement, each binding personal connection affects the historical psyche. Our relationships do not change merely you and me; they affect history. They are a form of culture. Their maintenance is also a first concern of the soul, required not only for its individual health but for the integrity of all human life and for the transference of psychological history to future generations.

Does all this mean, finally, that soul-making is only for those who have sat in the consulting room? Is the analyst the only one who can create psyche? The analyst is neither lover, nor daimon, nor creative demiurge, nor embodiment of culture. Moreover, analysis presents only one example of the creativity of any psychological relationship. It is a ritual, a new life-form, that fatherless has entered the history of consciousness without having uncovered what myth is being enacted and without having adequate hypotheses to account for its effects. Psychological creativity as the union of eros and psyche was dreaming within us long before analysis became a historical necessity for its realization. Freud in his later eros theory, Jung in his alchemical studies, and then Neumann have already adumbrated these ideas. How necessary the ritual of analysis was and is for psychological creativity is evident; how much longer its hermetic vessel will be necessary we do not know. And though necessary, it is questionable whether it is sufficient. Wherever transference takes place, an analysis is going on; and wherever these phenomena, formerly bound by the terms "transference" and "analysis," take place, soul-making is going on. The myth of Eros and Psyche, whose relevance for us has been rediscovered in analysis and experienced through transference, can no longer be bound to a prescribed ritual called the analytical method, in a special therapeutic place for a certain pair of persons, one "ill" and the other "well." Nor can we continue with a certain description of the psyche, divided into ill and healthy portions.

Analysis now points beyond itself; something else must happen, so that eros and psyche can find union in life and so that psychological creativity, including its psychopathology, can find adequate forms outside the consulting room.

PART TWO
On Psychological Language

Two Ways of Description

Early in our European tradition Parmenides of Elea set forth his poetic vision of the universe. One part is called the "Way of Truth," the other, the "Way of Opinion." The two ways of Parmenides have been much discussed since his time. Philosophical commentators ask why Parmenides found it necessary to describe his vision in two contrasting ways. One would think that the way of truth would be enough. Why bother with a second description? But the fact remains: one way of telling was not enough. Even our Bible begins with two differing tales of the Creation.

In the long tradition since Parmenides, descriptions divide again and again into two ways. This is not merely the influence of tradition. These divisions point to some necessity of the human psyche to tell two kinds of tales about the nature of things.

Jung tried to come to grips with this peculiar duality in the history of thought in his work *Psychological Types*,[1] where he showed that the division into two ways of description arises from the psychological bias of the observer. This bias for one or another attitude gives the observer his conviction that one method achieves a way of "truth," while another way is less valid and its descriptions are mere "opinion." In

1. *CW*, VI.

his biography (*Memories, Dreams, Reflections*)[2] Jung takes these conclusions one step further. The two ways of envisioning the universe are reflections of two personalities within the individual—the rational and the irrational, the logical and the mythic, the civilized and the primitive, the man and the child. He speaks of personalities number one and number two. This concluding insight into his life also places ultimate subjective limitations upon any description. Sometimes we may see life whole, but our description of it will always fall into halves.

Each half is represented by a personality, and each has its own language. Jung carefully discusses this problem of linguistic discourse in *Symbols of Transformation*,[3] in the section "Two Kinds of Thinking." During the same period Freud and Bleuler made similar contrasts between two systems of mental processes and their two languages.[4] Jung, however, differs from Freud and Bleuler. For them, rational, reifying, or thing-oriented language, even if a derivative and secondary process, was still the preferable "way of truth." Other psychic expressions were to be translated by the ego into the rational language of this "reality." On the other hand, if we take his work as a whole, we find that Jung gave primacy to the natural speech of the other personality. Reason and its definition of reality were never enough. Perhaps, because of his proclivity for the soul's speech, Jung was the first in our times to understand psychic reality as myth; this he learned from the tales told him by his psychiatric charges at Zurich's Burghölzli asylum. Freud saw the myth but did not leave it there; he turned it into conceptual language. Jung dreamt the myth along. Freud and Jung stand for a similar tale told in two cities, their societies and generations. Freud

2. London and New York, 1961.
3. *CW*, V.
4. E. Jones (*The Life and Work of Sigmund Freud* [London: Hogarth Press, 1955], II, 350), writes that Freud's distinction between two systems of mental functioning is his main theoretical contribution: "It was this distinction on which rests Freud's chief claim to fame: even his discovery of the unconscious is subordinate to it."

and Jung are also two ways of speaking. They are two ways in which the word of the soul, psychology, finds expression.

By opening this part of my book with Parmenides, I am intending to imply that there is a very old need in the human psyche to posit a "right way" to truth over and against another way. Conscious formulations seem to be the result of intense inner struggles between twin brothers. What appears to be a clear and distinct description is clear and distinct only because it can be limned against the shadow of another way of saying the same thing. We have two words for this: "language" and "speech." So, too, we have "psyche" and "soul." For the purpose of clarity we shall, in what follows, contrast the language of psychology with the speech of the soul. By making this contrast we are standing within the tradition of the problem of expression going back to Parmenides, formulated sometimes as mythos and logos, sometimes as idealism and nominalism, sometimes, as in the Romantic period, in terms of a day side and night side of the soul,[5] but always ex-

5. In G. T. Fechner (1801–87) an extremity of the two languages and two ways of perception were contained within one person. While pioneering the advance of scientific sensation psychology and opening the area of psychophysics to abstract laws and experimental investigations, Fechner at the same time spoke the other language of the "night side" of the soul—a favorite term of his. While writing and translating works on chemistry, physics, and electricity, he also wrote, under the pseudonym "Dr. Mises," studies in parapsychology, the soul of plants, and supernaturalism. He devoted himself to Eastern metaphysics, especially the *Zend-Avesta*, presaging Nietzsche. The inner struggle between two ways of perception resulted in a mid-life breakdown, lasting three years and particularly affecting his sight. (He was nearly made blind). When he had recovered and returned to work —still on both levels—an integration of the parallel paths of sensation-observation and intuitive vision came to him in a twilight state (while lying in bed on the morning of October 22, 1850) when he "perceived" a unified world of thought, spirit, and matter, which conjoined his inner twins. See K. Lasswitz, *Gustav Theodor Fechner* (Stuttgart: Fromann, 1902). The German philosopher Wilhelm Dilthey (1833–1911), whose major importance lies in his explication of the differences of method and language between explanation and understanding, dreamt, during a crisis in his life (1894), of the School of Athens, within which a chasm appears to separate forever the philosophers from the scientists.

perienced as an intense inner struggle with a shadow twin who sees and would say everything differently.

Is Psychology Ill?

TRANSFERENCE HAS BEEN A LESSON IN POINT, showing how the naming can distort experience. There are so many other examples that sooner or later one begins to doubt the words one uses about the soul and its processes. Doubts refer to the double nature of man, whose inner twins speak with different tongues. So, this part of the book begins in a mire of doubts about how to speak about psychology at all. These doubts form part of the subjective factor inherent in psychology, which always must begin and end with the insurmountable obstacle of oneself. We cannot climb above ourselves to get a clear, objective view of the phenomena lying, well lit and flat out (i.e., explained), on the plains below. There are no "plains" in depth psychology; its "levels" are a manner of speech, a fantasy for ex-plaining. Because the subjective factor is inherent and always intrudes, it becomes methodologically correct, and necessary, to recognize the subjectivity at the beginning. We then have justification for raising doubts, for seeing the possible subjective factor of other people in other times, as revealed through their language. In their "objectivity" will lie something subjective. Their language may be telling us not only about the objects they are describing but about themselves, the subjects making the descriptions.

My doubts concern psychological language, the descriptive apparatus the field has developed for engaging the human soul. I doubt the common conventions of the profession—the language of sense-perception theories, of the stimulus-response model, of projective and intelligence tests, of diagnosis, psychodynamics, psychosomatics, and of case histories. I question why so much that is perplexing and vital to psychology is placed outside its own preserve and described in the language of pathopsychology and parapsychology. I question both these notions and the way psychology defines itself so as to create these extrapsychological fields. I distrust the psychological language used to describe the learning process and education; I question the tales psychology tells us about infancy—those fantasies about babies' experiences at the breast; nor can I give credence to psychology's words about sexuality, since it treats sexuality as a separate, concrete function.

Above all else, I distrust the language of psychopathology, the description of the alienations, sufferings, and bizarre life of the soul. Because psychopathology is characteristic for psychology as a whole, its way of viewing what is both most difficult to understand and most unpleasant to experience; because it, of all parts of psychology, affects us each most closely; because it names those phenomena which are most threatening to the language and system of mind we call psychology, it is this aspect of psychological language that will mainly engage us here. In psychopathology, the language of the field and the speech of the soul seem to go most at cross-purposes.

We might look at some examples of the language of psychology: readings from journals, case reports, texts, research studies. But it would be boring—indeed, insulting! Why can we not read this stuff? Why is it so enraging? Let us put the question psychologically: what in us is bored, insulted, outraged? These emotions are telling us something, some emotional truth. The emotional self looks to psychology—that discipline which calls itself after the soul—to connect it with this soul. But this expectation for nourishment, for help in the psyche's struggle for awareness, is frustrated by psychology itself. The language of psychology insults the soul. It would sterilize metaphors into abstractions. We are made ill because *it* is ill.

Once depth psychology spoke with a living tongue. The origins of modern psychology in the introspective Reformation, in the Romantic imagination of Coleridge, or in the revolutionary activities of Philippe Pinel spoke from the soul of an age. The Viennese psychoanalysts let the soul freely associate and make its radical, uncouth statements; its fantasies soared. The establishment was shocked by its method and its language, but it unleashed a new psychological speech. Psychology was in touch with the soul. It had imagination. But today, psychology—even depth psychology—is a tool of the establishment. It is supported by government money; it is part of conventional education; it is the first thing one does with a spouse or child who becomes unmanageable. Its language is common currency. "Case material," "ego development," "psychotherapy"—even "animus-ridden" and "negative mother"—die on our lips. We can no longer give them belief; they have lost conviction; they no longer are speech that carries soul. This language is dead.

This conventional language divides personality number one from personality number two even further. The method cannot meet the madness. Because of its own language, psychology becomes antitherapeutic, an instrument of a new philistinism called "community mental health," spreading its kind of mental illness. The soul is again driven into hiding and forced to fantasy a new set of symptoms appropriate to this age, like the mass St. Vitus' dance and religious delusions of the late Middle Ages and Reformation, fainting sensibilities in the eighteenth century, hysteria in the nineteenth, anxiety and schizophrenia in the early twentieth. Today it seems to be psychopathy. We are in the age of psychopathy, an age without reflection and without connection, that is, without psyche and without eros, an age that acts out the soul's metaphors in the streets. This psychopathic behavior in the streets, which we have come to condone as "normal" for the underprivileged, the adolescent, and the revolutionary, is largely nonverbal, or verbal only at the level of chants, shouts, and slogans.

A language that no longer carries metaphor displaces the metaphorical drive from its appropriate display in poetry and rhetoric, or any symbolic form, into direct action. The body becomes the place for the soul's metaphors, and everyone who turns toward body for salvation is driven at once into the immediate action—stands, positions, gestures, styles—of psychopathic behavior.

Where is the dialogue? Especially, where is the *psychological* dialogue? We long for psychic experiences yet doubt psychological language. What has happened to this language of psychology in a time of superb communication technics and democratic education? Why has its language game departed from the soul's play? We no longer believe that psychology speaks for the soul. An early and primary root of sanity (the *sanitas* of Tacitus and Cicero) meant sensible speech, the appropriate use of words. Does not the converse suggest that when the words of psychology lose touch with the psyche, its "insanity" is partly the fault of psychology's wrong speech? Or is the matter yet more serious: is the soul abandoning speech altogether? If so, the very root of human culture is withering. If the Word is the beginning and divine, then does not its death to the soul demonstrate the death of God?

Let us inquire how things in psychology got this way. Let us present a "case history" where psychology itself is the case whose history will be exposed.

Names on the Land: A Brief "Case History" of Psychology

We start upon an excursion. The land we shall travel through is old indeed, and we can never leave it as long as we live. Yet we have never been able to map this land, the psyche, adequately or describe it fully in a guidebook. There are many maps and many guidebooks, which often tell us more about their authors than about the land.

Curiously, it has become difficult to speak of the psyche directly. We seem to require the markings given it through the years. These markings have become so familiar—the labels "depression," "perception," "ego," "projection," for instance —that our individual experience of these events is masked by the name. The land merges into the language.

The names on the land reflect various pioneers and civilizations. There is a Weber's law, a Ganser syndrome, and a Korsakov psychosis, named after their discoverers, just as mountain ranges or new-found stars were named after their nineteenth-century discoverers. But language is not an adequate archaeological tool for determining which aspects of the psyche have long been known and which are recent. Greek can be no guide. Some words—"mania," "hypochondria," "melancholia," "catalepsy"—have been with us since ancient Greece. But "pyromania" appears only in the eighteenth century, "schizophrenia" in the twentieth. Nor do the words—even the Greek words—fall into any system. "Mania" has its origins in religious states, and its first differentiation was given by Plato in a mythic-philosophical context (*Phaedrus* 244–45). "Hypochondria" and "melancholia" began as somatic descriptions referring to the actual physical body, and, as words, they grew through many variations with the centuries. "Schizophrenia," on the other hand, though Greek in root, is a Swiss construct applied to a variety of early twentieth-century man as viewed through the strong-ego lenses of his psychiatric contemporaries.

The special language of psychology is surprisingly new. Of course, psychological words are everywhere in our speech. But psychological culture can be expressed in speech other than the language of its own field. Also, gestures, styles of living, eating, dressing, courting, loafing, kinds of music and dance—all exhibit psychological culture independent of psychological language. Culture of the psyche may indeed require language, but not necessarily the technical language of psychology, which, as a systematic expression of a field, a specialism, is recent. This specialized language largely results from ninetenth-century psychological laboratories at German universities, while the language of psychopathology developed hand in hand with the development of psychiatric institutions during the same period.

Can we imagine the psyche without this language? Without "psychology," "psychiatry," "psychopathology," "psychopathy," "psychosis," "psychotherapy," "psychoanalysis"? Without "intelligence tests," "mental tests," "mental hygiene," "mental health"? Without "alcoholism," "autism," "catatonia," "claustrophobia," "environment," "folie à deux," "homosexuality," "hypnotism," "introspection," "introversion"? Without any of the "socio" or "bio" compounds? I could list a hundred more. None of these terms existed before the past century. Even "ego," "libido," "personality," "unconscious," "rationalization," "suggestion," "aberration"—in their contemporary psychological usage—are creations of this modern period. "Projection," such a favorite of psychology today, and on which depend "projective tests" and "projective techniques," originated in its contemporary usage only in 1895–96 through Freud.[6]

Our psychological language is largely post-Napoleonic. Its development parallels the industrial revolution, positivism, nationalism, secularism, and all that is characterized as the "nineteenth-century mind." Our language represents more specifically the academic and medical mind of the nineteenth century. Psychology and psychopathology are children of the late Enlightenment, the hopeful Age of Reason as it hardened into an Age of Matter.

In exposing our "case," we shall not be able to cite the usual histories of psychology and psychiatry, much as we may rely upon their data. We are obliged to write another sort of guidebook, because the existing guides are part of the "case" itself. They share the language that arises from the same aspirations of progress, positivism, and secularism of the nineteenth-century mind. They present psychology and psychiatry as a developmental conquest over the confusions of the mind and its aberrations. Even where they do attempt historical distance, they lack psychological reflection upon

6. S. Freud, "Analysis of a Case of Chronic Paranoia," *The Standard Edition of the Complete Psychological Works of Sigmund Freud*, translated under the general editorship of James Strachey (London: Hogarth Press, 1953——), III, 184. (The *Standard Edition* will hereafter be referred to as "*SE*.")

this history.[7] Hence we shall make a new start, rewriting psychology's history in our own way, a modest attempt at psychological hermeneutics. We shall leave aside the current conflicts concerning the methods and the point of histories of ideas and of specific disciplines like psychology—problems which lead ultimately into those tangled issues of historicism, the nature of historical reality and the philosophy of history—because we are not so much writing history as we are writing psychology.

A history of psychology belongs as much to psychology as to history; it reports not only historical facts but also psychological fantasies. History may be taken as one of the ways the soul muses, one of the ways in which it psychologically reflects life. The history which follows differs in intention from other histories of psychology, although it does not differ in respect for historical "facts." We are attempting to see by means of history beyond history; we are attempting to see through it, regarding it as a concatenation of events, like a dream with many themes calling for interpretive understanding. For us history is a psychological field in which

7. For a short and thorough review of the literature on the history of psychiatry and depth psychology see G. Mora, "The History of Psychiatry: A Cultural and Bibliographical Survey," *Psychoanalytic Review,* LII (1965), 154–84. For a discussion of theoretical and methodological problems in the history of psychiatry see G. Mora and J. L. Brand, eds., *Psychiatry and Its History: Methodological Problems in Research* (Springfield, Ill., 1970), a collection of lively papers by some principals in the field. In B. Nelson's paper in that volume, "Psychiatry and Its Histories," six ways for approaching the history of psychiatry are presented: (1) commemoration and laudation of the Great Men, (2) progressive evolutionary historicism—the present as better than the past, (3) history of ideas, or historiosophy (which Ackerknecht, in the same volume, exposes for its faults), (4) social and cultural history, (5) historiography, or the critical study of the history of the field, and (6) Nelson's own hope for a newer, integrative approach. As one line toward this integrative approach we use an archetypal perspective toward history. Our hope is that this approach makes history more relevant, gives it psychological impact, again in keeping with our point of view that a history of *psychology* forms part of *psychology* and should serve soul-making.

fundamental patterns of the psyche stand out; history reveals the fantasies of the makers of history, and at their back and within the fantasies and patterns are the archetypes.

The word "psychology" enters history through lectures given by Melanchthon (1497–1560) in the mid-sixteenth century and through his later contemporaries, Goclenius and Casmann.[8] Psychology coincides with the Reformation, just as the many new compound expressions of the self, reflecting a new inwardness ("self-regard," "self-conceit," "self-linking," "self-contained") also arise with the Reformation or at the end of the sixteenth century.[9] The term "psychology" did not quite catch on, despite Christian von Wolff's use of it in Latin in two book titles in the early eighteenth century (*Psychologia Empirica*, 1732, and *Psychologia Rationalis*, 1734). The subject matter of psychology was contained in essays on man, on the understanding, on the human mind or human nature, on anthropology, on the reason, the passions, and the sensations by the major philosophers of the seventeenth and eighteenth centuries. But none thought to

8. The first work to have "psychology" in its title is credited to Rudolf Goclenius (1547–1628) of Marburg, whose *Psychologia—hoc est de hominum perfectione* appeared in 1590. It was followed by Otto Casmann's *Psychologia Anthropologica* in 1594. A still earlier use has recently been discovered by K. Kristić in Yugoslavia in a manuscript referring to the work of Marco Marulić (1450–1524), with the word *psichiologia* in a title; see Kristić's discussion in English, *Acta Inst. Psychol. Univ. Zagreb*, XXXVI (1964), 7–13. Cf. E. G. Boring, "A Note on the Origin of the Word Psychology," *Journal of the History of the Behavioral Sciences*, II (1966), 167. Perhaps the first appearance of "psychology" in English is to be found in the rendering from the Latin of the "Discourse of James De Back," which was published in the English translation of Harvey's *De Motu Cordis* (London, 1653) as an integral part of that book. The passage which gives our field perhaps its earliest definition in English runs as follows: "*Psychologie* is a doctrine which searches out man's Soul, and the effects of it; this is the part without which a man cannot consist" (cited by P. F. Cranefield, "'Psychology' as an English Word," *American Notes and Queries*, IV, No. 8 [1966], 116).

9. O. Barfield, *History in English Words* (London: Faber Paperbacks, 1962), p. 165.

title his work *Psychology* or to speak of it as "a psychology."

Then the century turned, and suddenly there appeared: 1808, F. A. Carus, *Psychologie;* 1812, Maine de Biran, *Essai sur les fondements de la psychologie;* 1816, J. F. Herbart, *Lehrbuch zur Psychologie;* 1817, A. Eschenmeyer, *Psychologie;* 1824; Stiedenroth, *Psychologie;* 1824–25, Herbart again, *Psychologie als Wissenschaft.* Thereafter followed J. C. A. Heinroth, Carl Gustav Carus, F. E. Beneke; and, ever since, there has been an uninterrupted flow of "psychology" books. Even Kant, who was this period's most powerful and original thinker about the mind of man, turned to psychology proper only when the century was turning and when he himself was in his seventies. An eighteenth-century man, Kant called his work "anthropology" instead of "psychology." Subsequently, as psychology ascended, the word "soul" declined. By the mid-nineteenth century, "soul" had all but disappeared from the specialized language of psychology.

With the exception of Maine de Biran, the field of psychology—from Melanchthon to Christian von Wolff to Herbart—is mainly a creation of men working in the German language.

Herbart (1776–1841) brought out his first *Lehrbuch* in 1816. Herbart's psychology had perhaps the widest influence and was the longest lasting. He has been considered the father of all modern psychological movements. He attempted by means of an algebra of psychic reactions to express the soul in mathematical formulas. Herbart spoke from the chair at Königsberg. He was Kant's successor there and sat upon that throne from 1809 until 1833. His maps and guidebooks were authoritative. Everyone who entered the land of psychology began to talk in his words, to see things as he described them, and to teach others in his language. Lecture halls could not contain his crowds; Herbartian societies blossomed in Europe and America; his influence in wedding psychology to education cannot be overestimated, and we are still Herbartians whenever we consider teaching and learning to be primarily psychological activities. Herbart described the soul as follows:

> The soul cannot be a substance in Leibniz's meaning, for it has no original activity. The soul originally has no ideas, emotions, or desires. It has no knowledge of itself nor of other objects. It possesses no categories of thought and intuition, nor faculties of will and action. The soul has originally no predispositions whatever. The simple nature of the soul is wholly unknown and must remain unknown. Thus it cannot serve as a subject matter for either speculative or empirical psychology.[10]

The only quality ascribed to the soul was a *vis inertia*, *Selbsterhaltung*, the capacity to maintain itself. Stripped of all actuality and potentiality, the soul was completely beyond

10. J. F. Herbert, *Lehrbuch zur Psychologie* (Hamburg: Voss, 1816), Pt. 3, pp. 152–53; translated by B. B. Wolman in "The Historical Role of Johann Friedrich Herbart," in *Historical Roots of Contemporary Psychology*, ed. B. B. Wolman (New York: Harper, 1968). Herbart's view of the soul held through, and we are obliged to consider it representative, despite the controversies throughout the century on "Die Seelenfrage" (see J. T. Merz, *European Thought in the Nineteenth Century* [Edinburgh: Blackwood, 1912], Vol. III). The counterposition is represented by Herbart's contemporary J. Heinroth (1773–1843), whose book on psychopathology came out in 1818 (Herbart's appeared in 1816). Heinroth, whose background was theological as well as medical, was a strong advocate of the soul, and to its sins he attributed all unfree states, i.e., psychic disorders. Psychopathology is ultimately a statement of the soul's guilt. (Compare O. H. Mowrer's recent simple-minded confusion of sin with psychopathology in *The Crisis in Psychiatry and Religion* [New York, 1961].) Heinroth, incidentally, has been credited with inventing the term "psychosomatics" and with the first use in print of the word "psychiatry" (1818), although it has been attributed to Reil's lectures in 1808. Its popularization is even later (1845); we owe this to Ernst von Feuchtersleben (1806–49), the Viennese physician, poet, and academic reformer, who also introduced "psychosis" and "psychopathy" in their modern senses. Cf. the English translation by H. E. Lloyd and B. G. Babbington of his *The Principles of Medical Psychology* (London: Sydenham Society, 1847); cf. also W. Leibbrand and A. Wettley, *Der Wahnsinn* (Freiburg and Munich: Alber, 1961), pp. 493 and 666, and R. Hunter and I. Macalpine, *Three Hundred Years of Psychiatry* (Oxford: Oxford University Press, 1963), p. 952.

the realm of knowledge. It was, so to speak, "kicked upstairs," given full authority as a Kantian *Real*, a *Ding an sich*, but it was vain even to talk of it. As Hume had destroyed the notion of self, so Herbart removed the soul from the living center of personality. Although this soul is ever present and the ground of what happens to us, we can never come to grips with this ground. It is a soul created in the image of that Protestant God who is totally transcendent, unknowable, and beyond empirical and speculative theology, outside our human phenomenal world. This was the soul of the university specialism called psychology.

(*Nota bene:* When psychology becomes a specialism and the psyche is set forth in an academic textbook, the soul disappears. When the soul is taken over by the university in the secular spirit of enlightenment, it loses all actuality, all substance, and all relevance for life. Thus academic psychology has been a psychology without soul from the beginning. Perhaps it was meant to be this way, inasmuch as two ways are necessary for viewing phenomena. Perhaps the entire movement of psychoanalysis had to take place outside the academic world, and the original psychoanalytic training institutes had to be independent of the universities, since the universities would have nothing to do with psychoanalytic conceptions. Psychoanalysis put psyche back in the middle of psychology and conceived it as having full and autonomous power. Curiously, we note that, as psychoanalysis moves closer to the academic world and becomes affiliated with university clinics and departments, it seems to lose soul. Acceptance by the university or the clinic means being acceptable to the university or the clinic, means having a view of the soul, a psychology, that can be accepted in the existential world of academia and medicine. The university and the clinic are not merely buildings or people; they are a cosmos, a *Seinsweise*. To be acceptable there means to share in that ontology and to participate in its ritual. (Previously one might have said that acceptance means serving, or worshiping, the same Gods.) Our experience of the soul in analysis and the way Jung wrote of it have so far found little acceptance in academic or clinical surroundings. Evidently psychology still follows Herbart and still excludes the soul. The push within analytical psychologists to be academically or clinically accepted expresses both a tragic tension between psychology and the soul and an uncertainty within the psychologist whether he can stand up for his own experience. Freud was honored at a distance by the academic and clinical world but was never fully accepted. However, he did not want that acceptance and even in his old age warned against the amalgamation of psychoanalysis by academic and clinical psychiatry.)

Herbart's textbook appeared in 1816. In 1817, in Paris, Jean-Etienne-Dominique Esquirol was giving the first clinical psychiatric lectures, in which he carefully elaborated the concept of hallucinations (among other things), and our view of these convincing sense perceptions without corresponding public objects is today the same as that given by Esquirol.[11] Hallucinations are central to our point that psychology and soul speak different tongues. For centuries people have experienced various utterly convincing visions, sounds, and smells, the reality of which did not depend upon the sole criterion of correspondence with an outer object. Some cul-

11. Esquirol's lectures were written in 1817 and published in his *Des Maladies mentales* (Paris, 1838), pp. 159–202. Cf. J. Paulus, *Le Problème de l'hallucination et l'évolution de la psychologie d'Esquirol à Pierre Janet* (Liège: Faculté de Philosophie et Lettres, 1941). Esquirol's definition is: "Un homme qui a la conviction intime d'une sensation actuellement perçue alors que nul objet propre à exciter cette sensation n'est à portée de ses sens, est dans un état d'hallucination: c'est un visionnaire." (Also useful: T. R. Sarbin and J. B. Suarez, "The Historical Background of the Concept of Hallucination," *Journal of the History of the Behavioral Sciences*, III (1967), 339–58.) While Esquirol and French psychiatry were enlightening the night side of the soul with diagnoses and clinical categories, at the same time the magnetists and mesmerists were encouraging irrational productions through hypnosis, trance, and somnambulism. While Esquirol gave his clinical lectures, the Portuguese Jesuit Abbé Faria held his public lectures demonstrating magnetism (1813) and published his booklet thereon in 1819.

tures encourage and expect these events; they are necessary for initiation. Philosophers recognize the difficulties that hallucinations occasion for a theory of the real and for a theory of knowledge. Hallucinations put in question the materialist theory of sense perceptions; they are indeed dangerous phenomena for our epistemology and ontology, and so are preferably parapsychological or pathopsychological. Testing the reality of psychic events such as hallucinations today tends to mean testing only their outer objective reality. We are still influenced by Esquirol and the French Enlightenment. The demon and ghost are banished, but with them go the ancestor and the angel; they too enter the realm of psychopathology. Esquirol's observations were useful indeed for psychology, but they have had a reverse effect on the soul. They undermined the belief that the soul had private access to and communication with an "other world." This in turn undermined belief in that other world, since experiential evidence of it now had become pathopsychological or parapsychological. The soul lost its conviction in itself as a timeless intangible in vivid touch with timeless intangibles. In 1817 the evidence for such conviction became "hallucinatory." Public reality encroached upon private reality. The key word is "convincing": one could have these intimate experiences providing one did not give them real faith.[12]

12. Because so much of the "*puer* revolution" turns on the use of hallucinogens, hallucination has become a banner in a cause. Despite the noisy foreground, *puer* events always carry a new spirit because of the archetypal nature of the *puer* (as elaborated in my "*Senex* and *Puer*," *Eranos Jahrbuch*, XXXVI (1967) (Zurich: Rhein Verlag, 1968). Therefore, we are obliged to look at the hallucinogen for its meaning. Perhaps it signifies a desire to "save the phenomena" that have so long been declared aberrations and to readmit the banished modes of perception and, with them, another *Weltanschauung* and theory of the real based on a new theory of perception. This would indeed challenge the established epistemology and ontology with which Western man has been identified at least since Descartes—and identified to such a degree that he is largely unconscious that any other theory of perception could even be possible. It is a pity that this essential issue of metaphysics must be obfuscated by parent-child complexes and the *senex-puer* fight over legality, authority, and order.

In that same year, 1817, in which Esquirol in Paris was giving a pathological tenor to hallucinations, in England another superb—if not frightening—product of the Enlightenment, Jeremy Bentham (1748–1832: nearly an exact contemporary of Goethe), introduced another fundamental idea into modern, post-Napoleonic consciousness. In a minor, short, and late work, *A Table of the Springs of Action* (London, 1817), Bentham uses charts to sum up concisely his view of the basics of human ethics, psychology, and biography. He states: "Psychological *dynamics* (by this name may be called the science, which has for its subject these same springs of action, considered as such) has for its basis psychological *pathology*."[13] In 1817, long before Sigmund Freud, Jeremy Bentham found the mind a dynamic system, the source of whose dynamics lay in the mind's own sickness.

Jeremy Bentham was a prodigy of the Enlightenment. He recalled at the age of three being "seated at table—a reading desk upon the table, and a huge folio on the reading desk—a lighted candle at each side, . . . and myself absorbed in my studies."[14] He learned Greek and Latin and played Handel on a miniature violin by age five; by the time he had matriculated at Oxford, at age thirteen, he had mastered Locke's *Essay Concerning the Human Understanding*. He was the spirit of reason embodied. Bentham spiritually fathered the Benthamites; his "greatest good for the greatest number," based on the ultimate polarities of the pleasure-pain

---

The issue at the deepest level is not drugs. The issue is admission of a nonmaterialistic view of the real, the reality of private knowledge, and, ultimately, the reality of the soul.

13. J. Bentham, "A Table of the Springs of Action," *The Works of Jeremy Bentham*, ed. J. Bowring (Edinburgh, 1843), I, 205.

14. C. W. Everett, *The Education of Jeremy Bentham* (New York, 1931), p. 6. For a recent and careful exposition of Bentham's pioneering, but neglected, contributions to psychology see P. McReynolds, "The Motivational Psychology of Jeremy Bentham," *Journal of the History of the Behavioral Sciences*, IV (1968), 230–44 and 349–64, with bibliography. For Bentham's positivistic-materialistic view of language see O. Barfield, *Speaker's Meaning* (Middletown, Conn.: Wesleyan University Press, 1963), p. 52.

principle, also fathered the utilitarianism of the Mills. "Utilitarian" is his word. He inspired Mirabeau in France and Potemkin in Russia, the liberal movement, social and legal reform, and the best progressive ideals of the early nineteenth century.

Yet this same Bentham viewed the soul darkly indeed. The traditional "motions of the soul" could now be called "psychodynamics," and these dynamics emerged from "psychological pathology." Psychopathology, the shadow brother of psychology, soon became the major figure. Bentham characterized psychopathology as "the unseemly parts of the human mind." Because this cannot be overtly admitted, it is covered over, Bentham says, with a "sort of fig-leaves."[15] The image of "fig leaves" reveals Bentham's fantasy, which

15. Bentham, "A Table of the Springs of Action," p. 219. Comparable to the position of Heinroth against the rationalism of Herbart in German psychology would be the place of Coleridge against the mainstream of rationalism in England represented by Bentham. Coleridge's "Kubla Khan" was printed in 1816; it still remains—although bordering on the "hallucinatory"—the exemplary witness to the spontaneous creative power of the imaginal soul. In 1817 Coleridge published his *Biographia Literaria*, in which we find the modern definitions of "subjective" and "objective" and "intuition" and the differentiation between "delirium" and "mania" and between "fancy" and "imagination." Coleridge's impact upon our psychological language, especially through his public lectures and his personal relationships, has yet to be adequately investigated. J. S. Mill (*Mill on Bentham and Coleridge* [London: Chatto and Windus, 1950]) in 1838 first contrasted these two men as prototypes of fundamental opposites, "the two great seminal minds of England in their age." See, further, O. Barfield, *What Coleridge Meant* (Middletown, Conn.: Wesleyan University Press, 1971).

Fighting the same battle, and particularly through language, was Thomas Taylor, who singlehandedly brought all of the works of the major Greek philosophers into English. During this period (1816–21) he published his translations of Plotinus and Proclus and wrote on myth, alchemy, the Greek mysteries, and the Neoplatonists. His enemy in particular was soulless materialism, which he condensed into "Empire" (the growing British mercantile power) and against which he railed with as much fervor as Blake against Locke. (Between 1804 and 1820 Blake was working on his *Jerusalem*.) For Blake versus Locke cf. K. Raine, *Blake and Tradition* (Princeton: Princeton University Press, 1968), Vol. II, Chap. 20, "The Sensible World."

he shared with the Victorian period, at the beginning of which he stood. For it was then, too (1818), that the physician Thomas Bowdler (1754–1824) published his edition of Shakespeare, "in which those words and expressions are omitted which cannot with propriety be read aloud in a family." Bowdler perceived the relationship between the imaginal and language, and he attempted to control the imagination through the censorship of language. He went on to apply his method of "fig leaves" to Gibbon's *History*. His name has entered the *Oxford English Dictionary:* "to bowdlerize" means "to castrate."

Having been secularized by the Enlightenment, the soul no longer could hold spirit and eros together. The spirit was carried by the materialistic idealism of utilitarian progress. Eros devolved into bowdlerized sentimentality and pornography. Finally, at the century's end, they were reunited by Freud's sexual rationalism, a secularization, not only of the soul, but now of spirit and eros too.

During those same early years of the century the first specialized psychology journal appeared (1818) [16] and the

16. G. Zilboorg, *A History of Medical Psychology* (New York: Norton, 1941), pp. 383–84, lists nearly fifty such journals with dates of first appearance between 1818 and 1893. Earlier than the ones he records is the journal begun by J. C. Reil, *Magazin für psychische Heilkunde,* in 1805 and continued by his pupil, F. Nasse, an indefatigable editor and originator of professional publications. However, credit for the first truly psychological periodical belongs to Karl Philipp Moritz (1756–93), who, in association with Moses Mendelssohn, Marcus Herz, and Solomon Maimon, initiated a program of disciplined introspection resulting in a journal devoted to this "empirical soul-knowledge." The *Magazin zur Erfahrungsseelenkunde* ran in Berlin for ten years, beginning in 1783. Its contents covered a range of subjects which today no single "serious" journal could include. Moral philosophy, linguistics and semantics, sexual abnormality, child education, and parapsychology as well as psychotherapy and psychopathology all came under its purview. Within the short span of thirty-seven years this psychological pioneer moved through an amazing development. Moritz recapitulates in one man's soul the history of an age. He began as a Pietist, just as the new psychological journals may be seen to have had one part of their origin in the over five hundred moralistic and pietistic weeklies that appeared in Germany in the last

first technical histories and bibliographies were published.[17] One after another, syndromes were named. Sutton first described "delirium tremens" (1813), Parkinson "paralysis agitans" (1817), Gooch "puerperal insanity" (1819), Grohmann "moral insanity" (1819),[18] and, most important, A. L. Bayle, at the age of twenty-three, gave definition to "dementia paralytica" (1822). Naming the syndromes—neurological and psychological—continued throughout the century. The method was separation and isolation of phenomena through acute observation and description. Meanwhile, the synthesizers attempted to build the explorers' reports from the field

---

half of the eighteenth century. Pietism gave religious support to the introspective method Moritz was to develop. His program called for a study of the psyche based on exact self-examination in contrast to metaphysical speculation. Obsessive rumination about the states of the soul was a contribution of Pietism to the beginnings of empirical introspection, even if the ruminations tended to remain intrapsychic—reflection about reflection and without eros. Moritz took the ideas of feeling which were then in the air (owing to Rousseau, Goethe, Tetens, Herder, and Mendelssohn and to "sentimentality" and "sensibility") and found application for them in a stricter methodology, beginning with oneself, which refused categories and diagnostic names in favor of actual experience. He gave dreams an important place; he wrote on moods and fantasy; and he was continually involved in the problem of language. Sickly, obsessive, driven, full of ideas and feelings, Moritz, in the years before his death, discovered the importance of myth, as if his preoccupation with the psyche in its depths led him to its archetypal layers. His *Götterlehre, oder mythologische Dichtungen der Alten* (Berlin, 1791), intuited the intimate relation between classical mythology and human fantasy. Cf. G. Hinsche, *K. Ph. Moritz als Psychologe* (Halle, 1912).

17. U. Trélat, *Aliénation mentale: recherches historiques* (Paris, 1827); J. B. Friedreich, *Versuch einer Literargeschichte der Pathologie und Therapie der psychischen Krankheiten* (Würzburg, 1830). Also relevant is J. P. F. Deleuze, *Histoire critique du magnétisme animal*, 2 vols. (Paris, 1813).

18. In English the term "moral insanity" is attributed to the Quaker psychiatrist and anthropologist James Cowles Prichard (1786–1848), who did define this condition in his *Treatise on Insanity*, published in 1835 (his first publication on the subject was in 1833); however, J. C. A. Grohmann (1769–1847) had already described "moralische Insanie" as a symptom in 1819 (A. Wettley, *Von der "Psychopathia sexualis" zur Sexualwissenschaft* [Stuttgart: Enke Verlag, 1959], p. 57).

into one classificatory system, into one complete guidebook. In psychiatry, Kraepelin achieved the complete guidebook at the turn of the new century. There was now a classification into which every aberration could fit. Already in 1913, however, Karl Jaspers raised fundamental questions about diagnostic categories and psychopathological classifications. The terms have been continually questioned, and they are used in widely differing ways according to the personal preference of practitioners. Psychiatry is still struggling to achieve accurate operational definitions. Some existentialists would discard this attempt altogether.

The progress of diagnostic system-building can be compared with parallel developments in other fields during the nineteenth century. It paralleled medicine especially, at a time when medicine was making extraordinary etiological discoveries through the study of pathology. After all, the field workers in psychopathology were physicians. Their models of the nineteenth-century mind at work were Bernard, Pasteur, Neisser, Koch, Virchow. The success of this method in psychopathology preceded a similar development in psychology proper, which was also separating faculties of the psyche and studying them dismembered, piece by piece, with new techniques. But psychopathology had stolen the march on psychology itself.

Why did the advance of the field proceed through the shadow? What made psychopathology so fascinating just at this time of history? As Karl Jaspers, Erwin Ackerknecht, and Kathleen Jones each stress, psychopathology is a problem to which the human reason gave its attention relatively late. Psychiatry is the youngest full branch of medicine. The term came into existence through lectures by Reil only around 1805. Only then did it begin to be a separate and "teachable" specialty. Why did this concern with the pathology of the psyche wait until this moment to break out? Why so late, and with such vengeance?

Perhaps the Age of Reason had reached its last borders: the borders of reason itself, the mind and its own darkness.

The light, now turning toward itself, created a new science of the mind, psychology, and of the mind's shadow, psychopathology. Perhaps at its outset the nineteenth century was somehow aware of the shadow which the Enlightenment had been piling up within the soul—the same shadow that the same enligtened reason was piling up in other ways in the outer world. Perhaps Mary Shelley's *Frankenstein* (1818) belongs also to the history of psychiatry.

Eighteenth-century reason defined itself with such words as "arrange," "category," "classify," "method," "organize," "regulate," "system." [19] It was spellbound by "order," by "living in a 'clockwork' cosmos." [20] Perhaps the immense energy that went into ordering mental pathology was meant to hold mental disorder at bay. Why, we may ask, were the new continents of the psyche not named with more felicity? *Ir*rational and *un*conscious, like *in*sane, are negative signs, begrudgingly affixed by reason to what it does not comprehend. One might have called Uranus or Neptune "non-Saturn," Australia "un-Asia." Even that Kantian-style definition of the unconscious as a *negative Grenzbegriff* (negative borderline concept) [21] betrays the same pejorative bias toward the speech of the soul, whose expressions are simply imaginative, symbolic, fantastic, mythic—all words standing on their own, requiring no prior terms that are rational, conscious, and sane.

Not only was the science young, but it was the invention, to a surprising degree, of young men. Three of the most influential compendia of the nineteenth century were written by W. Griesinger (1817–68) and E. Kraepelin (1856–1926) in Germany and by H. Maudsley (1835–1918) in England. Griesinger was twenty-eight and Kraepelin twenty-seven when their volumes first were printed; Maudsley was thirty-two. When the massive work of Eduard von Hartmann

19. Barfield, *History in English Words,* p. 174.
20. *Ibid.*, p. 177.
21. C. G. Jung, *CW,* VI, par. 837; see, further, V. White, *God and the Unconscious* (London: Harvill Press, 1952), p. 37.

(1842–1906) appeared, which brought the "unconscious" into the book's title and thus out into the open at last, he was twenty-seven.

Other young physicians gave us these words: E. Hecker (1843–1909), "hebephrenia," age twenty-eight; G. Beard (1839–83), "neurasthenia," age twenty-nine; W. Sander (1838–1922), "paranoia" (in its present definition), age thirty. Influential works on psychic disorders, written before their authors were thirty, came from the pens of Falret (1794–1870), Georget (1795–1828), Brierre de Boismont (1797–1881), Billod (1818–86) in French; Vering (1796–1829), Hecker (1795–1850), Neumann (1814–84), Moebius (1853–1907), and Bloch (1872–1922) in German; Laycock (1812–76), Carter (1828–1918), and Issac Ray (American, 1807–81) in English. S. A. A. D. Tissot's inestimably influential work on the dangers of masturbation was written while the author was in his twenties. The essentials of Pierre Janet's system of psychopathology (*L'Automatisme psychologique*) appeared in 1889, when Janet was thirty. Bichat was dead at thirty. George Huntington (1851–1916), of Long Island, at the age of twenty-one first singled out and gave his name to inherited St. Vitus' dance, now known as Huntington's chorea.

It was particularly in this realm, organic psychiatry, that young men made their contributions. Bayle was twenty-three. Wernicke (1848–1905) did his investigations of aphasia at twenty-six; Hitzig (1838–1907) and Fritsch (1838–1897) discovered the electrical excitability of the brain, leading to localization of brain functions and to electroencephalography, before they were thirty and published their results when they were thirty-two; Wagner von Jauregg (1857–1940), who received the first Nobel award given for psychiatry (1927), wrote his earliest paper on fever therapy for progressive paralysis before he was thirty. Sakel (born 1900) began insulin shock treatments in his twenties. Hughlings Jackson (1834–1911) described the epileptiform seizures that bear his name at age twenty-nine. Also, at twenty-eight,

Lombroso (1836–1909) produced his influential book linking genius with insanity.

The French Revolution and the Napoleonic era had brought young men into positions of authority—even in psychology. Young authors became new authorities about the psyche and its states. In an expanding field, men were appointed at an early age to fill high posts in university clinics. They entered the guild of clinical psychopathology, wrote in the new journals, published the books and texts which established the new terms, and thus indoctrinated the generations unto our day. The profession created the language, and the language supported the profession. Clinic, university, and profession were joined in the fraternity of this new language.

"Sexualwissenschaft"

The last area to be claimed by the language of psychology in the nineteenth century was sexuality. Although there are no new sexual practices or fantasies not elaborated by the Greek and Roman imagination, although Galen gave us concepts such as "satyriasis" and "priapismus," although the actualities ruled by Aphrodite are less complicated and less various than many other domains of the Olympians, the latter part of the nineteenth century and this, our own century, have turned to Jeremy Bentham's fig leaf with considerable zeal and technical skill.

New words were coined: "vaginismus" by an American physician (J. M. Sims, 1861) during the Civil War; "homosexuality" in Germany in 1869; "exhibitionism" in France by E. C. Lasègue in 1877. In 1886 the Austrian, R. von Krafft-Ebing, through his remarkable book *Psychopathia Sexualis*, contributed "sadism" and "masochism." Havelock Ellis invented, at the turn of the century, "narcissism" and "autoerotism" and borrowed "erotic symbolism" from Eulenberg (1895); then Freud in 1905, with his *Three Contributions to the Theory of Sex*, gave us a rich lode of new terms and that marvelous mythical being, the polymorphous perverse infant.

A year later (1906) Ivan Bloch circumscribed the entire region with the appropriate word *Sexualwissenschaft:* both sexual and scientific.

Although sexuality had now become assimilated by psychology, it had not become psychological. Rather did this union sexualize psychology. Anxiety could be called "castration" anxiety; envy, "penis" envy. With the school of Melanie Klein, the affective ambiguities between mother and child became the "good" and "bad" breast. *Sexualwissenschaft* perceived accurately the sexual in the imaginal but then reduced the imaginal to the sexual. In his famous case of the sun-phallus, Jung had already seen the imaginal in the sexual.[22] Therewith he took a giant step beyond the nineteenth century, which always saw the sexual—whether in science, in classical studies, or in pornography—as only concrete biological activity. Sexuality was always sex. The step that Jung took has still to be taken by many even now. Jung saw that instinct has an imaginal aspect, a mythic factor, and that therefore the sexual is also an activity of the imagination, a psychological expression; the sexual is a way the soul speaks. *Sexualwissenschaft,* as a union of the two polarities, the sexual and the rational, still omits the psyche, still neglects the meaning *to the psyche* of sexual messages. Wherever in the eighteenth and nineteenth centuries we turn to writers on sexual subjects (Tissot, de Sade, Krafft-Ebing, or the pornographers), they miss the mythic factor—that the messages are fundamentally mythic and part of an archetypal pattern *that means something.* Thus "perversions," like the

22. Cf. C. G. Jung, *Psychological Types* (*CW,* VI, pars. 372–74), for a succinct presentation of Jung's position on the sexual and imaginal. Freud's insight into the sexual factor in neuroses partly arises from three similar offhand experiences which Freud (according to Jones, *The Life and Work of Sigmund Freud,* I, 273) had with Breuer, with Charcot, and with Chrobak. In all, "la chose génitale" (Charcot) was viewed as basic to the cause and cure of neuroses. Freud took literally this etiological hunch in the language of his time. He did not see clearly enough that "la chose génitale," like the psychoneuroses, has both a literal and an imaginal aspect.

words "abnormal," "deviation," and "*délire*," imply a true way, which one can be turned from (perverted, deviated), or not square with (abnormal), or be out of line with (*délire*). Whether this behavior or fantasy is perverse *per se* or perverse according to cultural norms, it will always require psychological illumination. It must be read for its meaning. Psychopathological definitions tend to beg the basic question; they leave us with the feeling that the meaning is contained by the definition. An example is masochism.

As Esquirol's definition of hallucinations was decisive for the visions of the soul, so was Krafft-Ebing's definition of masochism decisive for the sufferings of the soul. He tells how he derived the name:

> I feel justified in calling this sexual anomaly "masochism," because the author Sacher-Masoch frequently made this perversion, which up to his time was quite unknown to the scientific world as such, the substratum of his writings. I followed thereby the scientific formation of the term "Daltonism," from Dalton, the discoverer of color-blindness.[23]

The phenomena now scientifically named, in the fashion of the time, became appropriated by psychopathology through this language. They became perversions. Naming changes the thing named. (When Adam names the animals, they are then doomed to perform in accordance with their names; they take on the quality inherent in the name.) Thus did an immense area of the psyche become known as "masochism," for Freud and the psychoanalysts extended the

23. R. von Krafft-Ebing, *Psychopathia Sexualis* (Stuttgart, 1886); English trans., 12th ed. (New York: Pioneer, 1946), p. 132. The German original reads: "Anlass und Berechtigung, diese sexuelle Anomalie 'Masochismus' zu nennen, ergab sich mir daraus, dass der Schriftsteller Sacher-Masoch in seinen Romanen und Novellen diese wissenschaftlich damals noch gar nicht gekannte Perversion zum Gegenstand seiner Darstellungen überaus häufig gemacht hatte. Ich folgte dabei der wissenschaftlichen Wortbildung 'Daltonismus' (nach Dalton, dem Entdecker der Farbenblindheit)."

original area to emotions, fantasies, and character attitudes, well beyond Krafft-Ebing's actual "masochistic" behavior. Finally, this term—coined from the surname of a minor Austrian novelist of the latter part of the century (1836–95)—was used, first by psychoanalysis and now by the public, to describe the fundamental quality of feminine psychology. The archetypal background to that peculiarity in our tradition which again and again identifies the essence of so-called femininity with so-called masochism will be explored thoroughly in Part Three. The task here is merely to examine the psychological implications of "masochism."

Krafft-Ebing and Freud might well have turned to Bernard of Clairvaux rather than to Sacher-Masoch; they might have read Cistercian mysticism rather than *Venus in Furs*. The union of eros and suffering is a widely known religious phenomenon, especially among Christians, whose martyrs used a mystical speech drawn from the Song of Songs and the Passion to describe their fearful joys. (Our word "suffering" is originally sacred and derives from this source. It was the English for the *passio* of Christ on the Cross, retained still in our "Suffering Jesus.") But as Bentham said, nineteenth-century psychodynamics had its springs in psychopathology. Those crucial experiences of psychic life, eros and suffering and their union, had become, through the simplistic materialism of the nineteenth century, "nothing but" pleasure and pain, which Bentham might have liked to calibrate with his "felicific calculus," his fantasy for the mathematical formulation of pleasure and pain. And the small measure to which these themes had shrunk was yet further reduced: pleasure was sexual pleasure, and pain was physical pain. The new term for their conjunction was "algolagnia"—of course an "abnormality," since pleasure and pain are, by reason's definition, mutually exclusive. And this mean conceptual instrumentation was employed by *Sexualwissenschaft* to grasp the eros and suffering of the *gloria passionis* of great souls. Martyrs who might become saints in another age could now be scientifically named "masochists."

Let us listen to Bernard of Clairvaux describe the *gloria passionis:*

> For he [the martyr] does not feel his own wounds when he contemplates those of Christ. The martyr stands rejoicing and triumphant, even though his body is torn to pieces; and when his side is ripped open by the sword, not only with courage but even with joy he sees the blood which he has consecrated to God gush forth from his body. But where now is the soul of the martyr? Truly in a place, in the rock, in the bowels of Christ, where it has entered, indeed, through his open wounds. . . . And this is the fruit of love, not of insensibility [*Neque hoc facit stupor, sed amor*].[24]

Or hear Bonaventura, a man not said to be given to ecstatic transports, when he counsels a nun:

> Whosoever desires from God the waters of grace . . . let him draw them from the fountains of the Saviour, that is, from the five wounds of Jesus Christ. Therefore draw near . . . to Jesus wounded, to Jesus crowned with thorns, to Jesus nailed to the gibbet . . . and do not merely look at the marks of the nails in his hands, do not merely put your finger into the place of these nails, do not merely place your hand into his side, but enter wholly by the gate of his side right to the very heart of Jesus. And there transformed into Christ by the most burning love of the Crucified, fastened by the nails of the divine fear, transfixed by the lance of a heartfelt love [*lancea praecordialis dilectionis transfixa*], pierced by the sword of the deepest compassion, seek nothing else, wish for no other thing than to die with Christ on the cross . . . cry out and say, With Christ I am nailed to the Cross.[25]

The invention "masochistic," like the term "hallucination," placed in the shadow, on the side of psychopathology, one

24. Bernard of Clairvaux "Sermones in Cantica Canticorum" 61. 8, translated by E. Auerbach in *Literary Language and Its Public in Late Latin Antiquity and in the Middle Ages* (London: Routledge & Kegan Paul, 1965), pp. 70–71.

25. Bonaventura "De perfectione vitae ad sorores" 6; cf. Auerbach, *Literary Language and Its Public*, pp. 76–77.

way in which the soul is victim of the numinous and submits to the overwhelming power of the wholly other. This submission, in torture and mortification, is paradoxical: it gives both pleasure and pain. But it cannot be reduced to pleasure and pain. Psychological explanations formulated largely through the sensation function soon founder upon materialism, hedonism, and especially upon reductionism.[26] The basic sensation elements cannot account for the higher experiences, the simpler for the more complex. Masochism shows the reverse to be true: the complex molds the simple into a new meaning. Masochism shows that pleasure and pain are not ultimate opposites of a metapsychological polarity, as sensation psychology conceived them to be: irreducible basics of psychic life. In masochistic experience, pain and pleasure unite. Thus is masochism a paradigm, revealing the power of the psyche to transcend its so-called basics, pleasure and pain. The psychic qualities, eros and suffering, can transform their pleasure and pain components and join them. Masochistic phenomena can be seen against this background: the conjunction of opposites, which, as an *opus contra naturam*, seems from one point of view a perversion of nature.

In one respect some Freudians were right about masochism when they generalized it into a condition of the psyche as a whole. If it is an attitude of the person, then it is not merely a quirk or kink that should be treated as something gone

26. We find a curious repetition of sensationist psychology running from Locke through Cabanis, Herbart, Fechner, and Bentham to Freud. The similarity of emphasis upon sensation and the pain-pleasure polarity, resulting helplessly in materialistic hedonism, suggests an archetypal model influencing this line of thought. It could be called "Apollonic sensationalism" (see below, pp. 225, 288 f., on the term "Apollonic"), because, although stressing sensation, it always takes one away from the concrete and immediate through elaborate formulations into laws, principles, and mathematics. It differs altogether from the poetic intuition of the Romantics, like Keats and Blake, and like Moritz and C. G. Carus in psychology, who distrusted abstractions and for whom sensation was directly vivid, the stuff and filling of knowledge rising from imagination. Sensation experienced through the imagination and formulated by it is altogether different from sensation in the service of reason.

wrong and needing to be fixed. As long as masochism is regarded as a sexual anomaly only and sexuality is taken only as a concrete "function," the psychological import is reduced to piecemeal localizations in the sexual function or in one's personal history. Then, rather than an archetypal expression, it becomes something like a sore finger or twisted knee, calling for repair. The model is perfect functioning: sexuality as a smoothly running, conflictless apparatus. No pain—and especially no enjoyment of pain. One looks for its source in childhood beatings or whatever other adventurous fantasies the analyst and the analysand together concoct. But let us suppose instead that the source is *general* and not particular, local, or even sexual in the restricted sense. Suppose the source is not even in the past only, but, like all psychic phenomena, also refers to one's death. (Natural phenomena refer backward through their growth processes to their origins, whereas psychic phenomena refer, in addition, to their meaning for the soul in terms of death.) Suppose masochism to be related to dying, imagined as an ecstatic release, as something the soul wants and needs and which it receives through the discovery of an intense, overwhelming value of the flesh and its exquisite enjoyment, which is also our worst pain. Suppose masochism as a death experience and quite bothersome for life. Suppose, at the same time, that masochism makes possible a union of soul and flesh, impossible so intensely in any other way.

In other words, every pathological bias obstructs the possibility of metaphysical instruction; once experiences have been labeled and declared abnormal, we cannot learn from them or let them carry us beyond their immediate actuality. They are trapped by their names into mechanical performance. They lose their flight of fantasy. So, indeed, we want to rid ourselves of such symptoms, which are not the symptoms so much as the names. From them we truly suffer; whereas the phenomena themselves, freed from their labels, become modes of unusual experience. The unusual becomes abnormal only from the "normal" view, which one-sidedly judges in terms of "life." But every experience must be questioned also in regard to death, for then experiences take on soul and become truly psychological.[27]

If Passion mysticism—the mysticism of the cross and its stations, of the stigmata and the bleeding heart, of the flayed martyrs and the flagellants—becomes masochism, we have, by naming this after Masoch, turned passion into pornography. Let us remember that this same nineteenth century, for all its rational progress, also saw, as Stephen Marcus has shown, the high point of Western prurience and pornography.[28] The same debased mixture of eros and suffering—sentimentalized, secularized, sexualized—as it appears in nineteenth-century literature, is described by Mario Praz in *The Romantic Agony*.[29]

"Masochism," like so many of the words we have been discussing, reveals nothing of the underlying fantasy. Sacrifice, torture, passivity, the value of being a victim—we are told nothing of what these *mortificatio* phenomena mean to the soul. And these *mortificatio* phenomena existed long before the nineteenth century, as Krafft-Ebing himself notes. We find torture in primitive ritual; flagellation in healing, fertility rites, and ascesis; flaying in alchemy.[30] In this case scientific naming did not advance science, but it did degrade the experience, placing it within the framework of the century's *Anschauung*.

27. For a fuller discussion of the "death experience" and the "pathological bias" see my *Suicide and the Soul* (London: Hodder & Stoughton, 1964), Chaps. IV and IX.

28. S. Marcus, *The Other Victorians* (New York: Bantam, 1967), and G. R. Taylor, "Sex Denied," in *Sex in History* (New York: Ballantine, 1954).

29. M. Praz, *The Romantic Agony*, trans. A. Davidson (London: Fontana Paperbacks, 1960).

30. Cf. H. R. Schwarz, "Die medizinische Flagellation" (dissertation, University of Zurich, 1963); see also C. G. Jung, on flaying and on torture, in "The Visions of Zosimos" and "The Philosophical Tree" (*CW*, XIII) and, on sacrifice, in his "Transformation Symbolism in the Mass" (*CW*, XI). Jung gave a radical shift of meaning to "sadism-masochism" phenomena, which, on the model of alchemy, belong to the *opus*.

Therefore it might be legitimate to ask why "masochism" appeared at all. What was the collective psyche of the age expressing through this new psychopathological designation? Could it not have a meaning for the soul of the times, a statement from its collective levels? Perhaps masochism is a late Victorian and German expression for religious erotic passion, of a piece with the Romantic agony, the flood of flagellation pornography, *fin de siècle* art, the feminist movement: a personalized and profaned cry of the soul. The psyche had lost touch with eros, just as eros, having been excluded from psychology, was simplified and debased into pornography and sentimentality. Thus psychology discovered "masochism"; and psychology found masochism in the psyche, characterizing its femininity as masochistic. The "discovery" of masochism tells us that at that time the psyche craved to submit in some form, in any form, to eros—eros at any price—in order to disengage itself from the imperious materialist inflation of the nineteenth century's insistence that the psyche belongs only to the mind.

Psyche = Mind: Mind = Head

As the eighteenth century drew to its close, the head took on more and more fascination. The intuitive physiognomy of J. C. Lavater (1741–1801) spread through fashion and science. Men of both reason and romanticism were becoming head-hunters, looking to the head for the key to the nature of man. Until the time of Pinel and Bichat the "seat" of psychic disorder was often sought in the stomach, the bowels, and the ganglia of the midriff. But the abdomen was abandoned for the head—especially owing to Bayle's (too soon generalized) proof that psychic disorder = brain disease. By the mid-nineteenth century psychiatry had become what Ackerknecht calls "brain psychiatry."

When the Age of Light and Reason became the Terror, there was Dr. Guillotin (1738–1814), with his progressive blade for decapitation. Because it was mechanical, it was objective; because objective, it was democratic and humane. There was Mme. Marie Tussaud-Grosholz (1760?–1850), originally of Berne, who sculpted first the heads of the prominent leaders in Paris and then their decapitated heads and then went touring with her wax-head collection through England, beginning in 1802. Vicq d'Azyr (1748–94), the premier physician to a later victim, Marie-Antoinette, gave his name to a fiber pathway in the brain. F. J. Gall (1758–1828) in Vienna and Paris between 1800 and 1813 developed phrenology to establish a one-to-one, point-to-point correspondence between psyche and skull. "Gall's doctrine gave a new dignity to the brain. With him—see his famous slogan 'God and the brain'—it actually became an object of almost religious worship." [31] There was also the influential, romantic physiology of Joseph Görres (1776–1848), who, though not a physician, while still in his twenties produced several volumes (1802–6) giving priority, based on medicophilosophical assertions, to the brain as "Zentralwelt im Organismus." In Sardinia, Luigi Rolando (1773–1831) was experimenting, between 1804 and 1814, with electrical current on the brains of pigs, turtles, sheep, dogs, fowls, fish, goats, deer, and cats, while, in Germany, F. Tiedemann (1781–1861) was examining the brains of human fetuses. There were Charles Bell's beautiful anatomical drawings of the head (1802) and Goethe's theory of the skull (1806) and Oken's (1807). In 1809, two days after the funeral, "Papa" Haydn's skull was stolen from his grave. And there was Dr. Pierre-Jean-Georges Cabanis (1757–1808), in whose arms Mirabeau died and who probably did more than any other man to spread the sensa-

31. E. Ackerknecht, "Contributions of Gall and the Phrenologists to Knowledge of Brain Function," in *The Brain and Its Functions*, ed. F. N. L. Poynter (Oxford: Basil Blackwell, 1958), p. 150. Our contemporary notion of a psychological "function" derives largely from phrenology (a word coined in 1815 by T. Foster), that is, from the notion that a local section of the brain actively performs a specific task or governs the exercise of traits. See D. Bakan, "The Influence of Phrenology on American Psychology," *Journal of the History of the Behavioral Sciences*, II (1966), 207.

tion psychology of Locke into medicine and psychiatry (*Rapports du physique et moral de l'homme,* 1802). His view was that "this inner man is nothing but the brain" and that thought is a kind of organic "secretion." Dr. Cabanis studied the movements of decapitated bodies after execution; others studied the heads. Between 1796 and 1811 scientific arguments raged over the head as seat of the soul, over where, precisely, the steel knife should fall, and whether and how to use the head for experimental studies.[32] When in 1806 the University of Halle was closed by Napoleon, Reil (1759–1813) (to whom is attributed the term "psychiatry") profited from those two years by dissecting brains, in which he found that "island" named Reil. L. Rostan (1790–1866), a disciple of Pinel and one of the more influential French clinical teachers of the nineteenth century, "sees brain diseases everywhere"—so noted one of his students. In 1819, before he was thirty, Rostan published on *ramollissement du cerveau,* thereby giving authority to the fantasy of "softening of the brain." [33] In the sexual literature "brain softening" was directly related to venereal excess. A strong case was made (in three volumes and nearly 2,000 pages) by the Montpellier professor, M. Lallemand, an expert on brain research, that loss of semen represented physiological, moral, and social dissolution.[34] The sexual shadow was never far away in this period: Casanova; Mirabeau, revolutionary and

32. Cf. W. Leibbrand and A. Wettley, *Der Wahnsinn,* pp. 654–55, for references to sixteen of the many treatises in which the problems raised by beheading are argued in the scientific literature between 1796 and 1811. For the physiology of Görres see K. Rothschuh, *Geschichte der Physiologie* (Berlin, 1953), and W. Leibbrand, *Die spekulative Medizin der Romantik* (Hamburg: Claassen, 1956), pp. 121 ff. (The year of his birth is given variously as 1776 and 1777.)

33. E. Ackerknecht, *Medicine at the Paris Hospital* (Baltimore: Johns Hopkins University Press, 1967), pp. 111–12.

34. M. Lallemand, *Des Pertes séminales involontaires* (Paris: Béchet Jeune, 1836–42). The main figure in warning against seed loss and its effects on the brain was S. A. A. D. Tissot; cf. my "Towards the Archetypal Model for the Masturbation Inhibition," *Journal of Analytical Psychology,* XI (1966).

pornographer;[35] and de Sade (1740–1814), imprisoned and isolated, yet curiously always in the midst of the action, at the Bastille, then Bicêtre, then Charenton, elaborating his fantasies with scientific precision, describing each detail accurately, even to the number of strokes in a beating.

Cruelty was not confined to de Sade, and, as with him, it was combined with ideas of therapy in the minds of his contemporaries. Reil, for instance, was imaginatively searching for what he called "noninjurious tortures" for treatment of the insane. Benjamin Rush (1745–1813), father of American psychiatry and signer of the Declaration of Independence, advocated his favorite treatment for mental disorder: blood-letting, up to forty ounces at once. Broussais, an ex-sergeant and army surgeon, can be taken as typical of a main stream of French medicine of the period; he applied fifty leeches at a time.[36] Guillotin, Cabanis, Reil, and Rush were all optimistic and humanistic reformers, liberal revolutionaries even; yet they were caught by the same constellation of a psychology both sensationalist and secular.

Curiousy, the same Dr. Joseph Guillotin sat on the official commission that investigated mesmerism. Steel appears to have fascinated both men, for Mesmer reduced psychic suggestion and sympathy to a magnetic field that could be manipulated by iron rods and steel magnets. Steel was, during this time, a tonic prescribed for weakness. The Age of Iron

35. Mirabeau was of that same extraordinary generation born in the 1740's (1749–91). For his lascivious writings see his *Letters to Sophie*, *Erotica Biblion*, and *Ma Conversion*. For his death see Cabanis' little report, *Journal de la maladie et de la mort de Mirabeau* (Paris, 1791).

36. Cf. "Broussais" in Ackerknecht, *Medicine at the Paris Hospital*. For the implications of this tough-minded medical approach to psychiatry and the development of the ego-concept see "Broussais and Griesinger: The Introduction of Ego-Psychology into Psychiatry," in M. Altschule, *Roots of Modern Psychiatry* (New York: Grune & Stratton, 1957). As Herbart's soul was in the head, so was Broussais's ego: "The *moi* depends on a perfect brain, well-grown and adult" (*ibid.*, p. 28). We shall hear more of this, below, from Moebius, especially in regard to the comparison of the male and female skulls.

and Steel was already there in fantasy. Concretization—to use that hideous and appropriate word—was the approach, expressed equally in the psyche-equals-skull formula, the steel magnets of the mesmerists, the iron lightning rods of Benjamin Franklin (who also sat on the commission),[37] and the materialist psychiatry of Cabanis.[38] Iron was Cabanis' specific for that "green sickness," chlorosis, which included many gradations of weakness, from Romantic faintings to true anemia.

Philosophers of the eighteenth century had prepared the

37. It is from Franklin, by the way, that we have the terms "positive" and "negative," so fundamental to the electrical models of polarity used by psychology.

38. Cabanis is said to have affected even the philosophical ideas of Thomas Jefferson (1743–1826), who "had listened eagerly when he was in France to the lectures of Cabanis." In a letter to John Adams (1825), Jefferson tells him about the new research in brain localization. "In Jefferson's thought, which was highly representative of that of the leading intellectuals of his day, there was an intimate relationship between democracy and a rationalistic-materialistic view of the nature of man" (Bakan, "The Influence of Phrenology on American Psychology," p. 201). The blade of the guillotine was exemplary witness to this philosophy. Its mechanical impersonality made it the democratic tool par excellence. Under the blade all were equal. On the other hand, Jefferson, even if an abolitionist, had his racial views; and these, too, might be a resultant of identifying too much of human nature with "brain power," i.e., with ego. The head played an important role in the beginnings of physical anthropology. It became the symbolic focus of interest in the new "science of race," a theme which especially occupied German philosophers and Romantic writers. This "science" of race distinctions—and hierarchies—which was based mainly on the measurement and morphology of the cranium, implying that container determines contents, was to have immense influence throughout the nineteenth century on theories of degeneration in psychiatry, delinquency in sociology, and on rational justification of slavery, colonialism, and military conquest. The difference between superior and inferior peoples comes mainly "from the head," as perceived in a speculative and aesthetic philosophy of skull shape and skull size, from which conclusions were drawn about relative qualities of brains and values of psyches. Schelling (1775–1854) reversed the materialist order (skull determines psyche—container determines contents); instead, he viewed the skull as a shell, on the analogy of the snail, whose specifics are produced by the brain and, in turn, by the nature of its inborn psyche. See H. Blome, *Der Rassengedanke in der deutschen Romantik* (Munich and Berlin, 1943).

ground for the ascension of the psyche to the head. Voltaire (*Dictionnaire philosophique*, 1764) had already declared madness (*folie*) "a sickness of the organs of the brain." "A madman is a sick man whose brain is in distress, as the gouty man is a sick man who suffers in his feet and hands. . . . People have gout in the brain as in the feet." [39] Kant also considered psychosis a sickness of the head, even if, in the tradition of the eighteenth century, he placed the source of these diseases of the head in the digestive organs. A "head" for Kant was *pars pro toto* for one who understood much, that is, one who conceived, abstracted, and reflected.[40] Other symbolic aspects of the head—as the "top" of man, showing his spirit in aura, horns, and halo; as the expression of man, showing his "face," "smile," and "eyes"; as the place of cosmetic decoration and headdress as well as the animality of teeth, beard, and snout; as the carrier of taste, smell, sound, and sight; and in its alchemical meaning as *rotundum*[41]—all these significances faded before the dominant fantasy of a thinking and bodiless head, aloft, enlightened by Apollonic distance. Psyche = mind, and mind = head, could be pushed one step further: head = ego, in the modern sense of the controlling and ordering organ.

The head carried an archetypal fantasy; it had become the symbol through which the beginnings of the contemporary fantasy of a "strong ego" were being expressed. This new ego appeared in the fears of "softness" and the influence of Venus, in the strengthenings through iron, in the search in the brain for the essence of personality, in the notion of madness as a disorder of brain mechanisms and breakdown of control, in the doctrines of racial and male superiority, in the peculiar rationale of managed torture as therapy. This new

39. From the English translation by P. Gay of Voltaire's *Philosophical Dictionary* (New York: Basic Books, 1962), I, 276–79, *s.v.* "Folie."

40. R. Eisler, *Kant-Lexicon* (Berlin, 1930), *s.vv.* "Kopf," "Psychosen."

41. See "Rotundum, Head and Brain" (*CW*, XIV), pars. 626–28, with notes.

ego appeared also in the new—and confused—notion of democracy. Though the word referred to the Athenian ideal, its general use at the beginning of the nineteenth century neglected the psychological conditions on which classical democracy had been based. Then the psyche lived in terms of the Gods; now democracy had become the counting of heads of secular citizens under the reign of quantity. *Polis* always reflects *psyche* in both classical and modern democracies. Hierarchy, a principle so essential to the Greek psyche and expressed in both their psychological conceptions and their *polis* with its classes, was leveled by equality (and its psychiatric parallel, normality).[42] The soul, once a democratic reflection of the diverse Gods, where democracy was also an inner state of the psyche, with place for Hades and Zeus, for the Olympians, the Dionysian troop, the Gorgons and the heroes, and for nymphs and furies, too, was now a bundle of sensations in association. Federation was the political term for psychological association. The Lockean psyche and the Hobbesian state mirrored each other.

Most of the language of psychology developed within the same context which saw the rise of the modern ego. This language reflects its context, a psyche identified with the head and without eros, an "empire" of the hard, strong, materialized ego. Thus the descriptions and judgments in this language cannot help but reflect the point of view of this structure of consciousness, to which we are so habituated that we have come to call it "ego." Each of us accepts this collective structure so unthinkingly, so irrevocably, that each believes it to be his very own unique and private "I."

A First Summary

Our case history has covered great tracts of ground, and it has done so rather sketchily, because it has been mainly a

42. "Normal" comes from the Latin *norma* = carpenter's square, an instrument for making angles; in English normal meant originally

survey, aiming at psychological insight. To sum up the content of this insight, let us go back to the two ways of description, the contestation between two languages.

One of the many double ways of description comes from Plotinus, who in the *Enneads* II. 2. ii distinguishes between two kinds of motion in regard to human affairs and depicts the motion of the soul as circular: "The Soul exists in revolution around God, to whom it clings in love, holding itself to the utmost of its power near to Him as the Being on which all depends; and since it cannot coincide with God, it circles about Him." On the other hand, the motion of the body differs from the motion of the soul: "the forward path is characteristic of the body." [43] This passage gives some indication of why the language of psychology touches the soul only tangentially. The model of its discoveries and inventions follows the forward path of somatic research. Thus the grand accomplishments of positivistic psychology and psychopathology are limited by the nature of the psyche itself, which is continually revolving around the same fundamental paradox of its nature that it is at once embodied, mortal, and evolutionary yet is also centered around death and clings to the immortal. Each new psychological system is but one more amplification of this turning of the soul around the divine inscrutability at its center.

Man, it is said, was created in the divine image; the psyche of man somehow mirrors or clings to the divine. So, our psychological descriptions are also in some way descriptions of the divine. A textbook in psychology is also a kind of textbook in theology. If man is created in God's image, psychology as a positive, secular science is quite out of the question. We therefore cannot expect a closed field of operational definitions, nor can we have a true system of its aberrations. If a positivistic secular discipline of psychology is impossible,

"a right angle." "Squaring with a norm," and the concepts "normality" and "normalcy," enter the language in 1828 (*Oxford English Dictionary*).

43. *Enneads* II. 2. ii.

so too is psychopathology. We can have no theory of neurosis, no psychiatric nosology that is anything more than a heuristic aid, a kit of tools, a collection of insights and observations, purely nominalistic, a "way of opinion," empirical only, a language of *nomina* taken up and laid aside at will. The time of the textbook is past. These textbooks with their charts, diagrams, and cabbalism of statistics become bibliographical curios, to be regarded as we regard the textbooks of cosmology, geography, and alchemy of earlier times. The era of *Lehrbücher* in psychology which opened with Herbart now concludes, because we do not need either definitions or systematic explanations. The soul wants psychological insights to keep it on its circular course, insights that favor the circulation of the light.

We have been reflecting about these *nomina* in two ways: first, by means of historicism; second, by means of the hermeneutics of an archetypal psychology, asking what these *nomina* mean to the soul. This has been our method for gaining distance from the language. Historicism regards the language of psychology as an expression of a style. A style is the unity of all products of a historical epoch. Our approach to psychopathology is not new: Henry Sigerist, the great historian of medicine, pointed out forty years ago that the categories of psychopathology are relevant to time and place, that is, they are historically conditioned.[44] Hallucina-

44. H. Sigerist, "Psychopathologie und Kulturwissenschaft," in *Abhandlungen aus der Neurologie, Psychiatrie, Psychologie und ihren Grenzgebieten*, No. 61 (1930), pp. 140–46; see also Ackerknecht, "Psychopathology, Primitive Medicine and Primitive Culture," *Bulletin of the History of Medicine*, XIV (1943), 30–67, and L. Edelstein, "The History of Anatomy in Antiquity," in *Ancient Medicine: Selected Papers of Ludwig Edelstein*, ed. O. and C. L. Temkin (Baltimore: Johns Hopkins University Press, 1967). The major demonstration in recent years for the necessary interrelation between a culture and its definition of madness is that of M. Foucault, *Histoire de la folie* (Paris, 1961) (English trans. by R. Howard, *Madness and Civilization* [New York, 1965]). His book, ending with Pinel and Tuke and the French Revolution, provides a useful background for the study of psychopathology in the nineteenth century, our area of reflection.

tions, sexual "perversions," out-of-body experiences are normal and expected in some cultures and periods; our typical normal behavior might be judged quite mad at other times of history. History tells us that the style of each age and culture has its "psychology" and its "psychopathology." The nineteenth century had the one we are still familiar with; our age will have its own. Always, from the point of view of style, "alien" means "heretical." The alienated is the excommunicated, that which shows the behavior and beliefs of a soul that follows other Gods and is thus out of joint with the time and its prevalent *Anschauung*. As our *Anschauung* at the end of these two thousand years goes through a metamorphosis of the Gods, psychopathology, as a secular vision of heresy, will also go through its own metamorphosis.

Historical distance may benefit psychology. History is too often missing from its discoveries, else they might not be considered discoveries. Or history is misused: paraded forth as an outmoded "way of opinion" to be mocked and disowned or, on the contrary, to bring *senex* support to one's personal argument. But history is also reflection, a way of "doing psychology," an act of soul.[45] With history comes a sense of patience, and "in your patience is your soul." When psychology loses its historical connection, it loses soul. A psychology soon grows smug when it forgets that it, too, has a case history. It needs to take the historical point of view

45. History as reflection: "In 1934 Manfred Sakel of Vienna published his method of treating psychoses by producing a state of coma by means of insulin injections. That same year, Laszlo Joseph Meduna of Budapest reported his method of producing convulsive attacks through the injection of cardiazol. In 1935 Egas Moniz of Lisbon described his first leukotomy (prefrontal lobotomy), thereby introducing surgery into the psychiatric field and creating the new specialization of psychosurgery. And in 1938, Ugo Cerletti and L. Bini of Rome demonstrated their electroshock technique" (F. Marti-Ibáñez, *Centaur* [New York: MD Publications, 1958], p. 444). These four physically radical—even violent—technical methods of treatment for (against?) the insane all fall within that time of the mid-thirties when Europe (and especially Austria, Hungary, Portugal, and Italy) were in the throes of the Fascist problem.

toward itself, and not just toward the phenomena and documents of the past, which it interprets with such a sure hand. Much of the psychological language we have reviewed lacks this historical sense. This young language, so often a language of the young who made our field, neglects the pain which history has put into words. The self-struggle between two ways of description is forgotten. There is no inner wrestling; only one twin makes the statement. Then naming represents the conquest of "truth" over the way of "opinion."

When Plato attempted to encompass the soul, he was driven to myth as much as to careful, rational thinking. He needed two ways. Plotinus has recourse (*Enneads* IV. 3. 14) to myth when discussing the soul. Freud, too, used two ways. His rational language is interspersed with mythical images: Oedipus and Narcissus, primal horde and primal scene, the censor, the polymorphous perverse infant, and that grand vision of Thanatos, worthy of the pre-Socratics. Freud's language is inspired by mythic speech; it would be mistaken to consider his myths as empirical discoveries demonstrable through case histories. They are visions, like Plato's; missing only is Diotima.

If, finally, the language is a product of the nineteenth century's style and could as well be another language of another style, and if its necessity is given less by the phenomena it names than by the style which produced a necessity to name them, then we must question psychology's language game. Psychological language does not have the same reality as definitions in those fields whose validity is established largely by turning to public facts. Our words of psychology do not refer to things in the same way. Yet these words tend to become reified, to give us the belief that there are things to which the words refer. We pass judgments upon people and their souls through this language, group them, and treat them as if they had or were these things created by these words: "homosexuals," "suicidals," "depressives." Our language is but a view of the phenomena. (Remember Freud, attempting to convince his compeers that hysteria existed in men. But hysteria could not exist in me, one scoffed, because *hystera* means "uterus.") Words and names predetermine behavior.

Jung quite clearly regarded the diagnostic language of psychotherapy as mainly a professional convention to which he too paid his due:

> I have in the course of years accustomed myself wholly to disregard the diagnosing of specific neuroses, and I have sometimes found myself in a quandary when some word-addict urged me to hand him a specific diagnosis. The Greco-Latin compounds needed for this still seem to have a not inconsiderable market value and are occasionally indispensable for that reason.
>
> The sonorous diagnosis of neurosis *secundum ordinem* is just a façade; it is not the psychotherapist's real diagnosis. His establishment of certain facts might conceivably be called "diagnosis," though it is psychological rather than medical in character. Nor is it meant to be communicated; for reasons of discretion, and also on account of the subsequent therapy, he usually keeps it to himself. The facts so established are simply perceptions indicating the direction the therapy is to take. They can hardly be reproduced in the sort of Latin terminology that sounds scientific; but there are on the other hand expressions of ordinary speech which adequately describe the essential psychotherapeutic facts.[46]

Despite recognizing the two kinds of language—"Latin terminology" and "ordinary speech"—and that the scientific compounds of psychopathology have little to do with facts of therapy, Jung still leaves us with the dilemma of these opposites. We cannot rest with this split between two kinds of speech.

The relation between the clinical picture (*Zustandsbild*) of a psychological disorder and its etiology is also tenuous.[47] For centuries psychiatry has proceeded by assuming that

46. *CW*, XVI, pars. 195–96.
47. Cf. E. Fischer-Homberger, "Eighteenth-Century Nosology and Its Survivors," *Medical History*, XIV, No. 4 (1970), 397 ff.

classifications and descriptions had to be enough because causes were unknown, implying that it does not matter what "name" we give to a psychological disorder since the name has no real relation with the forces that bring the disorder about. To cut descriptions loose from underlying reasons (*aitiai*) is a nominalism where names and things have no inherent relation. This view of nosology is noxious; it implies that names have no power over our vision of the soul and how we take up and handle psychic events.

Is there no connection between terminology and ordinary speech? Between psychological descriptions and the roots of the suffering and disorder? If none, then what connections can words establish between an analyst, conceiving through his terminology, and the analysand, speaking of his soul in his ordinary speech? Must the analyst speak with two tongues, one to the analysand and the other to his colleagues about the "case"? And is not "cure" sometimes only a linguistic conversion, where the analysand has learned to handle his psyche through the names taken from the analyst?

It is not enough to point out two kinds of description, one adequate and one inadequate. If the language of psychology is inadequate to the soul and its therapy, then why continue with it at all? Surely the "market value" of these terms is not enough to justify their use, especially if this language is essentially a part of the sickness of the soul which occasions therapy in the first place. The choice would seem to be: either discard the whole lot or find some inherent *psychological* sense in it.

The language of psychopathology pretends to objective correlation with the psychic realities which it has named, become identified with, and even replaced. The authority to which this language pretends has been granted by history. As we have seen, it has resulted from historical necessities. But does this language have inherent authenticity? What, if any, internal relation exists between the categories of psychopathology and the unacademic speech of the psyche? Do these words have any reality except a nominal reality? Can these categories, this language, assume that reality and authenticity given by archetypal necessities? If we could fill in the archetypal background to the *nomina*, would these categories then fulfill their pretension to objective correlation with states of the soul? If we could, then the language would no longer be just empirical descriptions but *part of the inherent phenomenology of the archetypes.* Psychopathology would then be necessary to archetypal structures, and the language of psychopathology would be part of the way this necessity expresses itself through the fantasies of reason. Psychopathology's terms would no longer speak *about* the psyche, tell tales of it, call it pejorative names, but would be necessary to psychic life and speak *for* the soul. By "filling in" the archetypal background, the language would gain the authority of real substance instead of having only the authority lent to it by professional convention.

Let us then take these *nomina* of psychopathology to be expressions of a fantasy of the understanding. Psychopathology then becomes the reason's own mythic system, with which it grasps the demons of the soul, differentiates its voices, and produces an intelligible account. Psychopathology is mythic in the sense that it provides, in the manner of myth, categories and descriptions for the interrelation of the human and more-than-human powers. It tells tales of the origins, activities, and interconnections of these more-than-human powers, these syndromes which afflict the *dromena* (enactments) of the human realm and which the human realm tries to comprehend by means of these tales. It is related to the cult of therapeutic practice. The system also provides ways of propitiating the afflictions; it has a morale, rules of conduct, suggestions for sacrifice. Diagnosis tells to which category the afflictions belong, just as the oracle tells us to which more-than-human power we should attribute our fortune. The question is the same: to what category (God) does this problem of my soul belong? [48] Both recognize something un-

48. According to H. W. Parke (*Greek Oracles* [London: Hutchinson, 1967], p. 87), the favorite procedure for enquiring from the

known and powerful behind the experiences and offer a way of naming these forces.

Psychopathology as fantasy is now open, not only to doubt and skeptical questioning but to new reflection and new insights. This language becomes a road to consciousness; it, too, is a way of grasping the archetypes, since it is necessary to their expression. There must be psychopathology; the archetype must reveal itself in psychic afflictions. Thus the fantasy expressed in psychological and pathopsychological language can be reflected by the other personality, the twin who is at home with the mythic approach. This means we may insight the first system of object-oriented, literalistic fantasy—psychology or psychopathology or any scientific language—just as one may insight alchemy, which also conceived itself as object-oriented and as a literal description of real events. We view the first system through the second; thereby, first and second change places. The nineteenth century translated the speech of the unconscious into the language of reason. Our opportunity is to translate the language of reason into the archetypal background of the unconscious and its speech, to change concept back into metaphor. This metaphorical speech will be our next concern, but, as exemplary postscript to this history, let me tell one of the classically heroic stories in the history of psychiatry.

Philippe Pinel (1745–1826), a close contemporary of Bentham, Jefferson, and Goethe, is considered the great liberator of the psychiatric revolution which paralleled the end of the *ancien régime* in Europe and America. Pinel's *Traité médicophilosophique sur l'aliénation mentale* in 1801 inaugurated the new era. Pinel is also a legendary figure because he is remembered for removing, probably in 1794, the chains from the insane (although the Quakers had been doing this earlier, and in more quiet ways, in England, and it

---

Delphic oracle, to which one came at critical times, was "To what god or hero must I pray or sacrifice to achieve such and such a purpose?"

was done also in the Hospital of Saint Bonifacio in Florence).[49] We see him now at his task of liberating the insane, as told by Semelaigne:

> Le premier auquel Pinel s'adresse, est le plus ancien dans ce lieu de misère; c'est un capitaine anglais, dont personne ne connaît l'histoire, et qui est là, enchaîné, depuis quarante ans. Il est regardé comme le plus terrible de tous les aliénés;... Pinel entre seul dans sa loge, et l'aborde avec calme. — «Capitaine, lui dit-il, si je vous faisais ôter vos fers, et si je vous donnais la liberté de vous promener dans la cour, me promettriez-vous d'être raisonnable et de ne faire de mal à personne?» — «Je te le promets, mais tu te moques de moi; ils ont tous trop peur et toi aussi.» — «Non certes, je n'ai pas peur, puisque j'ai six hommes pour me faire respecter s'il le faut. Mais croyez à ma parole, devenez confiant et docile; je vous rendrai la liberté, si vous vous laissez mettre ce gilet de toile au lieu de ces chaînes si pesantes.»
>
> Le capitaine se prête de bonne grâce à tout ce qu'on exige de lui, mais en haussant les épaules et sans articuler un mot. Après quelques minutes, ses fers sont complètement détachés, et l'on se retire en laissant la porte de sa loge ouverte. Plusieurs fois, il se lève sur son séant et retombe; depuis si longtemps qu'il est assis, il a perdu l'usage de ses jambes; enfin, au bout d'un quart d'heure, il parvient à se tenir en équilibre, et, du fond de sa loge obscure, il s'avance en chancelant vers la porte. Son premier mouvement est de regarder le ciel, et il s'écrie en extase; «Que c'est beau!» Pendant toute la journée, il ne cesse de courir, de monter les escaliers, de les descendre, en disant toujours: «Que c'est beau!» [50]

49. Cf. G. Mora, "Vincenzo Chiarugi (1759–1820)—His Contribution to Psychiatry," *Bulletin of the Isaac Ray Medical Library,* II, No. 2 (1954), 51–104. Chiarugi not only pioneered as a reformer and as inaugurator of the model institution for the insane, but also, true to his times, he systematically studied brains in post mortem examinations. His main written work is *Della pazzia in genere, e in specie* (Firenze, 1793–94).

50. R. Semelaigne, *Aliénistes et philanthropes* (Paris: Steinheil, 1912), pp. 46–47.

Pinel took the chains off the insane but not off the insane phenomena. The imaginative phenomena of the psyche have become the new prisoners, restrained by the language which has grown up largely since Pinel. Part of our psyche is caught in that interlocking system and weighted down by concepts forged in the nineteenth century. The imprisoned inmates were freed from the chains of previous centuries. Psychic phenomena still await their liberation from the subtler chains of psychological language.

A Multiplicity of Souls

The year 1912 is frequently said to mark the end of the nineteenth century. Several significant psychological works appeared during this period (1911–13), which also marked the close of a period in psychology.[51] Among them was

51. Among many significant events in our field in those years of transition (1911–13): the last revised edition of Wundt's *Grundzüge der physiologischen Psychologie* (1911); the final number of *Virchow's Journal* (1913); the deaths of Alfred Binet, Francis Galton, and Hughlings Jackson (1911); and publications by O. Bumke (1912) and G. Genil-Perrin (1913) that Ackerknecht says represent the epitaph of the nineteenth century's degeneration theory (*A Short History of Psychiatry*, trans. S. Wolff [New York and London: Hafner, 1968], p. 58). Syphilis was at last proven to be the cause of general paralysis (Noguchi and Moore, 1913). In France, Semelaigne brought historical perspective through biography to the past century's psychiatry (*Aliénistes et philanthropes*, 1912), and A. Marie compiled the total sum of man's knowledge of psychopathology in the *Traité international de la psychopathologie*, counterbalanced by Jaspers' massive critique of psychopathology (1913). Schizophrenia now arrived at the center of the psychiatric stage with E. Bleuler's *Dementia Praecox oder Gruppe der Schizophrenien* (1911) and his lecture, "Autistic Thinking," at the opening of the Phipps Clinic in Baltimore (1912); the application of psychoanalytic theory to psychosis in Freud's publication of the Schreber case (1911); and Jung's *Wandlungen und Symbole der Libido* (1912). Also important were: Bonhoeffer's description of the acute exogenous reaction (1912); the appointment at the Boston Psychopathic Hospital in 1913 of the first "psychiatric social worker," a woman, and the invention of that field; by the Act of 1913 the British Parliament's giving official recognition to idiocy as a distinct class of psychiatric disorder, thereby paving the way for the new century's interest in mental retardation; and the

Wandlungen und Symbole der Libido by C. G. Jung. A new style began. Jung took the field as he found it at the beginning of this century, with its fascination with *Sexualwissenschaft,* psychiatric diagnosis, parapsychology, association processes; yet in all these areas—to which he too made his contributions—Jung remained true to the psychological point of view, a point of view grounded in the soul. His ontology could be formulated most simply as *esse in anima.* Jung did not, therefore, produce a theory of neurosis or a systematic psychopathology. He did not cleanly divide psychology from psychopathology, nor did he even divide neurosis from personality development. For him both normal and abnormal psychology were expressions of the soul, having their basis in the unconscious psyche. He viewed mental health and mental disease from one and the same standpoint. With the unconscious psyche and its expressions as his starting point,

---

founding of the Jean Jacques Rousseau Institute in Geneva (1912) and the important work by Thorndike (1911) on *Animal Intelligence,* which gave impetus to pedagogy—to education and learning theory. M. Wertheimer's experimental studies on the perception of motion (1912) was the starting point of Gestalt psychology. In 1911 Pavlov acquired the Reflex Tower in Leningrad, where his experimental method could be yet more independent of "psychic influences," i.e., where isolation of animal subject from experimenter and both from the outside world inaugurated an age of radical behavioristic materialism in psychology. In 1912 McDougall had defined psychology as "the science of human behavior"; publications supported this: M. Meyer, *Fundamental Laws of Human Behavior* (1911), J. B. Watson, *Psychology as the Behaviorist Views It* (1913), M. Parmalee, *The Science of Human Behavior* (1913). The years 1911–13 saw the crises in Freud's circle leading to the defections of Jung, Adler, and Stekel and thereby the extension of the psychoanalytic movement in both therapy and wider areas of culture (O. Rank and H. Sachs, *Die Bedeutung der Psychoanalyse für die Geisteswissenschaften* [1913], and Freud's *Totem and Taboo* [1913]). Indirectly bearing on the new century's psychology, psychopathology, and "speech" was the first "Blue Rider" group exhibition in 1911 and the music written between 1911 and 1913 by Webern, Berg, and Schoenberg—fragmentary, intensely abbreviated, discontinuous. Also: Husserl's *Phenomenology* (1913), Jane Harrison's *Themis* (1912), Einstein's General Relativity Theory, and the appearance in 1913 of D. H. Lawrence's *Sons and Lovers,* Mann's *Death in Venice,* and Proust's *A la recherche du temps perdu,* Part One.

Jung began a rectification of psychological language—the most difficult change to accomplish in a culture, since language is so basic. No wonder that Jung was not understood. He was speaking a new language and using an old language in a new way. His rectification of the language of psychology began with the expressions of the unconscious psyche as given in fantasy, dream, and emotion. He began with the manifest events, the phenomena as they appeared. His was thus an attempt to "save the phenomena," *der Inhalt der Psychose*,[52] the contents of the soul, at a time when the soul was believed to have no contents of its own, when its disorders were regarded as meaningless disturbances of function or structure. He turned to the soul itself and asked it to tell its tale in its own speech.

At another crucial time in psychological history, Tertullian did the same thing. He asked the soul to bear its own witness in its own language:

> I call in a new testimony, yes, one which is better known than all literature, more discussed than all doctrine, more public than all publications. . . .
>
> Stand forth, O soul . . . stand forth and give thy witness. But I call thee not as when fashioned in schools, trained in libraries, fed up in Attic academies and porticoes. . . . I address thee, simple and rude, and uncultured and untaught, such as they have thee who have thee only, the very thing pure and entire, of the road, the street, the workshop.[53]

Tertullian was rather sure of his witness; it would give the evidence he expected; it was naturally Christian. But can we be as sure of our witness? In the babble of internal voices,

52. *CW*, III, "The Content of the Psychoses." The German original, "Der Inhalt der Psychose" (1908), was augmented in 1914 by a preface which further emphasized the psychological contents of mental aberrations as meaningful processes in their own light, independent of their anatomical correlates in the brain.

53. Tertullian "De testimonio anima" 1 (English trans. in *Ante-Nicene Christian Library*, XI, 1 [Edinburgh: Clark, 1869]).

how do we hear the soul speaking? How do we recognize the soul and its authentic speech?

This is not a new problem. Porphyry, for instance, asks how we can distinguish among apparitions. How do we know whether we are in the presence of a god, an angel, an archangel, a daimon, an archon, or a human soul? [54] We might add many other soul voices to this list: a bush soul and a totem soul, the ancestral souls, and the soul or vital force within each organ or area of body consciousness (*cakra*), the soul as muse, as immortal protectress, as anima-image, as soul-spark of consciousness within each complex. All souls have voice; all these souls speak. The speech of these many souls gives cause for the many psychologies and their differing languages. The multiplicity of psychologies, the fact that there are so many different "psychological points of view," among which we cannot decide "who is right," reflects the multiplicity of souls and the states of these souls. All are necessary; none is sufficient. There can never be a single all-encompassing psychology encompassing all the psyche until there can be that utopia where the psyche—a complex of every opposite—becomes one, whole, and simple.

The multiplicity of souls is the basis of multiple personality and the dissociation of personality. However, the multiplicity of souls implies something else besides the possibility of pathology. The many voices of many souls make psychic differentiation possible.[55] We descend from the Tower of Babel. Babel not only images external differentiation into cultures; it also reflects an internal psychic reality. The babble of inner voices produces contradictions of will, florid fantasies, the spectra of viewpoints, the conflicts and choices; the inner

54. Cf. E. R. Dodds, *Pagan and Christian in an Age of Anxiety* (Cambridge, Eng., 1965), p. 54 n.; Porphyry, cited by Iamblichus *De Myst.* 2. 3 (English trans. by T. Taylor, *On the Mysteries,* 3d ed. [London: Watkins, 1968], pp. 85 f.).

55. Jung ("On the Nature of the Psyche," *CW,* VIII) has discussed "the dissociability of the psyche" (pp. 173 f.), which in turn provides ground for his hypothesis of the "unconscious as a multiple consciousness" (pp. 190 f.).

Babel means that *we cannot understand ourselves.* Our reason can never fully comprehend even our own internal dialogue, and therefore we can never become so integrated as to speak with but one tongue. The multiplicity of souls and their voices means that we will always be partly strangers to ourselves, estranged, alienated. From this inner self-alienation, psychopathological descriptions necessarily arise. Psychopathology is a result of Babel, the dissociated communication among the many voices of the soul.

The church had to face this question of multiple souls and multiple definitions of soul. The results of the church's labors are codified in a catechism (Questions 29 and 30) which the little child learns, so clear and simple it is. The catechism states: "The three powers of my soul are my memory, my understanding, and my will." These three powers are "the likeness to the Blessed Trinity in my soul" because "in my one soul are three powers." [56]

To know more precisely what these three powers are and which one of the three persons of the godhead each reflects is no easy matter. Is "Jesus the Imagination"—as Blake declared? [57] Does the memory reflect God the Father as the first term of the Trinity? Even Augustine, who more than anyone else developed this line of thought leading to the simple basics of the catechism, gives these powers differing names: *mens, notitia, amor* (*De Trinitate* IX); *memoria, intelligentia, voluntas* (*De Trinitate* X); and *memoria Dei, intelligentia, amor* (*De Trinitate* XIV).[58] Despite these difficulties in detail, Augustine did give us a *sacred* psychology. His trinitarian soul reflects a trinitarian God. All that takes place within the psyche reflects the divine. Psychology reflects theology. Or, in Jung's language, the archetypes reflect the Gods.

56. V. White, *Soul and Psyche* (London: Collins & Harvill, 1960), p. 244.
57. Cf. K. Raine, *Blake and Tradition*, Vol. II, Chap. 24, "Jesus the Imagination."
58. I am indebted to Father Frederick Copleston for these references to Augustine.

Depth psychology has been particularly concerned with one of these powers of the soul, one of the trinity of the catechism: *memoria*. We too are particularly concerned with this faculty, *memoria*, since it bears directly upon the speech of the soul.

Psychology's Loss of "Memory"

Freud began his talking cure by asking his patients to follow one basic rule: to let their souls speak without inhibition. (In the early years they were instructed to talk with their eyes closed.) When they thus abandoned voluntary control and the intelligibility of understanding, their associations led them into *memoria*. Analysis begins with the exploration of memory and its expression in speech.

The memories Freud collected through his talking cure seemed at first quite plain reminiscences. Memory seemed plainly to be a repository of past events—primarily, traumatic childhood events—but on closer scrutiny these events turned out to be not actualities but fantasies. In the world they had never happened at all, yet they happened in the memory. Memory, therefore, could not be quite so plain as it had seemed. It was not only a storehouse of what had happened. It also had a fantasy aspect that affected present and future. To things that never had existed and events that never had happened, memory could give the quality of remembrance, the feeling that they had existed, had happened. It was as if we recollected them: these things and events were familiar. Thus memory was truly not bound by time or place; it seemed quite independent of these categories of the external world.

The memory which Freud discovered seems much like the *memoria* of Augustine, which also was not limited to past and personal events. And the method in which Freud discovered or rediscovered *memoria* proceeds much in the manner of Plato: moving from concretely real and actual events to recollections extending far beyond the life of the personal individual. (This "far beyond the personal" was recognized early by some of Freud's pupils, who, owing to their nineteenth-century bias, sought to trace memories genetically to natal and intrauterine existence.) Freud names this region the *id*—a term coming from Nietzsche via Georg Groddeck. He described the *id* as prehistoric and prepersonal. Then Jung, in *Symbols of Transformation,* said that these "apparently infantile reminiscences" are in reality "archaic thought forms which naturally emerge more clearly in childhood than they do later." [59] Here Jung clearly implies the Platonic view that in childhood the soul is immersed in *memoria* and that *memoria* is the home of our first personality, the mythic and childlike. Thus the fantasies of *memoria*—and all that resides there and can be expressed there—may be considered the first speech of the soul. Personalities number one and number two must reverse their names. The natural, archaic, and symbolic twin is number one.

Though Freud rediscovered *memoria* and even referred to it as the "primary process," he remained suspicious of it; and his view has colored ours. The phenomena of *memoria* were neurotic unless subjugated to the will or sublimated into reason. Fenichel's authoritative compendium puts it like this: "The common denominator of all neurotic phenomena is an insufficiency of the normal control apparatus." [60] The possibility that the imaginal faculty might have its own, but different, control apparatuses, its own valid order, and its own laws—or art—is not sufficiently considered. Therefore, the imaginal realm of *memoria* must submit to will and reason or be diagnosed as neurotic. The language of psychopathology, which Jung in *Symbols of Transformation* explicitly warned us not to use in accounting for the speech of fantasy, becomes an instrument by which will and reason manage *memoria.* The independence of fantasy, its uncontrollability

59. *CW,* V, par. 38.
60. O. Fenichel, *The Psychoanalytic Theory of Neurosis* (New York: Norton, 1945), p. 19.

and primacy, its freedom of imagination and natural religious endowment, all were disallowed. *Memoria* was the realm of regression, of unreal childish pleasure.

If we further pursue these ideas of *memoria*, we arrive at a remarkable parallel between the "inner world" we speak of in our psychology and the "fields and dens and caverns" of *memoria* described by Augustine, "innumerably full of innumerable kinds of things, present either by their images, as are all bodies, or in themselves . . . or by certain notions . . . in and through all these does my mind range, and I move swiftly from one to another and I penetrate them as deeply as I can, but find no end." [61] What we today call "the unconscious" and describe in spatial metaphors, though it is boundless and also timeless, which "contains" "contents"—images, personages, and affects, now called complexes—and which has a collective historical aspect as well as an ahistorical archetypal structure, at the unfound center of which, and around which, all else moves, the *imago Dei:* this unconscious appears hardly to differ from what was once called by Augustine *memoria* or *memoria Dei* or the *thesaurus inscrutabilis.*

Augustine grasped the paradox of the objective psyche. He saw that the *memoria,* or the collective unconscious, as Jung called it, is both "in my mind" and yet far beyond me and the range of my mind. He too was struck by the multiplicity of souls in this unity called "I." Augustine says, in the same passage: "Great is the power of memory, a thing, O my God, to be in awe of, a profound and immeasurable multiplicity; and this thing is my mind, this thing am I. What then am I, O my God? What nature am I?" As Gilson says, in regard to Augustine's *memoria:* "Memory thus becomes the deepest hidden recess of the mind, in which God dwells by his light,

61. Augustine *Confessions* X. 17 (Sheed translation) (New York: Sheed & Ward, 1943). For further passages of Augustine on *memoria* see his *Confessions* X. 8–19; *De Trinitate* XIV and XV; *De Musica* VI. 2–9; and *Retractiones* I. 4. 4.

and where he teaches us as our 'internal Master.'"[62] The parallels to the unconscious of Jung are obvious.

The unconscious was not a new discovery of the 1890's. Why does psychology cling to this fable? L. L. Whyte has shown that the concept of the unconscious was already "topical" around 1800 and "fashionable" by 1870.[63] But the unconscious, so newly found, was in fact a palace left from antiquity and the Renaissance, still inhabited by the surviving pagan Gods and once called the realm of *memoria*.

This background to the unconscious gives us another approach to establishing its ontology. *Memoria* has the reality of a fundamental power of the soul. It needs no empirical proof. Yet the evidence for the unconscious has always been by negative demonstration; that is, the existence of the unconscious is demonstrated through its disturbing effects upon ego consciousness: slips of the tongue, forgetting, complex indicators of the association experiment, hysterical symptoms, multiple personality. Our modern evidence for *memoria* has been drawn from psychopathology! We have had to be sick to rediscover in felt experience the power of this imaginal faculty. Freud's psychology, and Jung's, and analysis itself all arise from the ontological ground of *pathological* imagination.

The tradition represented by Augustine and the Neoplatonists found another ground. This tradition said that *memoria* was a vestige or trace in the soul of one person of the godhead, or it was a reflection of the divine images and ideas, which is another way of positing substantial reality for this faculty of the soul. As a result, its images had to be considered as full realities, not mere fantasies, mere hallucinations, mere projections—not anything "mere" at all.

62. E. Gilson, *History of Christian Philosophy in the Middle Ages* (London: Sheed & Ward, 1955), p. 594, n. 32.

63. L. L. Whyte, *The Unconscious before Freud* (New York: Basic Books, 1960). Cf. C. G. Carus, *Psyche*, Part I, in English translation (New York and Zurich: Spring Publications, 1970), with my introduction, "C. G. Carus—C. G. Jung."

"Mereness" and negative proof reflect the failure of the understanding to grasp a power of the soul which is by definition outside its ken. The older tradition, beginning with Plato, never lost *memoria* or doubted its ontological position and the substantiality of its images, but during the nineteenth century in particular this faculty lost touch with ruling consciousness. We lost our imaginal ego, the ego which speaks for this aspect of the soul. Instead, we identified wholly with the rational, volitional ego. *Memoria* became unconscious. It became the Unconscious, hypostasized, spelled with a capital "U," experienced as a place; this was the new sign over the entrance to the halls and palaces of Memory. Meanwhile memory, spelled with a little "m," was shrinking to the limits of a modern case history.

Of all terms of analytical language that we have been reviewing, the unconscious is the first we should renounce. It is justified only within the limited context in which it arose, since it makes sense only within a definition of consciousness that excludes the memorial imagination. It is useful only within a fantasy of opposites through which the psyche is divided against itself between head and body, ego and shadow, day side and night side. Keeping this term helps keep the fantasy of opposites, which in turn helps keep us each a house divided: on the one hand, conscious, on the other, unconscious. It serves best the analytical mind, which works by taking and keeping things apart. What would analysis analyze were there no unconscious? How could it "make conscious" and how could we "become conscious" were there no reservoir of unconscious material requiring these modern procedures of enlightenment?

By questioning the term, we do not, however, renounce it in the manner of the existentialists. Our renunciation is neither philosophical nor semantic; it is, rather, psychological—even therapeutic. This term began as a heuristic concept, useful for accounting for various psychic processes. It was psychologically valuable, advancing the psyche's understanding of itself. By now the reverse seems true, since the term has come to cover over, to obscure, the imaginal. How does this term help us now? Already in Jung's usage the term was becoming inadequate. He had to speak of a consciousness in the unconscious, and he ascribed to the unconscious a superior, guiding intentionality—which is more fitting to divinities than to subliminal mental processes.

By questioning the term, we do not doubt the existence of unwilled and unreasonable psychic states, of dreaming and of subliminal creative activities, or of any of the disturbances that are called the psychopathology of everyday life, nor do we question their "inferiority" as "sub" forms of consciousness, as we now conceive consciousness; but we do insist that it would be therapeutically more profitable to reimagine these states in terms of their background in *memoria* rather than in terms of the everyday foreground which they disturb. We would carry them downward, as we did the erotic aspects of therapy; we would place them, as we placed transference and as, in Part Three, we shall place hysteria, against the imaginal realm and ask what is being spoken through psychopathology. To bring the peculiarities of psychopathology only upward, to the light of day and its bright ego, takes the color from these strange fish, and they expire in psychiatry's labeled baskets and stalls.

The term "unconscious" is suitable for describing states where consciousness is not present—coma, for instance; but to use the word for the imaginal region, for morally inferior or culturally ignorant behavior, for instinctual release reactions, and for a causal agent who "sends" dreams and to which one can turn to ask an opinion, is an erosion of categories. To personify it and regard it as one's inhibitory daimonic voice, or totem animal, or *familiaris* is not merely superstitious. Such habits are sacrilegious, because they deprive the Gods of their due. The unconscious is a concept, not a metaphor, even if what it represents is indeed the metaphorical and the source of metaphors. Thus we seem unable to avoid speaking in this peculiar, superstitious manner. But it is not good psychology to make a theology of the psyche or to psychologize the divine. By reserving the term for the absence of consciousness we do not mean the absence of the usual ego with which consciousness has identified itself. There are many things I do—such as dream, perceive and record, act habitually—which are indeed conscious though the ego is quite out of it.

Before continuing to use the term "unconscious" in therapy to mean a region of the soul and its deeper intentions, we might do well to reexamine what is meant by consciousness. (We shall turn to this in Part Three.) Perhaps the phenomena of the so-called unconscious which do not fit into our definition of consciousness and therefore have become "pathological" and "un"-conscious are better conceived as twisted paths into *memoria,* as ways leading back into lost areas of the soul, its imagination, and its history. Freud showed that symptoms lead to discoveries and that psychopathology is a vehicle for entering the depths.

The long loss of memory was experienced during the past decades as loss of soul. Jung reminded us of this, but his psychology was at variance with all the others. We had forgotten *memoria* because the ruling psychologies of the Enlightenment, from Locke through Cabanis, Herbart, and Freud, take their position from the will and reason, declaring the soul to be empty of imaginal remembrance. The unconscious is a waste bin of undigested sensations. Of course the mind is a *tabula rasa* if the mind consists only in will and learning. Of course we trail no clouds of glory as we come, remembering no Platonic a priori, if the imaginal memory is not considered an authentic region of the soul. Yet, when Freud followed the path of associations charted by Locke, he stumbled into the fields and caverns of impersonal *memoria,* innumerably full of innumerable kinds of things. Thus did Freud's discovery give us the opportunity to rediscover, as Jung did, the lost aspect of our souls. Thus can that exploration of the unconscious in therapy give us back a sense of soul.

Most important here is the word "innumerable." This

third person, this imaginal region of the psyche, does not submit to numbering. Kant, too, said that the unconscious, which he called the field of dark ideas in man, was "immeasurable." Yet the language of psychology initiated by Herbart is a language of quantity. Bentham suggested a "felicific calculus." Measurements cannot tell us about this aspect of the psyche; it is better comprehended as a storehouse of qualities and a movement of changing images that are the formal causes of experience, giving it shape, color, change, and significance. Therapeutic analysis which works wholly within the realm of qualitative change cannot be translated into measurements without failing somewhere. From the viewpoint of the imaginal realm, numbers themselves are qualities with a symbolic, fantasy aspect.[64] "Seven" is not just one more integer than "six." "Seven" is an altogether different experience, based on a different imaginal structure. By regaining our lost memory we should slowly be able to put an end to the dominance of quantity in psychology and the materialism which quantitative thinking brings in tow.

Freud and Jung have suggested that the unconscious enters into each mental act. This view of depth psychology gives further correspondence between the unconscious and *memoria*. Aristotle held that no mentation could take place without the mental images given by imagination, the basis of memory. The "imaginative phantasms" of Aristotle, the "phantasia" of the Stoics, and the "reminiscences" of the Platonists take part in all activities of consciousness.[65] In today's language: we

64. Cf. M.-L. von Franz, *Zahl und Zeit* (Stuttgart, 1970; English translation forthcoming from Northwestern University Press).

65. It is a task beyond the limits of this work to elaborate the differences between *memoria*, *phantasia*, imagination, fantasy, reminiscence, and related concepts. These ideas have undergone constant revision throughout the history of psychology; see M. W. Bundy, "The Theory of Imagination in Classical and Mediaeval Thought," *University of Illinois Studies in Languages and Literature*, XII (Urbana, 1927), for a thorough and excellent review. Within our context their conceptual differentiation is less urgent for contemporary psychology than is the appreciation of their basic similarity and their

cannot be conscious without at the same time being unconscious; the unconscious is always present, just as the past is always present. To say it another way: we cannot will (*voluntas*) or love (*amor*) or form a notion (*notitia*) or understand (*intelligentia*) without imaginal fantasies going on simultaneously. So, we never cease projecting. We are dreaming all the time. The dream is there; we can never leave it. Part of the soul is continually remembering in mythopoetic speech, continually seeing, feeling, and hearing *sub specie aeternitatis*. Experience reverberates with memories, and it echoes reminiscences that we may never actually have lived. Thereby our lives seem at one and the same moment to be uniquely our own and altogether new, yet to carry an ancestral aura, a quality of *déjà vu*.

These parallels between the unconscious and *memoria* are reflections of that brilliant and thrilling book by Frances

---

relevance as background to the concept "unconscious." Just as the "unconscious" has been in general judged pejoratively in comparison with the "conscious," so too, as Bundy shows, was the imaginal realm declared morally suspect and ontologically inferior by the Western rational tradition. Not only was the imaginal associated by this tradition with the passions and the illusions of bodily senses, but ever since Plato (*Sophist* 265A–B) the imaginal and the "way of opinion" merged. The predominant attitude toward the imaginal in almost every period and every writer is fear. Any psychology that bases itself primarily upon the imaginal must expect to be met with this same fear, and resisted. The reception Freud's theories got and Jung's still get from academic rationalism iterate the inherently anti-imaginal attitude of Western philosophical psychology in favor of intellect, the "way of truth." The war of the academic faculties reflects the conflict between the soul's faculties, between imagination and intellect. Psychopathology is only one more attempt in the recurrent campaign of will and reason against imagination. "In determining the attitude toward phantasy in any particular period one must always take into account this almost universal fear of the power in the moral realm—a fear only accentuated by the recognition of its freedom to recombine the materials of experience" (Bundy, p. 273). Psychopathology has become a moral weapon and a refuge for moralisms; it is a disguised way of denouncing behavior: "wrong" has become "sick" or "abnormal," thereby eroding the categories of true sickness.

Yates, *The Art of Memory*,[66] which will become a classic in psychology even though it is not aimed in our direction. This work shows that there was an *art* of memory. This art of remembering can order the *thesaurus inscrutabilis*. Yates describes the techniques used widely from antiquity through the Renaissance and up to Leibniz for the development of the *memoria* (shall we call this development individuation or soul-making?) through the disciplines of the imaginal life.

The Yates book also gives an account of the ways in which all the traits of the soul and the encyclopedic knowledge of the mind can be placed within an imaginal structure. An inner temple of fantasy was built, and in it stood statues of mythical figures. The art of memory presents us with a spatial "unconscious," like an amphitheater with a place for everything. If today we were to group the contents of the mind into one system, we should no doubt pigeonhole them by the letters of the alphabet, as on the covers of encyclopedia volumes or in "subject catalogues" in libraries, or according to a rational computer system with memory retrieval. The system would be purely nominal, without inherent relation to the contents. The art of memory, however, grouped all human knowledge according to meaningful categories, where content and system referred to each other. The principles of the imagination used as universals for this system were mainly the Gods and heroes and themes of classical mythology, the pagan pantheon, sometimes expressed as the zodiacal constellations. These rubrics alone seemed to provide enough scope for embracing all the phenomena of the psyche. Under the rubric of this or that God can be classified a vast assortment of passions, ideas, events, objects, all of which "hang together" because the archetypal configuration to which these details belong gives them inherent intelligibility. The archetype permeated the events grouped under it, and

66. F. A. Yates, *The Art of Memory* (London: Routledge & Kegan Paul, 1966).

the numinous power of the divine figures gave to each trivial fact in the halls of the mind a charge of emotional value. Things held together, not merely because of the laws of association, which are essentially external and even mechanical, but because of their inherent belonging within mythical meaning.

Using the terms of today, we might translate this art as a method for presenting the organization of the collective unconscious—and consciousness too—according to archetypal dominants. The archetypes would correspond to divine imaginal forms used as Aristotelian or Kantian conceptual categories. Rather than logical or scientific laws, mythical figures would provide the a priori structures within the caverns and dens of the immeasurable imagination. All psychic events might be placed in meaningful coherence by means of these mythical structures. In fact, the categories of logic and number, of science and theology, could themselves be reduced (i.e., led back) to more basic metaphors of myth. No concepts, no matter how general and abstract, could embrace the range of these archetypal metaphors. No concepts could encompass the psychological configuration of Apollo or Venus or the Moon. These personified universals had a visual attractive power; they were evocative living beings who synthesized the contents of the imagination rather than analyzed them into terms. An event to be remembered could be diagnosed through its mythical connection and the Gods to which it belonged.

Even if at times the art of memory devolved into a mere method for rhetorical brilliance (for having piles of facts at one's command) or into a technical device for learning, it was essentially—in the hands of such men as Albertus Magnus, Thomas Aquinas, and the Dominicans and for Renaissance scholars such as Bruno—a moral activity of the soul. Learning and remembering served psyche. This art can be seen, not merely as the compulsive accumulation of facts, but as a kind of *meditatio*, a training of insight into relevance, an elaboration of the imaginal propensity so that the mind could be familiar with all the regions of the cosmos and man's nature.

Moreover, these systems recognized the power of what Albertus Magnus calls *metaphorica*, "for the wonderful moves the memory more than the ordinary." [67] Conceptual language failed in its effect upon the soul unless ideas were fastened onto "corporeal similitudes" (see the discussion below of Thomas Aquinas). A language without body in it, *nomina* without physical imagery, doomed itself to extinction.

The details of these systems can be read in Miss Yates's book, but one general observation of hers should be remarked on here. We said above that the long loss of memory was felt as loss of soul. This is quite understandable, since *memoria* was considered by Cicero, among others, following Plato (*Phaedo*, *Meno*, *Republic*), to present evidence for the divine origin of the soul.[68] Through the imagination man has access to the Gods: through the *memoria* the Gods enter our lives. The secular psychology whose history we have traced had little place for imagination, soul, or the Gods.

A major implication of her work for us is that the language of this imaginal realm is nearer to the language of the arts than it is to the language of concepts, because a primary way back to the matrix of memory is through her daughters, the muses. Therefore, a language that would be a speech of the lost aspect of the soul may require forms given by the muses. Psychological language may thus have to find its kinship, not with the logics of scientific reason or with the exercises of a behaving will, but with the arts. Both the arts and the psyche at its primary levels speak first the language of *memoria*.

We may assume that this approach to psychological language will no longer give such prominence to sentences

67. *Ibid.*, p. 66.
68. *Ibid.*, p. 44.

concerned with "how," which have become the curse of modern psychology. How can I formulate psychological laws (methodology); how can I technically effect psychological cure (therapology); how is the psyche put together, how does it work, how did I get this way, and how can I resolve my problems? If the "why" of wonder is the mother of philosophical thinking, then "how" is the generator of problem-solving, technical thinking. "How" belongs with the psychodynamics of Bentham, pragmatic and utilitarian. The will and understanding ask "how," but *memoria* neither asks "how" nor answers it. The problems of "how" are superseded by fantasy.

The discipline of imagination instead asks "where"—where to place this happening; and by asking "where" and fantasying in terms of place, the psyche enlarges its interiority, the space by which it carries meaning. We assume from the beginning that there is a place for everything, that everything can somehow belong to one God or another. The search through the caverns of the soul extends our capacity, whereas the search for "how" solutions reduces us to fixers. Whenever the "how" question arises under the guise of "Let's be practical," a movement goes upward out of the psychic realm into the world of coping consciousness. The complexes are not placed and rooted in their archetypal homes but are dealt with as disturbances. But perhaps this is all that modern therapeutic analysis has become: a branch of the practical intellect where the analyst is a sophistical teacher about "how to cope." But from another classical point of view there is only one valid "how," which supersedes all others and leads one quite away from "how" altogether, and that is: "How to die?" This "problem," which has no practical, analytical solution, makes a ridicule of "problems" and "hows." It returns us again to imaginal fantasy.

But let us not believe that fantasy is an easy business. When Freud's patients lay down and began to reminisce, they found their fantasies embarrassing. Freud also found them embarrassing. Alone with each other and these fantasies, teller and listener did not look at each other. Their eyes did not meet. Why are our fantasies embarrassing to tell, and why are we embarrassed hearing the intimate tales of another's imagination? Is interior life really a matter of the fig leaf?

The shame about our fantasies gives testimony to their importance. This shame is now called professionally "resistance," but what function does resistance perform? I do indeed resist telling my daydreams, my scorching hatreds, my longings and fears and their uncontrollable imagery. My fantasies are like wounds; they reveal my pathology. Resistance protects me. Fantasies are incompatible with my usual ego, and because they are uncontrollable and "fantastic"—that is, away from the relation to ego reality—we feel them alien. We are not embarrassed in the same way by our will and intelligence; indeed, we proudly exhibit their accomplishments. But what breeds in the imagination we tend to keep apart and to ourselves. Imagination is an inner world—not spatially inside, but kept in, esoteric, the inner aspect of consciousness. These affections and fantasies are the imaginal or unconscious aspect of everything we think and do. This part of the soul that we keep to ourselves is central to analysis, to confession, to prayer, central between lovers and friends, central in the work of art, central to what we mean by "telling the truth," and central to our fate. What we hold close in our imaginal world are not just images and ideas but living bits of soul; when they are spoken, a bit of soul is carried with them. When we tell our tales, we give away our souls. The shame we feel is less about the content of the fantasy than it is that there is fantasy at all, because the revelation of the imagination is the revelation of the uncontrollable, spontaneous spirit, an immortal, divine part of the soul, the *memoria Dei.* Thus the shame we feel refers to a sacrilege: the revelation of fantasies exposes the divine, which implies that *our fantasies are alien because they are not ours.* They arise from the transpersonal background, from nature or spirit or the divine, even as they become personalized through our lives, moving our personalities into mythic enactments.

Psychopathology Reimagined:
(1) Toward an Imaginal Ego

Jung started us toward a new psychopathology by basing his approach on the archetypal structures of the imaginal world. His rediscovery of *memoria* as the collective unconscious made possible a separation of unconsciousness in the narrower senses (stupor, trance, coma, habit, and forgetting) and the unconscious in the older sense of *memoria*. That they were intertwined was due in part to our one-sided ego formation; they were not intertwined per se, either necessarily or logically. He perceived the mythic memorial factor behind or within psychopathological phenomena, but psychopathology was neither the only nor the necessary road to the collective unconscious. One did not have to be neurotic in order to dream, nor did one have to be in analysis to experience the archetypes.

Nevertheless, Jung turned to the unconscious (as *memoria*) in order to transform unconsciousness (as pathology). By taking the dream ego with utter seriousness and by training consciousness to think symbolically or psychologically, he attempted to develop a new kind of ego consciousness, which I have called, stimulated by Henry Corbin, the "imaginal ego." Jung thus seemed to make war on merely rational thinking, and thus he relegated the will to a smaller role. These powers of the soul, and the ego attitudes derived from them, prevented awareness of another sort. He had found that therapy in depth depended upon just this other sort of ego consciousness, an imaginal awareness that leads to another sort of ego attitude.

Despite Jung's emphasis upon the imaginal, there nevertheless remains an inconsistency within analytical psychology that appears in the name "analytical" itself. Jung pointed beyond the ego concept of the nineteenth century with its emphasis upon head, will, and reason. But analytical psychology has yet to work out a concept of the ego corresponding with Jung's psychological *Anschauung*, which puts such stress on imaginal consciousness—dream, vision, fantasy—and on a life-style (the symbolic life) in which the ego lives and behaves primarily in terms of this imaginal consciousness. The old concept of ego development is anachronistically retained.

The model of thinking is nineteenth-century: a primitive Darwinism of evolution, dominant over recessive; a psychological imperialism, colonizing the unconscious or the id with a reality-coping ego consciousness. We still tend to think of "development" as a progressive march, whose retreats are only for a better leap forward (*reculer pour mieux sauter*), and which is modeled upon the hero's opposition to an irrational imaginal world beyond his powers of control. Ego and unconscious thus tend to be opposed, a priori; ego and Self come to terms in the language of will (submission) after "having it out" (*Auseinandersetzung*), or in the language of reason (*sacrificium intellectus*). Perhaps we are obliged to abandon the notion of development, since it has become a linear idea, requiring continuity. Besides, our own lives tell us that the ego does not move like a hero on his course; this sort of ego is a superego in whose shadow loom the complexes of inevitable psychopathology. As we have already reported, the conceptual structure of psychopathology has arisen parallel with the specific ego development of the past century and a half.

The imaginal ego is more discontinuous, now this and now that, guided as much by the synchronistic present as by the causal past, moving on a uroboric course, which is a circulation of the light *and* the darkness. It includes the downward turns, the depressions, recessions, and fallings-away from awareness. Psychopathology has its place; it is necessary. Does this not accord with our experience? The movement of the imaginal ego should be conceived less as a development than as a circular pattern. Circularity still receives from the old ego a rather pathological description: the return of what is repressed, the repetition compulsion, and the ever recurring cycles of the negative mother complex. But the psyche insists on repetition. Are we so sure it is negative? Or is the negativity a view taken from an ego who must progress and develop? The psyche insists on the same figures and situations, bringing them back in dreams through many years. Work, ritual, remembrance, and style return to the same ground again and again. The ego of will and reason, recognizing itself by development, feels caught, compelled, or to blame in the circularity of repetition. This old ego can take part in the process of circulation only by abandoning itself, by forgetting, self-surrender, *metanoia*, etc. It is not an ego based on the alchemical goal of *circulatio* or *rotatio* but one which is fundamentally at a tangent to the motion of the psyche as a whole. The "strong" ego, that first aim of psychotherapy, is thus opposed to and then overwhelmed by the numinous Wholly Other.

The idea of an imaginal ego gives conceptual form to what actually happens in Jungian psychotherapy, where adaptation to the unconscious, or *memoria*, is reflected in the changed ego personality of the analyzed person. His adaptation is primarily to "psychic reality" (Jung), to the "imaginal world" (Corbin). As will and reason conceived adaptation in terms of controlling and understanding reality, so the adaptation of the imaginal ego is in terms of imagining reality. Its consciousness is of its fantasies first, its "psychopathology" and what is now called, by reason and will, the "unconscious" psychic life. These fantasies and psychopathologies have been the hardest and last thing to come by in therapy, requiring special techniques for lowering the ego's threshold. An ego conceived mainly as will and reason has small place for fantasy, other than repression beyond the threshold. No wonder fantasy is so "hard to get"; it blocks the way of linear purpose. Should fantasies break in during a breakdown, they are to be controlled or interpreted. But if the ego is patterned upon circularity (which is the motion of the soul, as Plotinus said), then it will be less estranged from its own fantastic otherness. Because of this circular pattern, the imaginal ego is driven to be faithful to itself; it is stuck with the self-same repetition, the ever recurrent themes of its afflictions. But this faithfulness to the compulsive repetition and its specific fantasies, habits, and familiar symptoms is also being true to form, true to the *causa formalis* of one's own mythic pattern. Repeated remembrance of things past leads to the memorial core of these remembrances, their archetypal meaning and necessity, and to the scintilla of insight in that core. The vicious circle is also the *iteratio* of alchemy and a way of becoming what one is. The purgatory of faithful repetition of the same mistakes is also their redemption into individual style.

Each of these tiresome cycles compels us to recognize the force of that which coerces us, a force which feels stronger to us than a "syndrome" or a "problem" and which we tend to personalize, perhaps even to name and to talk with, as with a tormenting demon. Even the strongest ego, hard and toughened through its repetitious coping with its "problem," is forced ever and again to submit to imaginal powers. As if to a living God, the I is forced to serve. In this manner the I is drawn into the halls of *memoria*, becoming itself but one more of the many particulars that finds its place in association with an archetype. My fantasies and symptoms put me in my place. No longer is it a matter of where they belong—to which God—but where I belong, at which altar I may leave myself, within which myth my suffering will turn into a devotion. Though imagination seems to be inside me, as a faculty of my soul (or a compartment called "memory" inside my brain), it is also possible to experience myself inside the imaginal, where the ego is no longer an independent factor, carrying consciousness like a lamp or knife or knot between the eyes. At this point the usual ego fades into the dream ego.

The dream ego is another name for the imaginal ego. It is that aspect of the ego complex which takes part in imaginal reality. There are discrepancies between day ego and night ego; usually what we do in dreams shocks the waking ego. But perhaps what we do during the day is equally disturbing to the I of our dreams. Therapeutic analysis generally tries to bring a *rapprochement* between the two. It attempts to bring about a correction in the dream ego, much as it tries to transform the waking ego into attitudes that take more account of what is happening at night. So far, so good, concerning the night blindness of the day ego: of course it must learn from dreams. But must the dream ego also be corrected upward in the light of our day vision? Here, the idea of the dream as compensatory corrective gets us into trouble, for it assumes that the I in our dreams should react with the values of day consciousness. From this vantage point dreams become "good" and "bad," and we judge the wrongs and rights of dream behavior. We return from sleep to the analyst with a punishment or a reward. But must everything psychic be put at the altars of the biblical personages and their warnings? Do dreams belong to Moses and Jesus and Paul, or to Night and her children (Oneiroi, Hypnos, Thanatos, Old Age, and Fate) and Hades? [69] Is soul made with guilt? Rather, I think, responsibility for the behavior of the dream ego and attempts to correct it strengthen the old ego of will and reason. When we take the dream as a corrective to the leftovers of yesterday or as instruction for tomorrow, we are using it for the old ego. Freud said the dream is the guardian of sleep. And indeed the dream ego belongs to the family of Night (Nyx), serves there regularly, and takes its instruction in terms of its own "family," from its mother and its brother and sister phenomena. Perhaps the point of dreams is that, night after night, year after year, they prepare the imaginal ego for old age, death, and fate by soaking it through and through in *memoria*. Perhaps the point of dreams has very little to do with our daily concerns, and their purpose is the soul-making of the imaginal ego.

We have needed a more complete view of the ego in order to adapt to Jung's later psychology, which, though it began

69. *Iliad* XIV. 259; XI. 241; XVI. 853; Hesiod *Theogony* 211 f.; Cicero *On the Nature of the Gods* III. 17.

as analytical, became archetypal. "Already in 1912," as I have mentioned elsewhere,

> Jung placed analysis within an archetypal frame, thereby freeing the archetypal from confinement to the analytical. Analysis may be an instrument for realizing the archetypes, but it cannot embrace them. Placing archetypal prior to analytical gives the psyche a further chance to move out of the consulting room. It gives an archetypal perspective to the consulting room itself. After all, analysis too is an enactment of an archetypal fantasy.[70]

The ego of an "analytical" psychology gives insufficient adaptation to archetypal reality. Jung presented us with this new reality, and we do injustice to the archetypes of *memoria* with a nineteenth-century concept. An "analytical" psychology offers "analysis" of *memoria*, but Jung said we must dream the myth along. The old ego offers a one-sided adaptation; it is inadequate to archetypal psychology because it restrains and ignores the imaginal part of the ego complex. This is why the anima holds such sway with its promise of emotion and fantasy; this is why the Self becomes so Wholly Other and is experienced magically through the images of the unconscious, through things irrational and unwilled. We have had no ego of the imagination to serve as familiar in the imaginal realm. Our concept of the ego has placed that which would heal us beyond the threshold.

Further, this accounts for why we have become so obsessed with symbolic images, confusing archetypal reality with visual imagery. When we have lost the imaginal, the archetypes first re-present themselves to the soul by pictorial configurations. But symbolic images are not the only way the archetypes may manifest themselves. We overvalue the study of symbols, believing that we will find archetypal reality there. Iconoclastic breaking of these vessels may be required to free the psyche from this first level of archetypal appearance

70. "Why 'Archetypal' Psychology?," *Spring 1970* (Zurich and New York: Spring Publications, 1970), p. 216.

so that it can perceive fantasy in behavior, in the subtler forms of style, voice, body carriage, and the living enactment of myth. An imaginal ego does not mean an ego filled with drug-caused images or one filled with the knowledge of images. It rather means behaving imaginatively.

Jung called one main method for preparing the imaginal ego "active imagination," a term describing the subtle balance between the three faculties: an active will, an interpretive understanding, and the independent movement of fantasies. Again we find parallels between the art of memory and active imagination as instruments for reordering the psyche at its objective levels.

In active imagination one enters the *thesaurus inscrutabilis* of Augustine, and in his words: "When I enter there, I require instantly what I will to be brought forth, and something instantly comes; others must be long sought after . . . others rush out in troops. . . . These I drive away with the hand of my heart . . . until what I wish for be unveiled." [71] Like Augustine and the subsequent memory techniques, active imagination stresses the activity of consciousness. *Notitia, voluntas,* and *amor* are applied to *memoria.* The art of memory is a work; thus does it require the will power of ego development. Especially important in this work is love. The images are best activated by the emotion of love—our love turned toward the imaginal world: *amor* in service of *memoria.*

Not only does archetypal psychology experience the *memoria* and practice an "art of memory," but we learn a psychology of the *memoria* very much like the systems described by Frances Yates. We learn characteristics, groups of images and symbols. Of the Great Mother, for example, we learn her principal forms in fairy tales, myths, and pictures, in objects and conventions; we learn the typical ideas, attitudes, and reactions occasioned through her and the elements, body

71. Augustine *Confessions* X. 8, quoted from Yates, *The Art of Memory*, p. 46.

zones, animals, people, and places associated with her. Thus we proceed, as through the halls of memory, circumscribing archetypal figures. Where once these figures were Gods, each with an assemblage of attributes, they now are archetypal figures: the divine child, the anima maiden (*kore*), the magician, the *senex*. The root idea is the same as in the art of memory: the archetypals or universals of the unconscious psyche are to be found in myth. Myths are *universali fantastici*, said Giambattista Vico, and they can reorder the imagination. Myths become the new universals of fantasy for an archetypal psychology. Furthermore, these universals are not mere *nomina*, because myth is the a priori given with the soul itself. Fantasy is the primordial force of the soul that would take everything back into its prior condition, ritualizing all occurrences, turning events into mythemes, fixing the trivia of each case history into the precise details, seemingly so irrelevant, of a legend, continually confabulating our lives into patterns that we can neither understand with our minds nor manage with our wills but which we can love with an *amor fati*.

Psychopathology Reimagined: (2) Myth and Mental Illness

A task for us who try to follow Jung is to take his implications for psychopathology through to the end. We need to inquire with precision into the archetypal constellations and their effects upon disorders of personality and upon its individual development. Then we shall have both psychology and psychopathology within the same description. A pathography then becomes a necessary part of each archetypal configuration, somewhat as disease belongs to complete physical health. Special forms of torment and bizarre behavior are an inherent part of the myth. At once our view of psychic illness changes. No longer is psychic illness that which does not fit in, that which is alien, deviate, *délire*, *entgleist*—all terms shot through with shadow, judgments against the phenomena made by the baffled understanding and the frustrated will. Rather these fantastic and alien events are expressions of moments within a mytheme *which cannot be better expressed or lived in another way*. They belong to its suffering, its pathos, its pathography. The archetype is an affliction; it makes us suffer. A pathology of the psyche is an integral, necessary part of psychology because suffering the archetype through our complexes is an integral, necessary part of psychic life. The imaginal is also emotional, else what human reality would it have? How could it affect us? The great images are great passions; the palaces and caverns of *memoria* are also arenas of the inferno.[72] The self that stands behind or within the great archetypal images is after all a human self, an expression of our humanity—not only a God-image or an abstraction of completion through conjunction. Does not the goal of self mean just being human, human-being, a man; is the Anthropos not Man? Archetypal images portray our human emotions, our all-too-human complexes, which produce the affliction of just being human, each human being living the experiment of human Being.

Faith in the old psychopathology is gone. As an inadequate shadow to a psychology which gives too little place to imagination, its *nomina* lose conviction. The nosologies are written anew in each century; system after system rises, holds sway, comes down. All the French *délires* and *manies*, all the diagnostic acuities of German psychiatry, dissolve back into the matrix. To what do the signposts point? Except for a score or so of adjectives, like "*débile*," "senile," "manic," the language does not hold.

But what have we instead? In the art of memory, myths and their figures represented universals under which all aspects of learning and nature could be grouped. Jung showed us how myths could be applied to psychology. If our task is to draw the ultimate consequences from Jung, then does

72. Yates, *The Art of Memory*, p. 95.

he not suggest that psychopathology can be based altogether upon mythology and that mythology itself can become a new psychopathology? May we not search for the myth of mental illness?

Once it was fashionable to take myth as a mental illness, a kind of infantile primitive madness for explaining things. Now it has become fashionable to speak of mental illness as a myth, as only a fable, something not real or true, a delusion that helps the ruling classes or a ruling philosophy. But I would bring "myth" and "mental illness" together in another manner. I mean that psychopathology is so real and so true, the fantasy of illness so necessary, that only something equal to its strange reality and strange truth can provide adequate background.

Neoplatonism studied myth, and the Renaissance under the influence of this philosophy wrote and painted the classic stories of the Gods and heroes and their human associations. Was this mere entertainment or an antique conceit? Or could there be a significant relationship between the return to classical myth and the extraordinary quality of the Renaissance psyche? The purpose of myth was to relate the soul to what the Neoplatonists considered to be its divine nature and even to "heal the maladies of our phantasy." [73] Mistaken and peculiar fantasy could be led onto a right path through frequenting the metaphorical truths in the images of myth. As wrong reasoning and weak will are corrected through their own principles, myth becomes a discipline for fantasy.

I do not mean that we shall now return to Greece and schematize psychopathology into classical mythology, finding the divine root for each syndrome. This would be to take the syndromes literally and the Gods as emblems of them or as causal machines behind them. This would be making use of the mythic, which means nothing less than using

73. Cf. T. Taylor, notes to *Pausanias* (London: Richard Priestley, 1824), III, 302.

the Gods.[74] We are not in search of a new pathography based on mythical figures—the Trickster, or Pan, or Saturn, say—though a specific pathological motive is part of each mythical gestalt. Let us not begin in the old way by inventing, with the understanding, another set of descriptions. Rather the task is first to rethink or, rather, *reimagine* psychopathology by examining behavior with a mythical eye and by hearing reports as tales. It means hearing as a story what is told when we say, "Tell me about it." It means "case material" as a tale. Or maybe it means returning to a case as a *Fall*, as the word was originally understood: the way things fall, *cadere*, from Heaven perhaps, the hap and chance of undiagnosed life.

Case material is itself a fantasy, a new style of fiction developed during the past century, written by thousands of hands in clinics and private practices, sometimes published as empirical evidence for a theory but mainly stored in the archives of asylums and the attics of analysts. These fictions, with their conventions of style, derive not only from the medical model of following the course of a disease. They develop also from the fantasy of fiction-writing, of the fictional vision which composes life into a story. A "case writeup" in the hands of a social worker places a person within the imaginal world of the writer who creates a fictional personage, a kind of hero carrying a fate. This writeup is usually the first stage in therapy. By means of anamnesis and case history the details of life are given a vision, and an imaginal ego is prepared at a first level. The therapeutic situation unfolds in terms of this fiction called "a case history." Inadvertently, therapy devised a form through which life could be translated into a tale.

Mythology provides basic patterns for the tales of lives. "Mythologems . . . belong to the structural elements of the

74. The Jesuits used the pagan Gods as emblemata for moral edification during the Counter Reformation. Cf. J. Seznec, "Theories Regarding the Use of Mythology," in *The Survival of the Pagan Gods* (New York: Harper Torchbooks, 1961), p. 275.

psyche. They are the constants whose expression is everywhere and at all times the same." [75] Yet we return to Greek mythology, not seeking a skeleton for a new psychopathology, but because one returns necessarily to the classic roots of our culture whenever one is in search of imaginative sources for a new beginning.[76] We go to Greece for an archaeology of fantasy.

Classical mythology as it comes down to us gives us one insight that will be essential for grasping the sufferings of the soul. Classical mythology is a collection of highly interrelated families of tales with much precise detail *but without schematic system* either in the individual tales or among the tales as a group. Psychopathology, too, is a family of interrelated problems that are precise in detail yet cannot be systematized. The Gods, like the sufferings of the soul, melt into one another. Classical mythology would have us abandon our insistence upon cubbyholes for each difficulty, each difficulty with a name, each name with a prognosis. Mythology shows us that each difficulty can belong to several Gods and can be fantasied in various ways. The will to fight, for instance, can be guided by Ares, by the warlike aspects of Aphrodite and Athena, or by Hercules. And what differences there are in the psychic styles of these fights! Even milk and suckling, which one would think must belong exclusively to the Great Mother, appear as essential phenomena in the tales of both

75. *CW*, XVI, par. 207.

76. Nearly every classicist and mythographer has expanded at some point upon the importance of returning to Greek and Roman mythology for rekindling the imagination. See, for instance, M. Grant's Foreword to his *Myths of the Greeks and Romans* (New York: World, Mentor Books, 1962) and B. Snell, *The Discovery of the Mind* (New York: Harper Torchbooks, 1960), pp. 258–63. The reasons for the return are not historical, nor do they lie in imitation or worship of the past or even in an effort to get to the roots of culture; the reasons are to be found rather in the observation that Greek and Roman myth presents, explicitly and with subtle differentiation, the archetypal patterns of our Western existence; and, as Snell says, we "are constantly forced to revert to the archetypes of Greek thought."

Zeus and Dionysus. Modern psychotherapy does not have the flexibility of myth; it believes its diagnoses and the ultimate root in childhood. But even the child can belong, now to this myth, now to that. Only within the Great Mother cult must childhood be understood as modern therapy regards it (which implies that reductive analysts are her priests).

Just as psychological diagnoses can change and vary, so too mythology lets things stay in flux or in process. A myth is a description of a process; it is itself a process. It unfolds, moves, and at its different joints leads off into various possibilities, which lead into other mythemes. Its structure is dramatic; myths resolve themselves. The pathology and the cure are there together. The problem, the ways of working it through, the forms in which a myth is lived and plays itself out in suffering, the *passiones animae* making us ill, the prognosis as the expectations with regard to its *lysis:* all are presented by the tale. The tales themselves have a psychopathological aspect because the mythical propensity follows certain absurd and bizarre patterns. For instance, myth is precise—the way sadism is precise, the way compulsions or hypochondriac worries or confabulations are precise—and yet dereistic, altogether away from reality. Their precision is that of fantasy.

Psychopathology reimagined may also give a mythical background to those areas we have profaned and debased with the term "perversion." A mythological approach offers the possibility of reuniting the profane and the sacred, the behavior with its mythical meaning. By giving this sacred background to a "case," to the way things "fall," psychology again reflects theology. The behavior of the psyche reflects the acts of the Gods, because we are created in the Gods' images and can therefore do nothing that they have not already made possible in their behavior. Psychodynamics thus does indeed have its source in the hidden recesses of the mind (Augustine), its unseen parts (Bentham). These hidden invisibles are the divinities. They are the ground of our fantasies. If our fantasies are "God"-given, our attitude toward them must necessarily be religious. Again, psychology reflects theology, but a pagan and polytheistic theology.

By regarding psychopathology from the viewpoint of mythology, we shall in turn be taking a fresh look at mythology through the eyes of psychopathology. Seznec and Wind have shown how the pagan Gods and their myths lived on into the late Renaissance. Our civilization has turned to them again and again for humanistic, aesthetic, and moral inspiration. Not only the Romantics, but even Freud made this return to classical mythology.[77]

However, we have yet to look at mythology from the perspective given by psychopathology. Mythology's moments of anxiety, bestiality, and possession, its extraordinary nonhuman imaginal happenings, can be newly illumined through our own corresponding experiences. Mythology can then reach us, and we it, in a fresh way because it bears directly on our pain. More: *our pain becomes a way of gaining insight into mythology*. We enter a myth and take part in it directly through our afflictions. The fantasies that emerge from our complexes become the gate into mythology.

This way suggests a new method for the study of mythology, a *method of fantasy*. This method would be a truly and wholly psychological approach, unconstricted by scholarly supererogation, which keeps the psyche a handmaiden of intellect, allowing it to fantasy only in accordance with the texts and the historical evidence. The "science of mythology" must yield to the "art of memory." Mythology as a science assumes the Gods to be of the Greeks, of another time and another language, dead and not ours, whose last statements have been made, thus constituting a dogma accessible to interpretation only through scholarly method—a preserve of the academic *senex*. On the other hand, the art of memory as we can develop it within ourselves by the method

77. G. Tourney, "Freud and the Greeks: A Study of the Influence of Classical Greek Mythology and Philosophy upon the Development of Freudian Thought," *Journal of the History of the Behavioral Sciences*, I, No. 1 (1965).

of fantasy, which includes active imagination, shows the Gods to belong not only to the Greeks but as living right now and speaking through our fantasies and afflictions, continuing to declare themselves through the *dynamis* of the imagination. Since this method produces participation and thus new knowledge (as well as releases the divine figures themselves from their antique conventions), it is also therapeutic. Entering into the divine archetypal core of the complexes, we can be cured *of* what ails us *by* what ails us. The problem is redeemed by its own fantasy, since the fantasy makes transparent the archetypal core of the complex.

The art of memory indicates that pathology plays a special role in mythology. I quote now from the *Ad Herennium*, which Frances Yates says is the main source for the classical art of memory. The author of *Ad Herennium* is advising us how to set up our images so that they can be recollected. They have most effect if they are "active (*imagines agentes*); if we assign to them exceptional beauty or singular ugliness; if we ornament some of them, as with crowns or purple cloaks . . . or if we somehow disfigure them, as by introducing one stained with blood or soiled with mud or smeared with red paint . . . or by assigning certain comic effects to our images." [78] An example of a complicated legal proceeding can be remembered by means of the following image: "The defendant at the bedside, holding in his right hand a cup, in his left, tablets, and on the fourth finger a ram's testicles." [79] "Testicles" are introduced to remind one of *testes*, witnesses. This kind of association—between an abstract idea and a sexual body image—carried only by the sound of the word, is familiar enough in what we today call schizophrenic thinking.

Another example comes from the fourteenth century. An English friar, John Ridevall, invented "invisible memory images, held within the memory, not intended to be externalised, and being used for quite practical mnemonic purposes."

78. Yates, *The Art of Memory*, p. 10.
79. *Ibid.*, p. 11.

Ridevall describes "the image of a prostitute, blind, with mutilated ears, proclaimed by a trumpet (as a criminal), with a deformed face, and full of disease." [80] This image, said to represent "Idolatry," follows the rules, according to Miss Yates, in that it is "strikingly hideous and horrible." Pathological detail helped engrave in the mind the ideas and principles which the mind was to recall.

Here the art of memory referred to a rule given by Thomas Aquinas: "Simple and spiritual intentions slip easily from the soul unless they are, as it were, linked to some corporeal similitudes." [81] Pathological similitudes are especially favorable for helping us enter the halls of memory; to attach these extraordinarily hideous or comic or glorious details to the images of people we know is more helpful yet. Peter of Ravenna gives an example of this last principle. His work, published in 1491, "became the most universally known of all the memory textbooks." [82] The details of Peter's astounding memory, his method of interiorizing external places into inner space, and so on can be read in *The Art of Memory*. Here I want only to present another example of the reliance of the technique upon peculiar, personal idiosyncrasy. Peter introduces the image of a young girl, Juniper, "who was dear to him when young and whose image he finds stimulates his memory." In his variation of the lawsuit image, she appears and tears up the will. Miss Yates comments: "We are baffled as to why such an image, even if Juniper is a destructive girl, should help Peter remember." But we know, from the analytical practice of active imagination, the power of anima figures and their role as *imagines agentes*.

Frances Yates suggests that the art of memory may be one explanation for the medieval love of the grotesque. Perhaps the strange figures decorating medieval manuscripts and ubiquitous in medieval art are a reflection not so much of a

80. *Ibid.*, p. 96.
81. *Ibid.*, p. 74.
82. *Ibid.*, p. 113.

"tortured psychology"[83] as of methods used for maintaining an imaginative consciousness, for helping the imaginal ego to keep the mythology of the soul in order. In any event, tortured psychology and reminiscence belong together; the path to recollecting the imaginal seems to lie in the complexes, which move the psyche as Peter of Ravenna's soul was moved by the image of his Juniper complex.

The rules for ordering the imaginal so that the images have "ridiculous movements, amazing gestures"[84] are very close to the dynamics of what we today call psychopathology. Are the exaggerated and bizarre details—"things remarkably beautiful or remarkably hideous"[85]—merely technical aids to recollection? And even if the grotesque, obscene, and horrifying are introduced merely as stimuli, they show to what depth and with what power the pathognomonic awakens the imaginal.

Because this is still a wholly new vision for the field of psychopathology, we can draw only general conclusions. First, exact pathological details are an inherent part of fantasy figures; if the details are not originally in the mytheme, the image will take on "sharpened expressions," a pathological distortion, in order to bring the pathological into the mythic. Second, the easiest, first, or best way to see into these figures, to gain entry into the imaginal and mythic, is through the "sharpened expressions" of personalized pathology. Third, merely because a memory or fantasy is "tortured," exaggerated, or obscene does not imply that it needs therapy. The damaged and queer figures who emerge from our complexes do not necessarily indicate that something has gone wrong and that the ego should set it straight. These shapes are dynamic, and their pathological detail is a goad to vivacity and insight. They are the active agents of the imagination, its vanguard, leading to profounder psychological insights. The en-

83. *Ibid.*, p. 104.
84. *Ibid.*, p. 110.
85. *Ibid.*, p. 109.

tire field of depth psychology began in pychopathology; modern psychological consciousness was led into existence through the crazy distortions shown to Freud by Charcot and to Jung at Burghölzli. Every fantasy released by every complex is an example of the soul's naturally "tortured" psychology, just as every myth shows peculiar and pathological distortions.

"Distortion," "tortured," "torment"—these words refer to the twisted nature of the psyche, its complexity, which Jung placed at the fundament of psychic life. Our complexes are a twisting-together of opposites. Etymologically, "twist," "wrestle," "wreath," and the "writhing" of our torment belong together. We are twisted in soul because soul is by nature and of necessity in a tortuous condition. We cannot be explained, nor can we be straightened out. Psychopathological distortion is the primary condition given with our complexity, the crowning wreath of thorns or laurel garland we wear always on the tortuous path through the labyrinth that has no exit. For, as Jung said, the complexes are life itself; to be rid of them is to be rid of life.

At this juncture, apt examples might be called for. But every myth is an example. Think of the pathological detail in the tales of Persephone, of Hercules, Dionysus, or Apollo. Classical mythology is a textbook, if you will, of pathopsychology; it is all there if we but read it in this light. Depth psychology in fact begins with Freud's fundamental insight that the mythic and the pathic belong together. Freud proposed this link with his Oedipus model. Jung's archetypes are in each case examples of the interplay of myth and behavior. Take for example the bitch, the bitterness, the salt, and the mooniness in the alchemical study of Luna.[86] The tale of Psyche and Eros is one example of mythopathopsychology. The *senex-puer* figure, which I have examined elsewhere, presents the negative and pathological within the same configuration as the mythic. We have seen how the

86. *CW*, XIV.

mythic accounts for the pathic—that, for instance, the suffering of psyche belongs within the Eros-Psyche tale, that Persephone and Eleusis tell about rape, or how a study of Saturn can tell us as much about depression and its possibilities as depression can tell us about Saturn.

No, we do not need examples. Rather we need clarity about first principles. We need a new way of looking, an imaginative way, a way that starts from within the imaginal itself, so that everything we look at becomes an example. In this way we would experience ourselves through the third faculty of the psyche, by means of an imaginal ego consciousness that is not estranged from the imagination and its fantasies; and the conventional ego and its usual views would also become objects of this new consciousness. We could then see through our habitual ego, see the myths working within it to create our so-called ego psychology and its usual psychopathology. We might also be less threatened by the grotesque, horrible, and obscene, since, from the imaginal perspective, the bizarre would simply belong.

Thus our notions of psychological insight would change. Insight would no longer mean translation, no longer mean the reformulation of imaginal speech into psychological language, mainly through understanding our fantasies, interpreting our dreams. We would let the insight contained within the fantasy appear of itself, in its own "intrinsically intelligible" speech.[87] For, try as we may, we cannot make insights with reason or will. Something imaginative is needed. Fantasy products need to be insighted against an imaginative background, transformed into imagination. (The transformation of fantasy into imagination corresponds with the development of the anima, as discussed in Part One.) This imaginative background is given by *memoria*, as a kind of natural

87. See Kathleen Raine's paper, "Poetic Symbols as a Vehicle of Tradition," *Eranos Jahrbuch*, XXXVII (Zurich: Rhein Verlag, 1970), 373 f., where she discusses Coomaraswamy's notion that the archetypal symbols of the *memoria* need no "translation" since they are "intrinsically intelligible."

light that yields a consciousness about fantasy according to principles different from the effort of will and the constructs of understanding. The imaginal ego reflects this imaginative background and this kind of consciousness. It is unlike the Cartesian ego, based on the *cogito,* or the ego of will, with which we are all too familiar.

As we do not need new examples for reimagining psychopathology, so do we not need new psychopathological classifications or even explanations. The search for explanations is again a problem of the understanding. The imaginal does not explain; myths are not explanations. They are bound to ritual happenings; they are stories, as our fantasies are, which project us into participation with the phenomena they tell about so that the need for explanation falls away. The myth both involves us and, at the same time, through its ritual precision, detaches us. Therefore, finally, since we need neither new examples nor new systems, the old ones may well be kept.

The old language may be kept—but *not believed in* in the same way as before. The *nomina* become objects for new insights. By shifting the position of consciousness, we arrive at a radical nominalism and can begin to insight the old diagnostic language with a new imaginative vision. We view the so-called factual from the archetypal. The archetypal has provided a perspective for the study of other fields and other periods, and we shall now use this same perspective to see mythic factors at work currently and closer to home: in psychology. By insighting this psychological language, we are seeing into, seeing through (*Durchschau*), seeing within and from within, catching the fantasy, the imaginal potential, of that concatenation of the ways things have fallen which we call a syndrome.

We need not discard these *nomina* of psychopathology as the operationalists, existentialists, and radical pragmatists implore. Nor need they be revised and retranslated into an up-to-date new language. Rejection or revision is not necessary because the categories of psychopathology are not merely *nomina.*

A field must have a language of its own; in fact, a field is its language. It defines itself through its particular language game. Psychology needed a manner of speaking adequate to the peculiar realm that was being discovered. "To work through," "to act out," "to constellate," and "to integrate"— these inventions of psychotherapy arose in answer to needs of the psyche to speak of events for which there were no other terms. We cannot do without the very words which we have taken to task since they fulfill a function within the psyche itself. They allow it to present itself by means of a game of symbolic counters that were coined concurrently with the growth of modern psychological consciousness. It is not the words with which we find fault but psychology's literalistic relation with them: its belief that its words refer directly to things. Rather, the words refer to the game called "psychopathology," and they make sense within its fantasy.

Psychiatric language has, for all our scorn, two signal virtues. In the first place, those men of the nineteenth century were earnestly concerned with mapping the mind and curing disease. Whether disease of the psyche exists as they then conceived it, where its limits begin or end, whether it exists at all—be this as it may—neither their searching nor their accomplishments should be forgotten. To throw out the past leaves only a new lacuna. Even the residual blunders we inherit from history are better than no history, that vacuity and illusion of a clean slate, the new, the now. History undigested only repeats, sour.

In the second place, these predecessors of ours observed keenly. Their mistaken language results from a kind of consciousness in which we each have a share, but their descriptions also belong to the psyche's phenomenology. Their terms can be saved if we strip them of their portentous and final diagnostic authority. We must merely clean from them their nineteenth-century context and take them as precise verbal fantasies mirroring certain details of psychic behavior. We need not assume them to be "realities" of "mental illness" or factual conditions in a positivistic sense. They are names which can be reemployed in the mood of this century.

Nomina are mere inventions picked out of the air—but this air is fantasy. Thus *nomina,* too, are expressions of the mythical imagination; or, as we said above, psychopathology is a mythic system of the reason. As such, these *nomina* of psychopathology are also archetypal expressions. The reason of the Enlightenment took the fantasy to itself, rationalized it, rigidified it by severing it from its mythic root. The system it developed was thus dogmatic, based on mere descriptions, and so quite empty. Yet there was a dynamic fantasy in the creation of psychopathology that cannot be neglected. Unfortunately, it was stopped short in a historical period and became identified with the form of that period. But the kind of fantasies that led to the language of psychopathology, fantasies in both the patient and the doctor, have not stopped. These "crazy" manifestations continue, as they mythically must. They go on springing from archetypal roots, even if reason sees first a pathology in the fantasy, names it such, and thus perpetuates its own rational fantasy, which it takes so literally. Since the fantasies have not stopped, we are not stopped from imagining and insighting them and the language in new ways.

Imagination can give old terms new life; by reimagining psychopathology, we can recreate this language by *giving back to the* nomina *their archetypal substance.* The terms thereby lose their purely descriptive nominalism. They are no longer only empirical "opinions" but are now "ways of truth": concepts as metaphors. The two ways of description come together as the terms fill up with the stuff of mythic meaning. If "masochism," "depression," "suicidal panic," "hysteria," and "rape" belong to precise moments of mythic behavior and feeling and are archetypally necessary to the expression of this mythic behavior and feeling, then they have a real a priori basis in psychic reality. Thus the *nomina* of the old language change their ontological status. The *nomina* of psychopathology also have their *esse in anima* given to them through the myths in which these patterns of behavior and feeling are necessary components.

Concluding Reflections: A Speech of the Soul

There has been a concealed urgency in this essay, underlying its rhetoric and polemic and its compulsive collection of information. I like to think that this urgency arises from the soul itself, whose emotions ask the psychologist to remember psyche. What place has psyche in psychology? Do its statements speak for the soul, call it forth? Do its descriptions reflect Psyche, to whom we devoted so much of the last essay? And has Eros touched psychology with joy and passion, so that psychology, too, may become a place of soul-making?

Psychology, as the specialty named after Psyche, has a special obligation to the soul. The psychologist should be a keeper of the great natural preserve of memory and its innumerable treasures. But the nineteenth-century psychologist (and the nineteenth century is a style of mind not confined to the last century) laid waste this area of the soul with his inroads and signposts. While other nineteenth-century investigators were polluting the archaic, natural, and mythic in the outer world, psychology was doing much the same to the archaic, natural, and mythic within. Therapeutic depth psychology shares this blame, since it shares nineteenth-century attitudes. It gave names with a pathological bias to the animals of the imagination. We invented psychopathology and thereby labeled the *memoria* a madhouse. We invented the diagnoses with which we declared ourselves insane. After subtly poisoning our own imaginal potency with this language, we complain of a cultural wasteland and loss of soul. The poison spreads; words continually fall "mentally ill" and are usurped by psychopathology, so that we can hardly use them without their new and polluted connotations: "immature," "dissociation," "rigid," "withdrawn," "passive," "transference," "fixation," "sublimation," "projection" (the last three notably different in alchemy), "resistance," "deviate," "stress," "dependence," "inhibition," "compulsion,' "illusion," "split," "tranquilized," "driven," "compensation," "inferiority," "derange," "suppression," "depression," "repression," "confusion"—these words have been psychologized and pathologized in the past one hundred fifty years.

So Psyche requests the psychologist to remember his calling. Psychological remembrance is given by the kind of speech that carries remembrance within it. This language is both of culture and uncultured, is both of art and artless. It is a mythic, metaphoric language, a speech of ambiguities that is evocative and detailed, yet not definitive, not productive of dictionaries, textbooks, or even abstract descriptions. Rather, it is a speech that leads to participation, in the Platonic sense, in and with the thing spoken of, a speech of stories and insights which evoke, in the other who listens, new stories and new insights, the way one poem and one tune ignite another verse and another song. It is conversation, letters, tales, in which we reveal our dreams and fantasies—and our psychopathology. It evokes, calls forth, and creates psyche as it speaks. It speaks of mood: of "sadness" and "despair" before "depression"; of "rage" before "aggression"; of "fear," "panic," and "anguish" before "anxiety attacks." This speech is "not fashioned in schools," and it will be "simple and rude," as Tertullian said. It will have "corporeal similitudes," that is, body images, speaking from and reaching to the imaginal body in order to provoke the soul's movements. It must be speech that works as an "imaginative agent," stirring fantasy. Such speech has impact because it carries body in it; it is speech alive, the word itself alive, not a description about a psychic state by a psychologist, not carefully defined, but freely imagined.

Yet this speech cannot be uncultured and unhistorical. The grunt and slogan of an anticulture will not do, because such simplicity and rudeness do not reflect the psyche's needs. Verbal stupidities are merely the obverse of academic verbiage, a reaction against the old ego and its literalness, its lack of imagination. Although not fashioned in schools, this language will be fashioned and schooled, it will be a rich and full speech, a tongue of metaphor, of poetry and myth, for it is obliged to reflect Psyche's beauty, pregnant with voluptuousness. Its aim will always be soul-making.

Emphasis upon the making of "soul" rather than "self" keeps us in the tradition of language that works as an imaginative agent. "Soul" retains corporeal similitudes. Its immanence in my body or in my environment (bush soul and totem and clan) echoes the primitive substantial sense of soul as a power of life. It is experienced as a living force having a physical location, and the old words for it in Greek, Latin, and Germanic carried emotional impact. In Greek thought soul and body were generally indivisible. We cannot speak of soul without evoking values, importance, love, and the deepest anxieties over the possible loss or destruction of the soul. It is a matter of life or death. As soul (in the anima definition of Jung) is the archetype of life, self is the archetype of meaning. Its analogies tend to be drawn from philosophy (self-actualizing entelechy, principle of individuation, the monad, the totality) or from the images of mystical theology and the East (Atman, Brahman, Tao). The differences between "self" and "soul" compare with the distinctions we made in Part One between spiritual and psychological creativity. The former moves toward transcendence and abstraction; the latter, psychological, requires involvement. Myth involves the soul because its dynamics are personified. Its life-metaphors are physical and emotional, whereas self-dynamics more easily lend themselves to diagrams, numbers, and paradoxes.

"Speech and myth are one and the same. Myth means

originally the true word . . . speech about that which is,"[88] said Walter F. Otto (whom we shall hear again in Part Three). Such speech meets every human at the ultimate levels, beyond education, age, or region, just as the themes of our dreams, panics, and passions are common to all humanity. If the language is of the street and workshop, then psychology has already taken another step out of the consulting room. The soul's confusions and pains need words which mirror these conditions through imagination. Adequate descriptions of the soul's states will depend less upon right definition than upon accurate transmission of style.

First among the terms that have no anguish in them and so make us ill are "positive" and "negative." How cool and superior they are in their diagnostic certainty about what is good and bad for the soul: a "positive" mother complex and a "negative" animus; the "good" breast and the "bad"; a "good" dream and a "bad" dream; a step forward in analysis and a "regression"; the "positive" father role and the "negative" restoration of the persona. Analysis is stuffed with these judgments; and so it must be, since analytical consciousness, as an instrument of the practical intellect,[89] proceeds by making divisions. But within the art of memory there is room for the seven deadly sins and for the seven planetary Gods, and their separation is not quite so easy. Since the earliest pre-Socratic psychology we have known that psychic conditions are always mixed states; the psyche is a middle thing between heaven and the underworld, a harmony, a bow, a lyre, and its physical locus was imagined near the midriff of *phrenes* and *thymos*. The archetypes which the psyche transmits to our consciousness are also *dei ambigui*,[90]

88. W. F. Otto, "Die Sprache als Mythos," in *Mythos und Welt* (Stuttgart: Klett, 1962), pp. 279 and 285.

89. Aristotle *De Anima* III: "The speculative intellect thinks nothing that is practical and makes no assertions about what is to be avoided or pursued."

90. E. Wind, *Pagan Mysteries in the Renaissance* (Harmondsworth: Peregrine, 1967), p. 196 (term from *The Dream of Poliphilo*). Compare Jung (*CW*, IX, i, par. 80) on the archetypes: "The ground

figures undivided into positive and negative. These poles are necessary inventions of the Cartesian ego by means of which the psyche can be more exactly modeled upon mechanics and logics. By using this division into contradictories, the ego keeps its blade sharp for performing surgical divisions on our psychic substance.

Despite its preference for ambiguities, I tend to believe that the psyche is not against stern precision and exactitude. I do not think that the psyche itself has an inscrutable smile, half-closed eyes, and a fake indefiniteness that is but a comforting converse of scientism. The psyche as it appears in therapeutic practice responds to precision, and the images which the psyche produces are precise. To confront them and distill insight from them calls for refined, precise intensity and accuracy of insight. I believe that the psyche's affinity for precision expresses its affinity for spirit. To what else can we attribute that remarkable quality of psychic exactitude inherent in the linguistic acts of consciousness, including its fascination with precise psychiatric classifications and the "naming of the animals"?

Precision is an attribute of the psyche prior to all its manifestations. It is expressed in the craft of art, the fact of history, the procedure of ritual. Precision is not the preserve of science or exclusive to its method, since the same precision occurs in the smallest child's concentrated intensity, in the acute differentiations of primitive language, in the tiny detail of fairy tale and superstitious recipe. In other words, the imaginal ego, even though it arises from the *memoria*, can have the Cartesian ego's clear and distinct virtues. The art of memory shows that the imaginal realm presents itself with exactitude and requires qualitative precision in its handling. This precision is nothing else than a religious quality, for it

---

principles, the *archai*, of the unconscious are indescribable because of their wealth of reference, although in themselves recognizable. The discriminating intellect naturally keeps on trying to establish *singleness of meaning* and thus misses the essential point" (italics added).

shows care—caring about what we feel and do and say. At the same time, this psychological precision is not intellectual definition, because it never loses sight of the paradoxical aspect; thus it retains the ambiguity that is present in all psychological and symbolic events. Exact methods show care for the thesaurus of *memoria,* the storehouse of the imaginal. This exactitude is not borrowed from the methods of natural science or of scholarship. The precision of psychology stems from the psyche's own native precision, the indigenous exactitude of fantasy, to which reason shows its faithfulness by means of the exact methodologies of scholarship and science.

Science has unfortunately confused precision with measurement, confusing the quality with one of its instruments. But we shall not find psychological precision through the *wissenschaftliche Weltauffassung,* the conceptualizations of natural science. This contemporary representative of the Enlightenment carries the specter of the eighteenth and nineteenth centuries into our own day. Its main target is our words. Its proponents would reduce language by stripping away all ambiguities, emotional undertones, and historical associations to make each word mean one thing and one thing only. Intelligibility is extrinsic, given by machine-adapted, man-made definitions.

If our words are our primary psychic tools, before fire and before things, and if each one of our words contains its own sound and echo of history and its own culture, then the rectification of language in the manner of operationalism destroys the linguistic basis of culture. George Orwell warned against this possibility in his book *1984,* in which the language of the future is called Newspeak, while Oldspeak is scoffed at for "all its vagueness and useless shades of meaning." Orwell reveals the true aim of language control with this passage:

> Don't you see that the whole aim of Newspeak is to narrow the range of thought? In the end we shall make thought-crime literally impossible, because there will be no words in which to express it. Every concept that can

> ever be needed will be expressed by exactly *one* word, with its meaning rigidly defined and all its subsidiary meanings rubbed out and forgotten. Already . . . we're not far from that point. . . . Every year fewer and fewer words, and the range of consciousness always a little smaller.[91]

There are many ways to destroy words. We have been examining psychology's part in this destruction. Curiously, while inventing words and seeming to add new dimensions to the psyche's understanding of itself, psychology has at the same time been impoverishing the soul by these inventions. The principal way our field has harmed language is by turning sound terms into illnesses. Part of contemporary "mental illness" is the sickness of psychology's speech; the words in our minds have lost body and soul. We know not what we say and therefore have no language for what we do.

I believe the destruction of speech masks an attack upon the soul, especially against its "third person," its unquantifiable faculty of the imaginal, which, like the spirit, despite its precise qualitative descriptions, can never be wholly measured, wholly controlled, by the understanding and the will. Surely this narrowing of language is not what Confucius meant when he spoke of renewing culture through the rectification of language. For him this rectification was to be accompanied by the restoration of ancient ritual.

If ritual and right language belong together, perhaps they also express together the same imaginal realm. Upon this refound power of the soul, the imaginal *memoria*, of which we have been so long unconscious that it became confused with the unconscious and was named the unconscious, and upon the imaginal speech in this power of the soul, the life of our psyche and our culture depends. If ritual and right language belong together, I believe that, for the psyche, right language is as holy as ritual and that speech is ritual. And I believe that psychology—the practice of which was first

91. G. Orwell, *1984* (London: Penguin Books, 1954), p. 45.

known as the "talking cure" and which is thus a ritual of speech—requires, for its renewal and cure, a prior renewal and cure of its speech. To bring reflection to bear upon this speech has been my aim in this second part of the book, attempting in the traditional way to "save the phenomena" where the phenomenon is the word.

This critique of psychological language has gone deeper than a rejection of the conventions of a profession, deeper than a rejection of nominalism and operationalism. Through questioning the language of analysis, we have been led to question the very mode of analytical consciousness which necessitates this kind of speech without soul. Our critique thus issues finally into a new psychological question: What is the nature of this consciousness which no longer speaks for Psyche, having lost its relation with the feminine ground of soul? What is the archetypal background of analytical consciousness? To a study of these questions we shall now turn.

PART THREE

On Psychological Femininity

The Abysmal Side of Bodily Man

Our design in Part Three will follow the pattern laid down in the first two essays. First we shall review in some detail a specific problem—the physiological demonstrations of female inferiority—showing how history has resulted in a distortion of contemporary psychic values. Then we shall penetrate the historical and narrowly academic aspect of the problem to its more basic fantasy, aiming to reveal the archetypal background of the idea of female inferiority. At this level we shall come to myths which hold out hope for rectifying our perspectives for the sake of the soul.

In 1938 Jung gave a lecture at the Eranos Meetings that was called "The Psychological Aspects of the Mother Archetype." In a revision of this paper, issued in 1954, Jung appended four paragraphs of afterthought stimulated by the papal encyclical on the Assumption of Maria, which elevated the Christian version of the feminine principle to a radically new position.[1]

Jung writes (par. 195): ". . . the question naturally arises for the psychologist: what has become of the characteristic relation of the mother-image to the earth, darkness, the abysmal side of the bodily man with his animal passions and instinctual nature, and to 'matter' in general?" In part, this question was both raised and answered by the Assumption of

1. *CW*, IX, i, pars. 148–98.

the feminine. Now "even her human body, the thing most prone to gross material corruption" (par. 195) is not only beneath us but also above us. The abysmal side of bodily man with his animal passions and instinctual nature now also assumes a higher position. As Jung points out, matter and spirit can no longer be such polar extremes, because the dogma heralds their union: earth and the feminine body have been elevated to a higher place. This elevation of the below in turn relativizes the above: spirit may no longer reign absolute. It has been lowered, but lowered for the sake of a new relationship with the feminine, for the possibility of a new unity. As Jung says (par. 197): "The dogma of the Assumption . . . reflects the strivings of science for a uniform world-picture."

The uniform world-picture presaged in the dogma of the Assumption may not find its first realization in the realm of science and a new picture of matter. The matter-spirit relation and the difficulties of their harmony reflect, from the psychological point of view, prior difficulties in the harmony of those opposites we call mind and body or, even deeper, male and female. For in just this metaphor of male and female the religious dogma of the Assumption puts the whole question. In other words, the uniform world-picture will depend on the male and female images of the psyche, for even world-pictures are also in part psychological phenomena.

I would like to put the problem yet more psychologically and more directly. It is very well to talk of new theories of matter, of the relativity of matter and spirit, of the end of materialism, of synchronicity and *unus mundus*, and of the possibility of a new, universal science, where matter and spirit lose their hostile polarity, but these are all projections of the intellect unless there is a corresponding change of attitude in regard to the material part of man himself, which has, as Jung says, always been associated in our tradition with the feminine. The transformation of our world-view necessitates the transformation of the view of the feminine. Man's view of matter moves when his view of the feminine moves

—"even her human body, the thing most prone to gross material corruption"; and this change regarding the feminine refers not merely to rights for women, or "the pill," or marriage for priests, but a movement in consciousness in regard to bodily man, his own materiality and instinctual nature. The uniform world-image in metaphysics requires a uniformity of self-image in psychology, a conjunction of spirit and matter represented by male and female. The idea of female inferiority is therefore paradigmatic for a group of problems that become manifest at the same time in psychological, social, scientific, and metaphysical areas. Paradigmatic ideas with such ubiquitous reverberations we now call, after Jung, archetypal. But by "archetypal" we do not mean *only psychological;* the archetype does not belong only to psychology or only to the psyche. The archetype is a psych*oid* phenomenon; in part it stands completely outside the psyche. It thus influences the psyche and the field of psychology, as it influences other fields and sciences, as a primary given. Psychology has no more privileged access to the archetype and knowledge of it than any other field has. The individual psyche, however, does have one form of knowledge of its nature that is not given to any field, not even to psychology, and that is the psyche's reflective subjectivity, its own afflictions, pathologies, and fantasies, where the archetype can speak individually and directly, where our psychopathology is a revelation, a gnosis.

First Adam, Then Eve

For male primacy and the secondary, derivative nature of woman the *locus classicus* in our culture is the Adam and Eve story in the Genesis creation myth (Gen. 2). Whereas Adam was fashioned in God's own image, Eve was made only from Adam. Whatever is divine in Eve comes to her secondhand through the substance of Adam. "First Adam, then Eve" can be expanded from this tale in several ways. First, the male is prior in time, because he was created first. Second, the male is superior, since he alone is said to be created in the image of God. Third, the male is superior in consciousness, because Eve was extracted from Adam's deep sleep, from his unconsciousness. The sleep of Adam is a fallen state. For example, Jacob Boehme believed that the original Adam had no eyelids, was always awake.[2] His sleep resulted in Eve; Eve is man's "sleep." Fourth, Adam is substantially superior, since Eve is preformed in Adam as part to whole. Adam is perfect at the beginning, a mirror image of God's own perfection. The existence, essence, and material substance of Eve depend on Adam. He is her formal cause, because she is preformed in him; he is her material cause, since she is made of his rib; and he is her final cause, since her end and purpose is help for him. The male is the precondition of the female and the ground of its possibility.

Moreover, the metaphor is physical; the arguments build on images of anatomy, physiology, reproduction, and embryogeny.

The psychological history of the male-female relationship in our civilization may be seen as a series of footnotes to the tale of Adam and Eve. Of the specific commentators who did actually write footnotes, Sforno's Renaissance commentary to Genesis 2:21 equates man and woman: they are the same; only in regard to sex does woman differ from man. (Others have agreed: Berdyaev places the sexual in the woman; she carries sexuality in the world; man is less sexual than woman. The main difference between man and woman is sexual.) This implies that, if sex is the specific area of difference, then sex is the specific area for demonstrating this difference and the priority of Adam. The difference between man and woman thus becomes differences between male and female—a sexual difference; the battle between man and woman becomes a sexual battle; and the conjunction of

2. (*Von den drey Principien Göttlichen Wesens*). See E. Benz, *Adam, der Mythus vom Urmenschen* (Munich, 1955), pp. 16, 56 ff.

masculine and feminine principles becomes a sexual union. This special line of demonstrations of the male-female difference—sexual, reproductive, physiological—will be our first topic, not only because it is the most persistent and the most pernicious to the possibility of conjunction but because just here the most obdurate and refractory psychological questions lie. Just here, "in the abysmal side of bodily man," psyche is buried in *physis,* in the dark embrace of female matter, as the alchemists would have said it; and so we tend not to see that all these sexual, physiological, and embryogenetic question are also psychic and that, in this "alchemical sludge," psychological questions of the most profound sort lie waiting to be released from centuries of concretization.

As long as the physical represents the feminine, the physical will go on receiving antifeminine projections. This is familiar enough to us in that tradition—often condensed into the word "Manichaean"—that asserts that matter, evil, darkness, and female are interchangeable concepts. The material aspect of the feminine, "her human body, the thing most prone to gross material corruption," will have a *doubly* negative cast. The more female the material, the more will it be evil; the more materialized the female, the more will it be dark. Upon the physical body of the feminine the fantasies of female inferiority become most florid, since just here "the abysmal side of bodily man with his animal passions and instinctual nature" is constellated.

In what follows we will do well to bear in mind a remark of the eminent medical historian Ludwig Edelstein: "The theory of the human body is always a part of philosophy." Every theory of the female body is part of philosophy. And the investigations themselves are not merely physiological. They are philosophical. Edelstein says further:

> In Hellenistic philosophy . . . the theory of the human body—which forms an intrinsic part of philosophy—is not a matter of scientific investigation but is philosophy

> based on the insights gained by science. Facts are cited in order to demonstrate the school's philosophy.[3]

Galen states the same idea:

> . . . the study of the function of the various parts of the body is useful not to the physician alone, but much more so to the philosopher, who strives to acquire an understanding of all nature. To this end all men, collectively and individually, who worship gods must, in my opinion, be initiated into this mystery.[4]

Even for Galen the "study of the function of the various parts of the body" is a philosophical activity, a kind of mystery initiation. We are thus engaged, not in an academic investigative study, but in a kind of *theoria*, in a psychological rite whose aim is the transformation of consciousness in regard to the subject matter of the study.

We might paraphrase Edelstein's statement and say that the theory of the human body is always a part of a world-picture, remembering that such pictures are framed by fantasy, have fantastic frameworks, even when cut away from their fantasy structures and formulated in the abstractions of philosophy. The theory of the human body is always a part of a *fantasy*. It is the mystery of ourselves, of our nature, as imagined by the *memoria*, whose possibilities of imagination are governed by archetypal patterns. Theory-forming is thus as free and fantastic as the imagination; it is limited perhaps even less by observational data than by the archetypal a priori dominants of the imagination, the preformations of ideas acting as preconceptions that determine how and what one observes.

Fantasy especially intervenes where exact knowledge is

3. L. Edelstein, "The History of Anatomy in Antiquity" in *Ancient Medicine: Selected Papers of Ludwig Edelstein*, ed. O. and C. L. Temkin (Baltimore: Johns Hopkins University Press, 1967), p. 265.
4. Galen *De usu partium* XVII. 1.

lacking; and when fantasy does intervene, it becomes especially difficult to gain exact knowledge. Thus a vicious circle forms, and the mythical usurps theory-forming; furthermore, the mythic is given fantastic witness in observation. Seeing is believing, but believing is seeing. We see what we believe and prove our beliefs with what we see. This is familiar enough when we look at old beliefs, such as a flat earth around which the sun revolves. By looking back into history, we can see the influences of fantasy upon observation quite easily. It is harder to see these influences on observations closer to our own times. Thus we turn to history to train the eye; it gives perspective. History lets us see through facts into fantasies. History provides an entrance into the imaginal; it is like an avenue down which we can look into the archetypal. To stop with the historical itself, as facts and explanations, is the blind alley of historicism, that fantasy of "what really happened" and that search for "historical reality." History must not be limited to a method for understanding the past or the present; for us it is mainly a psychological discipline for gaining archetypal perspective. Thus we can more easily see through to the archetypal factor in the female-inferiority theories of our own time by seeing these factors at work in other times. By looking back over the field of conception theories and embryology we can see the fantasy factor affecting not merely theory-forming but the observational data, the evidence of the senses. Let me offer some examples of these florid fantasies, as a foretaste:

1. During the seventeenth and eighteenth centuries reasonable scientific men (Dalepatius, Hartsoeker, Garden, Bourget, Leeuwenhoek, Andry), while empirically studying the problems of fertility, conception, and embryology, "asserted that they had seen exceedingly minute forms of men, with arms, heads, and legs complete, inside the spermatazoa under the microscope." Zypaeus and du Hamel saw minute embryos in unfertilized eggs; Gautier saw a minute horse preformed inside the semen of a horse and a cock inside the semen of a

cock.[5] (Details with drawings of these fantasies are given by Bilikiewicz.)[6]

2. That genius, William Harvey, after famous dissections upon the uteri of the does of King Charles, came to the "conclusion that semen could not enter the uterus and therefore was not necessary for conception."[7] Buffon's experiments produced as their main result the impossible "discovery" of sperm in the *liquor folliculi* of the ovaries of nonimpregnated female animals.[8] Male seed was produced even by females!

3. In the examination of eggs, during the sixteenth and seventeenth centuries, a triad of bubbles was perceived. These were conceived as the primordia of liver, heart, and brain, like a Platonic trinity, later to become the three-faculty system of the psyche. Sides were soon taken between those who gave priority to one or another of these nodular organs. Observational data were then used to substantiate a philosophical position of the priority of heart over liver, of brain over heart, etc.[9]

4. According to the pneumatic theory of penile erection subscribed to in various ways by Aristotle (*Hist. animal.* VII. 7), Galen, and the Stoics, the air element both ejects the semen and, as *aura seminalis,* is the first cause of generation. The theory was also based on evidence: erection originates in the airy element of man's *imaginatio* as a movement of the "animal spirits"; so of course, as Galen said, there was air in the *corpus cavernosa.* Leonardo da Vinci, "the father of embryology regarded as an exact science,"[10] shows in his ana-

5. J. Needham, *Chemical Embryology* (Cambridge, Eng., 1931; 2d ed., 1959), I, 169, 199, 201.

6. T. Bilikiewicz, *Die Embryologie im Zeitalter des Barock und des Rokoko* (Leipzig, 1932).

7. A. W. Meyer, *The Rise of Embryology* (Stanford: Stanford University Press, 1939), p. 163.

8. *Ibid.*, p. 150.

9. H. B. Adelmann, *Marcello Malpighi and the Evolution of Embryology* (Ithaca: Cornell University Press, 1966), p. 755; J. Needham, *Chemical Embryology*, I, 194, on A. von Haller's discussion of this controversy.

10. Needham, *Chemical Embryology*, I, 110.

tomical notebooks sectional drawings of *two* urethral passages: one for the seminal fluid and a second one for the *pneuma* or *aura seminalis*.[11] His drawings are based on "observed" data from actual dissections.

5. In 1827 Karl Ernst von Baer published his discovery of the female ovum (*De ovi mammalium et hominis genesi*, Leipzig), ending finally the ignorance of centuries and opening the new age of modern embryology. According to medical historians, von Baer both thought profoundly and observed meticulously. His was a "mind of equal intellectual power with Darwin's." [12] Yet von Baer did not envision the conjunction of egg and sperm as necessary for conception. He coined the term "spermatazoon" but seemed to be so strongly influenced by the ovist theory of generation (that the embryo develops out of the egg alone) that he continued to classify sperm as a kind of variform parasite and to enter it under the category of *chaos*, recalling the rubric where Linnaeus, too, had grouped these *animalculae*.[13] Even though Prévost and Dumas had, some years before, established experimentally Spallanzani's conviction of the necessity of sperm for fertilization, his view was unalterable.[14] Final experimental demonstration that sperm penetrates egg and that from this conjunction the new individual results did not come until 1875 (O. Hertwig).

The point of these tales may be taken from Paracelsus, who said that imagination fertilizes the embryo; but imagination fertilizes also the theories of the embryo. It is important to realize how very late in history our scientific understanding of female functioning is. Not until 1827 was the human egg discovered, and not until the turn of the present century was the cyclical relation between menstruation and ovulation

11. C. D. O'Malley and J. B. de C. M. Saunders, *Leonardo da Vinci on the Human Body* (New York: Schuman, 1952).

12. J. M. Oppenheimer, *Essays in the History of Embryology and Biology* (Cambridge, Mass., 1967), p. 223.

13. Meyer, *The Rise of Embryology*, p. 152.

14. V. Brunner, "Der Genfer Arzt Jean-Louis Prévost (1790–1850) und sein Beitrag . . ." (dissertation, University of Zurich, 1966).

clearly established. More: only a few years ago there were still conflicting theories concerning the origin of the vaginal exudate, the source of which was repeatedly and inadequately attributed in standard anatomy texts to the Bartholin glands and the cervix.[15] Feminine darkness encourages fantasy.

Because embryology is a logos of beginnings, it will be influenced by creation mythemes. Because theories of generation reflect the differences and union of opposites, these theories will be influenced by *coniunctio* fantasies. Perhaps still more fundamental are the fantasies which afflict the male in regard to the female when male is observer and female is datum. We encounter a long and incredible history of theoretical misadventures and observational errors in male science regarding the physiology of reproduction. These fantastic theories and fantastic observations are not mere misapprehensions, the usual and necessary mistakes on the road of scientific progress; they are recurrent deprecations of the feminine phrased in the unimpeachable, objective language of the science of the period. The mythic factor recurs disguised in the sophisticated new evidence of each age.

We have already noted one of these mythic factors: "First Adam, then Eve" in Genesis. Another, though less known, is perhaps more relevant. In the *Eumenides* of Aeschylus (ll. 658–63) the mythic factor appears as the divinity Apollo, who presents a theory of reproduction. Apollo says: "The mother is no parent of that which is called her child, but only nurse of the new-planted seed that grows. The parent is he who mounts. . . . There can be a father without any mother."[16] This passage has been interpreted, following Bachofen, as the assertion of patriarchy over matriarchy. Apollo supposedly represents the patriarchal principle of paternity. But the social-historical context which we might try

15. W. Masters and V. Johnson, *Human Sexual Response* (Boston: Little, Brown, 1966), p. 69.

16. *The Eumenides*, trans. R. Lattimore, in *Complete Greek Tragedies*, ed. R. Lattimore and D. Grene (Chicago: University of Chicago Press, 1953), Vol. I.

to establish and then use for interpretation is again subject to fantasy. We do not know why Apollo made the speech or why Aeschylus put it in his mouth. It is a statement of an archetypal position representing a world-view which can be attributed to Apollo and may be called Apollonic.

The Apollonic fantasy of reproduction and female inferiority recurs faithfully in the Western scientific tradition. We call it "Apollonic" because, unlike "Adamic," with its overtones of the natural *Urmensch*, mystical man, and androgynous man, "Apollonic" evokes the purified objectivity and the scientific clarity of masculine consciousness. The Apollonic view of the feminine appears to be inherent in the same structure of consciousness as the methods by which the fantasy is supposedly proven. I use the word "scientific" to distinguish the material we shall be examining from the overtly symbolic materials on the bisexual theme that have already been spoken of at the Eranos meetings in years past.[17] We shall proceed in a different direction, turning to theories of embryogeny, physiology, and reproduction, exploring them, too, for psychological content, and seeing how the same imaginal mythemes appear in scientific language. We should expect to find Apollo especially in the language of medical science, since Apollo is the father of Asclepius, God of medicine. Our examination of medical theories, like that of psychiatric ideas in Part Two, should show typical attitudes of Apollonic consciousness.

Female Seed

Inasmuch as we may regard procreation theories as creation mythemes projected on the level of physiological processes, partly observed and partly conjectured, the interplay of observation and fantasy nowhere shows itself more clearly and more importantly than in the question which concerns all ancient writers on embryogeny in the Western tradition.

17. See note 2, above. On bisexuality in "primitive" myth, ritual, and religion see H. Baumann, *Das doppelte Geschlecht* (Berlin, 1955).

This question is the issue Apollo declaims upon, the role of the female in reproduction, formulated as: "Does the female have seed?"[18] The question raises ontological issues; in it can be heard the doubt about woman that recurs in later Christian centuries in the question *Habet mulier animam?*

The questions raised by "female seed" extend beyond Western tradition, since the idea of female seed—its affirmation or its denial—appears in noncivilized theories of conception as well as in the *Rig-Veda* and the *Laws of Manu*. This much may be said in sum: in our tradition, wherever it was conceded that there was female seed, or where the even rarer concession was made that such seed was necessary for reproduction, female seed was inferior. The problem is vast because so many philosophers took a position upon the question and often argued it in meticulous detail.[19] We may remember that the concern with conception in antiquity (Aristotle devoted 37 per cent of his biological writings to generation) was part of philosophy and not merely a problem in a minor branch of physiology.

From the viewpoint of social anthropology one might suppose that matriarchal and matrilineal societies would affirm female seed. Yet correlations between the role of the female in theories of conception and the role of the female in the social structure have yet to be established. From the psychological viewpoint it is questionable whether such correlations, even if established, could explain fantasy by social pattern. A specific theory of female seed is not a necessary and logical consequence of a certain kind of society. Fantasy need not be congruous with or compensatory to collective doctrine. There are many kinds of fantasies in our tradition that show

18. W. Gerlach, "Das Problem des 'weiblichen Samens' in der antiken und mittelalterlichen Medizin," *Sudhoffs Archiv für Geschichte der Medizin und der Naturwissenschaften*, XXX (1938), 177–93.

19. H. Balss, *Die Zeugungslehre und Embryologie in der Antike* (Berlin, 1936).

parallels to the fantastic notions of conception in noncivilized societies.

These parallels often fit more closely with one another than they fit into the structure of male or female domination in the society. Examination of field workers' evidence suggests rather that fantastic notions of conception are cross-cultural.[20] An ovist theory, for example, that emphasizes the female, was a position strongly held and supported by the science of the "fathers" in our predominantly patriarchal society of western Europe. Parallels to ovism occur in many noncivilized societies having social structures of varying forms. Thus, fantasy about female seed does not fit into social forms. We may still assume a relative independence of fantasy which gives structure and contents and *dynamis* to

20. Human Relations Area Files, No. 842 (Conception). See C. S. Ford, *A Comparative Study of Human Reproduction,* Yale University Publications in Anthropology No. 32 (New Haven, 1945). Ford writes (p. 44) that eight societies hold the belief that the womb is a mere vessel and that female sexual secretions do not matter; the male seed is the essential stuff. Of these eight societies, two are matrilineal, the others patrilineal. Other societies believe that both female and male secretions play an important part in conception. Of these societies some are patrilineal, some matrilineal, some dual, some bilateral, and others are patrilineal in groups and matrilineal in marriage regulation. Parallels to extreme ovism can be found in the Arunta and the Trobrianders, who are ignorant of physiological paternity; see Ford, p. 34; also, M. F. Ashley-Montagu, "Ignorance of Physiological Paternity in Australia," *Oceania,* XII, No. 1 (1941), and "Ignorance of Physiological Paternity in Secular Knowledge and Orthodox Belief among the Australian Aborigines," *Oceania,* XI, No. 1 (1940); L. Austen, "Procreation among the Trobriand Islanders," *Oceania,* V (1934–35). A parallel to the "First Adam" view occurs in Diodorus Siculus: "The Egyptians hold the father alone to be author of generation"; also, the Indians of the Gran Chaco (Toba, Mataco) consider the newborn infant to be formed solely by the father (see Ford). Parallel to the Aristotelian view: "East Bay people believe that conception resembles the planting of seeds in the ground. The semen is the seed containing all of the material which eventually will grow into a foetus. The womb is the soil from which the developing organism draws nourishment" (W. Davenport, "Sexual Patterns and Their Regulation in a Society of the Southwest Pacific," in *Sex and Behavior,* ed. F. A. Beach (New York, 1965).

theories. Sociology and anthropology do not account for imagination.

The recurrent questioning about female seed in our tradition obviously expresses a recurrent doubt about female essence. The problem had therefore to be repeatedly encountered, and female seed had in some way to be accounted for, in order to maintain the image of female inferiority. It is incompatible with a theory of female inferiority to affirm the importance or value of female seed. Aeschylus through "Apollo" has already made this point. Let us hear Aristotle do it more scientifically.

Aristotle

Aristotle gives our tradition's first carefully elaborated argument for female inferiority. In his work *On the Generation of Animals,* "the first great compendium of embryology ever written,"[21] his position is: "the female does not contribute semen to generation" but does contribute the matter of the catamenia [menses], or that which is analogous to it in bloodless animals (*De gen. animal.* 727a–b). Besides the physiological evidence for his view (cessation of menses during pregnancy, indicating that this material was now being used in the building of the embryo), Aristotle characteristically removes the question to a metaphysical level:

> . . . there must needs be that which generates and that from which it generates, even if these be one, still they must be distinct in form and their essence must be different; . . . If, then, the male stands for the effective and active, and the female, considered as female, for the passive, it follows that what the female would contribute to the semen of the male would not be semen but material for the semen to work upon. This is just what we find to be the case, for the catamenia have in their nature an affinity to the primitive matter.[22]

21. Needham, *Chemical Embryology,* I, 61.
22. Aristotle *On the generation of animals* 729a22.

The female provides the *prima materia,* the nourishment, and the place for the developing embryo. She has her necessary role. But the active, formative, generative principle comes wholly from the father. His is the better part. It would seem to be an equality in the sense of a parallelism or symmetry of function, but if we look a bit deeper we see the prejudice at work.

The female contribution is menstrual blood, which, after all, is widely held to be a taboo stuff, a wastage, or at best a cleanser. Its inferiority to male semen is explicitly explained in Aristotle's theory of semen.[23] Semen was the superlative form of blood, a highly concocted froth or foam produced from it through a transformation process called *pepsis*—digestion or cooking. The blood which the female contributes to the reproductive process has not yet gone through *pepsis.* It has not yet reached the higher form of actualization. And so must it be, since the female is the cooler sex, not having the innate heat necessary to cook the blood into its higher state. The female contribution is therefore physiologically inferior. Besides, having no seed, she is without the *causa formalis* that can generate her own essence out of herself. Her essence is thus subject to the male, in whose essence is male and female both. As in the Genesis myth, in the male is the preformation of the female. First Adam, then Eve.

The Aristotelian view is both representative of his own time and causative of the later Catholic view of the Thomists. Perhaps the prototypical denial of female seed by means of physiological arguments, reflected later by Aristotelians and Thomists, comes from Diogenes of Apollonia, one of the last Ionian natural philosophers, of the latter half of the fifth century B.C.[24] In his cosmos, air is the major element; and, in

23. E. Lesky, "Die Zeugungs- und Vererbungslehren der Antike und ihr Nachwirken," *Akademie der Wissenschaften und der Literatur, Abhandlungen der Geistes- und Sozialwissenschaftlichen Klasse,* XIX (1950), 120.

24. K. Freeman, *The Pre-Socratic Philosophers* (Oxford, 1946), p. 282; Lesky, "Die Zeugungs- und Vererbungslehren der Antike," pp. 121–22.

his theory of seed, air plays the major role. Air is the pneumatic aspect that concocts the blood into the rarefied substance of semen, which is lighter, whiter—and more soulful. Air is also mind and intelligence. "The father, not the mother, provides the offspring." Woman, because she lacks the pneumatic element and has inferior seed, also has less soul and less mind.

The biological inferiority of woman presented by Thomas Aquinas depends greatly on the Aristotelian theory of reproduction. Woman is *ignobilior* and *vilior* than man in the view of Thomas Aquinas. She is on a lower plane. The reasons are, first, biogenetic, in the sense of Aristotle; second, she is qualitatively inferior because she is not able to transform blood into sperm and is therefore unable to bring forth a human being; and third, she is functionally inferior because she provides only the passive principle of the uterus and the nourishment for the embryo.[25]

Saint Thomas states with characteristic succinctness: "Semen mulieris non est de necessitate conceptionis," because female seed "nihil facit ad generationem." [26] Female exudate is an imperfect analogue to male semen. Owing to inherent female weakness or inferiority, it has not been "digested" or concocted to its ripeness. During the Scholastic period the determination of female sterility was based altogether on this theory. The *impotentia generandi* of the woman is admitted only when the menstrual blood cannot be delivered to the embryo.[27] Her contribution is this inferior product.

In the writings of the Church Fathers misogyny is particularly virulent in regard to the *body* of woman. Maria had not yet been liberated by the dogma of the Assumption, and so the "abysmal side of bodily man with his animal passions

25. Lesky, p. 134 (following A. Mitterer).

26. *Sent. lib.* 3. d. 5. q. 2. a. 1; see J. Löffler, "Die Störungen des geschlechtlichen Vermögens in der Literatur der autoritativen Theologie des Mittelalters," *Akademie der Wissenschaften und der Literatur, Abhandlungen der Geistes- und Sozialwissenschaftlichen Klasse* (Wiesbaden), VI (1958), 39.

27. Löffler, "Die Störung des geschlechtlichen Vermögens," p. 77.

and instinctual nature" is felt to come into man from woman. The Jahwist and Pauline views of woman derive particularly from arguments of the physiological kind. Woman is closer to matter, and her inferiority is described as filth (see John Chrysostom, "An Exhortation to Theodore after His Fall"; Tertullian, "On the Apparel of Women" and "On the Veiling of Virgins"; and the "Two Epistles Concerning Virginity" attributed to Clement of Rome). Even Jerome, of all the Fathers of the Church said to be one of the mildest in regard to woman and female company, nevertheless was violent when it came to their bodies (see his *Letters* 22, 52, 54, and 107 and *Against Helvidius*).

The other side of this repression is fascination—and prurience. Vesalius thus "alludes to Scholastic theologians, among whom, he says, there is more frequent disputation as to generation than among medical men, and who attend his lectures in crowds whenever the genital organs are to be shown."[28] (Another subject which fascinated pious minds at the Sorbonne was the use of syringes for baptizing infants *in utero*.)

White-Red

The concoction of blood into seed provides the background for another contrast between male and female based on fantasies of physiology. A passage from *Aristotle's Masterpiece* points this up nicely. *Aristotle's Masterpiece* was not written by Aristotle. It is a compendium of popular physiology, gynecology, and psychology which began as a folio printed in Venice in 1503 and subsequently enjoyed an immense circulation, especially in England. It contains misrepresentations of Aristotle, along with accretions from Avicenna, Galen, Albertus Magnus, and other "authorities." But the book is indeed authoritative, since it is an authoritative representation of collective fantasy, having proceeded through at

28. Vesalius *De humani corporis fabrica* V. 15 (L. Thorndike, *A History of Magic and Experimental Science* [New York, 1941], V, 526).

least sixty-six editions during five centuries of our culture. The information is presented in the form of a catechism:

> Q. Why is a man's seed white and a woman's red?
> A. It is white in men by reason of great heat and quick digestion, because it is rarefied in the testicles; but a woman's is red, because her terms corrupt the undigested blood, and it hath its color.

The red-white pair as representative of male and female is familiar from alchemy, but there red is male. In Jewish tradition one finds the reverse: in the embryo, the bones, tendons, nails, contents of the head, and whites of the eyes come from the father, "who sows the white"; skin and colored parts are derived from the mother, "who sows the red." [29]

Female inferiority, i.e., red inferior to white, is not inherent in this symbolism, since, as colors, both red and white have ambivalent values, neither being only positive or only negative. However, when the idea of concoction enters, as in Aristotle and in the "masterpiece" named after him, the female red is merely an incomplete, prior state of male white.

Ripe-Unripe, Sphere-Ovoid, Right-Left

Before proceeding to Galen, let us review a few other bits of physiological "evidence" for female inferiority.

The basic superiority of white semen over red blood is that the former is more fully concocted. It is drier and more coagulated and thus acts as a coagulant upon the female substance (a cheese simile going back to Aristotle). Because it is in a more advanced state, the male principle is at the outset

29. Needham, *Chemical Embryology*, I, 93. A "primitive" parallel comes from the Barenda of East Africa, who believe that the white elements of the embryo come from the father, the red from the mother. Red and white were used also in sex-determination tests of pregnant women in European folklore. One advice said: "Store a woman's urine for a few days; if the particles that form are red, the child will be a boy, if white, a girl" (T. R. Forbes, "The Prediction of Sex: Folklore and Science," *Proceedings of the American Philosophical Society*, CIII, No. 4 [1959]).

more mature than the female. That the male is more active, requiring less "perfection time" (as Needham calls it), influences theories of sex determination. The boy child in the womb will quicken first because it ripens first. In the Hippocratic school, for instance, it was said that boys were completely formed in thirty days and girls in forty-two days. The male fetus was superior to the female because it ripened sooner, requiring less "perfection time." [30]

Pliny the Elder said that the fetus of the boy quickened in forty days, that of the girl in ninety days. He also said that the mother was heavier in the legs when carrying a girl child. A mother with a boy, on the contrary, had better color, owing to the quickness or warmth or ripeness of the male spirit within her. This idea recurs so often that our tradition must be specially fond of it. In 1859 a physician reported to the Obstetrical Society of Berlin that a rapid pulse in the mother indicates a boy fetus; and in 1878 fifteen gynecological cases were reported in support of the idea that a cheerful, joyful, sweet pregnant mother is diagnostic of the birth of a boy.[31] Such was the preparation for the girl's birth: to be conceived out of inferior substance, carried in paleness, and delivered from the depression of her mother.

Male superiority entered canon law in this specific manner: the time of quickening of the embryo. The male soul entered earlier: ". . . the canon law as finally crystallized recognized first the fortieth day for males and the eightieth for females as the moment of animation, but later the fortieth day for both sexes." This idea lingered on until Goelicke disproved it experimentally in 1723.[32]

We look at eggs for our next example: the choice is between the spherical *versus* ovoid form of the hen's egg. The examination of hens' eggs and the development of the embryonic chick has been a main basis for the study of

30. Needham, *Chemical Embryology*, I, 199; H. Graham, *Eternal Eve: A History of Obstetrics* (London: Heinemann, 1950).
31. Forbes, "The Prediction of Sex," p. 539.
32. Needham, *Chemical Embryology*, I, 91–92.

embryology. An unbroken line of tradition, beginning in ancient Egypt and continuing through the Greeks and Renaissance science in England and Italy up to modern scientific biology, has used the egg for its empirical study. Since the egg is also an extraordinary symbol, observation was of course prey to the fantasy released by this passive, silent, feminine object of investigation.

Of these many fantasies springing from the egg, the one relevant to our theme concerns the comparative value of eggs judged morphologically. Aristotle held that the male chick develops from the sharp-pointed or ovoid egg. That egg which is most true to the nature of eggness, most ovoid in shape, most perfected and actualized as egg, naturally produces the male chick.

> In the sixth book [of *De animalibus*] Albertus [Magnus] contradicts Aristotle's opinion that the male chick develops out of the sharp-ended egg . . . ; he goes on to say that . . . really Aristotle agreed with Avicenna in saying that males always develop from the more spheroid eggs because the sphere is the most perfect of figures in solid geometry.[33]

No matter how this is argued, the superior egg is always the male egg. If the form of the sphere is more perfect, then the spherical egg is male. If the ovoid is more perfect in its eggness, then the ovoid egg is the male one. The Apollonic prefers perfections and discovers perfection in form. Horace held for the Aristotelian view, for in one of his satirical verses on gastronomy (*Sat.* II. 4. 1. 12) he says that long eggs are the sweet and white ones and are male. Leonardo is an example from the side of Avicenna and Albertus Magnus; he writes in his notebook: "Eggs which have a round form produce males; those which have a long form produce females." [34] The controversy ended only in the eighteenth century, when experiments disproved the idea that egg form

33. *Ibid.*, p. 99.
34. O'Malley and Saunders, *Leonardo da Vinci on the Human Body*, p. 506, note on drawing 213.

indicated sex of egg inhabitant. Whichever side one held to —long or round—the female was always proved inferior. Even the egg, the female symbol par excellence, had superior and inferior aspects, and could be used to adduce female inferiority.

The left-right pair is another example: "On the right boys, on the left girls." This statement, attributed to Parmenides, was passed on to us by Galen. It compares to a similar one from Anaxagoras, passed on by Aristotle. As Lesky says: "Of all theories of conception in antiquity, none persisted so through the millennia as the belief that the male arises from the right side of the body and the female from the left." [35]

There is, of course, the usual implication of female inferiority in the left-right theory. In our tradition, "the power of the left hand is always somewhat occult and illegitimate; it inspires terror and repulsion." [36] Aristotle formulated the inferiority of the left after observing the dominance of the right in crab claws (*De part. animal.* IV. 8. 684a26), supporting the metaphysical position (*De incessu animal.* 706a20, 706b14): "the right stands higher in value than the left." The superiority of the right side and its maleness is a notion so widespread and so well known that we need not spend time on it here. It reflects a deep level of popular fantasy. We find it in Artemidorus, where dreams of the right hand and eye refer to male relatives, left to female. We find it in early Hindu medicine, which states that boys come from the right side of the uterus and girls from the left. We find it in eighteenth-century France, where noblemen would bind or even excise their left testicle to ensure male offspring.[37]

35. Lesky, "Die Zeugungs- und Vererbungslehre," pp. 39, 41, 53.

36. R. Hertz, "The Pre-Eminence of the Right Hand," in *Death and the Right Hand* (London: Cohen & West, 1960), p. 105; cf. Baumann, *Das doppelte Geschlecht*, pp. 293–310.

37. Graham, *Eternal Eve*, p. 41. Graham also relays this excruciating piece of folklore: "to this day certain Indian peasants practice assiduously a technique based on this belief. At the moment of ejaculation the wife seizes her husband's left testicle and squeezes with all her might" in order to prevent female offspring.

We find it again in the comparatively late work of Seligson, who published a work in 1895 called *Willkürliche Zeugung von Knaben und Mädchen.* He attempted to place on an experimental basis the ancient idea "boys to the right, girls to the left" handed down via the Hippocratic collection of medical aphorisms. Seligson claimed that all tubal pregnancies showed a male embryo in the right tube, a female in the left, and that by means of one-sided castration of rabbits he could determine sex in offspring. In 1913 experimentation was still being reported on the left-right theory of conception.[38]

In her excellent little book, *Left and Right in Science and Life,*[39] Vilma Fritsch has collected and documented a great range of discussion focusing on this basic pair. Despite Bachofen, whose strenuous and brilliant efforts raised the hypothesis to an accepted truth, left = female is not a universal law. The Andaman islanders, for instance, associate left with male.[40] Nor is left inferiority as widespread as we, standing within our right-oriented tradition, might believe. For many examples we may turn to Fritsch, to Granet on China,[41] to Jewish mystical tradition, or even to the Delaware Indians, among whom "left is holy, right unholy."[42]

The fantasies of laterality are perhaps even more complex than those of the male-female pair, with which they have been merged. This problem is not our task. But when considering laterality and the arguments and observational evidence for the equivalence of left inferiority with female inferiority, we do well to remember a caution from Fritsch: "the frequent preference entertained by scholars for the right side."[43]

38. Lesky, "Die Zeugungs- und Vererbungslehre," p. 69.
39. V. Fritsch, *Left and Right in Science and Life* (London: Barrie & Rockliff, 1968).
40. Forbes, "The Prediction of Sex," p. 538.
41. M. Granet, *La Pensée chinoise* (Paris, 1934), Bk. III, Chap. II, "Le Microcosme."
42. Fritsch, *Left and Right,* p. 38.
43. *Ibid.,* p. 36.

This line of thought, beginning with the Beginning (Genesis) and with Apollo and developed by men of science and reason, has had a Manichaean effect upon the investigation, tending to bias it to the "right" in favor of male superiority. Consciousness is right-handed, or right-eyed, tending to be twisted into specific perspectives by its underlying archetypal structures. We see things as the dominants would have them seen. Our sight reflects their vision of things. Our sight, even scientific observation, is unreliable, not just because of the senses and their well-known capacity for sensory illusions, but because of the psychic structures on which it is based. Behind the vision of sense is the vision of the archetypal, and we are unreliable when we lose the inward sight—insight—toward the subjective factor which influences our observations. We are unreliable, not because we are insufficiently "objective," but because we are impious, losing "sight" of the Gods and their influence upon the subjective factor in our views.

Galen

It would seem that Galen (129–99 a.d.), the next in our series of scientific men looking at the female, saw her differently from his predecessors. Galen seems to open a new tradition which gives the female a physiologically equal place in generation. First, he maintained, against the authority of Aristotle, that there was indeed a female seed, having its functional uses in generation. Second, his anatomical research suggested to him a morphological similarity, even a parity, of organs between male and female. By recognizing female seed he gave recognition to a creative potential in the female. By drawing parallels between male and female generative systems, he gave scientific substance to an equality of the female.

But when we regard more closely what Galen said, we find that his opinions retain a misogynist bias. (Perhaps one must see his ideas also within their Roman setting and the mental climate of Marcus Aurelius, Commodus, and Septimius Severus, the emperors he served.) Compared with male seed, he finds the female to be "thinner," "colder," of "higher viscosity," "weaker," "quantitatively less," and finally of an "inferior tonus."[44]

Not only the seed, but the generative apparatus itself is inferior in the woman. Galen (IV. 158) writes: "All parts which are present for the male can be observed in the female genital tract with only one difference: the female organs are within, the masculine outside, that region described as the perineum."

As Lesky rightly points out, the masculine genitalia in this theory are an "extraversion" of the female. For Galen, this extraversion represents a further stage, a more complete achievement. What is a culmination in the male exists in only an early form in the female. "Thus Galen is able to say that the male individual is perfect, while the female represents an imperfect stage."[45]

The parity of male and female is thus not a true one. Galen's anatomical research discovered an analogous morphology of the organs of generation. But the model for the analogy was the male system. The male was the prototype, the female the analogue. First Adam, then Eve. The ovaries are inferior testes; female seed is inferior to male. Ontogeny here merges with ontology, that is, the male is the realized, perfected, actualized. The female remains still *in nuce*, within the perineum, only potential, not yet ripe. She does not have the innate heat to come to ripeness in either anatomy or seed. We shall later return to the idea of female slowness.

FREUD

THERE ARE STRIKING SIMILARITIES between Galen and Freud. They do not depart from past notions; but by means of the

44. Lesky, "Die Zeugungs- und Vererbunglehre," p. 180; Gerlach, "Das Problem des 'weiblichen Samens,'" p. 188.
45. Lesky, "Die Zeugungs- und Vererbungslehre," pp. 184 f.

helpful authority of a large corpus of written words, the past is reassembled into a new organization, so that the old is retained within the new system and influences it from within. Observation and imagination merge and lose distinctness. Thus is created an integrated system concerning the female which seems to take its departure from observation; yet, when we take a closer look, we may see that it springs more from imagination. Most decidedly in both, "the theory of the human body is always a part of philosophy." Specific to our theme is Freud's main evidence for female inferiority, which, like Galen's, is argued in terms of comparative anatomy.

Of Freud's many masters, he was most attached to Wilhelm Fliess, who provided the foil for Freud's consciousness during the period of his most intense self-analysis (1887–1902). Fliess was interested in the right-left polarity—so interested that the theme of bilateralism is said to be the cause of the two men's subsequent estrangement.[46] Fliess believed that the left side of a person expressed his contrasexual side, his own dominant sex belonging to the right. Where "a woman resembles a man, or a man resembles a woman, we find emphasis on the left side of the body." [47] Fliess gave the right-left polarity a sexual turn. Where the left side is markedly manifest, the traits of the opposite sex will be evinced. Or, as he says: "Since degeneracy consists in a displacement of the male and female qualities, we can understand why so many left-handed people are involved in prostitution and criminal activities." [48] Here the genetic idea of dominant versus recessive, the sexual contrast of male versus female, and the ethics of social uprightness versus moral degeneracy are all expressed by the right-left polarity. No wonder Fliess was so fiercely argu-

46. S. Freud, *The Origins of Psycho-Analysis: Letters to Wilhelm Fliess; Drafts and Notes, 1887–1902,* ed. M. Bonaparte, A. Freud, and E. Kris, trans. E. Mosbacher and J. Strachey (London, 1954), p. 241 n.

47. Fritsch, *Left and Right* (quoting from Fliess, *Der Ablauf des Lebens* [1st ed., 1906; Leipzig and Vienna, 1925]).

48. *Ibid.* For Freud and left-handedness see also E. Jones, *The Life and Work of Sigmund Freud* (London, 1955), II, 389, 496.

mentative over his "discovery." He was taken utterly by a symbol which combined so many strands—biological, sociological, moral, sexual—and which expressed in metaphysical form the "battle of the sexes." Therefore, even before Freud wrote his own view of female inferiority in his theories of infantile sexuality, he knew through Fliess of the left-right system aiming at the same theme—woman is the lesser. A second grouping of ideas that associated the feminine with the hysterical were also familiar to Freud through another of his masters, Charcot, and the controversies centering around his views of hysteria.

In 1905 Freud published his *Three Essays on the Theory of Sexuality*. "The accent falls, as throughout his writings, on the importance of the male impulse." As Jones goes on to say: "He maintained that the female child's libido is more male than female, because her auto-erotic activity concerns predominantly the clitoris. He even made the obscure suggestion that perhaps all libido, being like all impulses in its nature active, is essentially male." [49] This implication is rather devastating for woman: if the life-force, being active, is principally male—the old equation of male = active, which we can find in Aristotle and Galen too—then woman is an *opus contra naturam*. Her penis envy merely reflects her more fundamental lacuna, her defective life-force and her inborn structural inferiority.

Freud's principal argument for female inferiority, like Galen's, is based on morphology. The basic model for the human being is Adam. Freud writes: "The assumption that all human beings have the same (male) form of genital is the first of the many remarkable and momentous sexual theories of children." [50] The observation—or is it fantasy?—that little girls regard their genital form as a deprivation and unnatural is the basis for all his subsequent views of the essence of woman. In 1924 Freud wrote in regard to women: ". . . the

49. Jones, *Sigmund Freud*, II, 326; cf. Freud, *SE*, VII, 219–21.
50. Freud, *SE*, VII, 195.

morphological distinction is bound to find expression in differences of psychical development. 'Anatomy is Destiny,' to vary a saying of Napoleon's."[51] Her impaired genital is "ground for inferiority." The anatomical difference has its psychical consequences, as he shows further in a paper dedicated to this theme (1925).[52] Finally, in Freud's last writings, written when he was eighty-two and published posthumously in 1940 as *An Outline of Psychoanalysis*, we find the original view restated:

> A female child has, of course, no need to fear the loss of a penis; she must, however, react to the fact of not having received one. From the very first she envies boys its possession; her whole development may be said to take place under the colours of envy for the penis. She . . . makes efforts to compensate for her defect—efforts which may lead in the end to a normal feminine attitude. If during the phallic phase she attempts to get pleasure like a boy by the manual stimulation of her genitals, it often happens that she fails to obtain sufficient gratification and extends her judgement of inferiority from her stunted penis to her whole self.[53]

Both Galen and Freud assume the male genital as prototype. Galen observes this empirically in dissection of corpses; Freud observes this empirically in analysis of fantasy. Both observe evidence of female-organ inferiority. Inferiority is incontrovertible when presented in terms of comparative morphology. The inferiority is irreversible because it is in the very *physis* of female nature. Anatomy is destiny: look, and you shall see what the senses observe! Yet the actual observational basis in both men is shaky: we have no evidence of Galen's ever having dissected a woman's body or of Freud's ever having analyzed a little girl. Galen's conclusions about

51. Freud, "The Dissolution of the Oedipus Complex" (1924), *SE*, XIX, 178.

52. Freud, "Some Psychical Consequences of the Anatomical Distinctions between the Sexes" (1925), *SE*, XIX, 243 ff. See, further, "Female Sexuality" (1931), *SE*, XXI, 223 ff.

53. Freud, *SE*, XXIII, 193–94.

the female body are drawn from animals, Freud's conclusions about children from adults.[54]

Nota bene this blend of observation and imagination. Freud's fantasies about the sexual satisfaction and theories of

54. "Galen's anatomy was for centuries the standard, but was in many ways inaccurate, and this, in addition to technical imperfections and inexactitudes, because it was based upon dissection of animals only" (W. Riese, *Galen on the Passions and Errors of the Soul* [Columbus: Ohio State University Press, 1963], p. 14). See, further, G. Sarton, *Galen of Pergamon* (Lawrence: University of Kansas Press, 1954), pp. 39–60. Conclusions about humans based upon animals have long been a sore point. Thomas Aquinas and Spinoza objected strongly (cf. my *Emotion* [Evanston: Northwestern University Press, 1964], p. 106 n.). Concerning Freud and the analysis of children, Jones writes (*Sigmund Freud*, III, 145): "I had later several talks with him on the subject of early analysis, but I never succeeded in making any impression on him beyond his admitting that he had no personal experience to guide him." His famous case history of child analysis was of a *boy*, "Little Hans," on whom he wrote in 1909 (Jones, II, 294): "I never got a finer insight into a child's soul." But this five-year-old *boy* was analyzed by his father; Freud saw the child for only one interview (*ibid.*, p. 289). Jones says (p. 292): "The brilliant success of child analysis since then, and indeed inaugurated by the study of this very case, prove that here Freud's customary insight had deserted him. It seems a curious thing to say of the very man who explored the child's mind to an extent that had never before been possible that he should nevertheless have retained some inhibitions about coming to too close quarters with it . . . , and to the end of his life he displayed certain reservations about the limits of what it was possible to accomplish in child analysis." If Freud did not take his theory from empirical data only, then, as suggested by M. D. Altschule (*Roots of Modern Psychiatry* [New York: Grune & Stratton, 1957]), perhaps he was influenced by the folklore of female genital inferiority that had entered the anatomical thinking of the nineteenth century via the medically eminent and anatomically authoritative Meckel family; cf. A. D. P. Callisen, *Medizinisches Schriftstellerlexicon* (Copenhagen, 1843), Vol. XXX. J. F. Meckel (1781–1833) "concluded from his own studies that woman, as contrasted to man, was a sexually undifferentiated human organism" (Altschule, p. 113). His brother, Albrecht Meckel (1790–1829), at the age of twenty presented his inaugural thesis on "The Analogy of the Genitals and the Intestines," a fantasy concerning the "abysmal side of bodily man" found often enough today in psychotherapeutic case histories. However, the *historical* background for Freud's perspective need not be directly traced, provided we accept the *archetypal* influence of fantasy upon anatomical theory, whether in Galen, the Meckels, or Freud.

anatomy of very little girls are presented as observation. So, too, are the conclusions of a supposedly psychological nature that these imaginary small children draw from the supposed insufficient satisfaction. Freud's fantasy *of* the little girl's mind becomes a Freudian fantasy *in* the little girl's mind. Freud's basic fantasy—"the assumption that all human beings have the same (male) form of genital," his "First Adam" theory (of 1905)—is put into the mind of children as *their* fantasy. The child, like the "primal horde" of the prehistorical past, is an unknown *tabula rasa* or *prima materia,* upon the ground of whose emptiness one may freely propound one's fantasies without contradiction or even response. When we parade forth the child, the primitive, the animal, or the archaeological past—and, I would add, the patient—as observational *basis* for psychology, in order to support a theory by grounding it in "origins," nowhere could we better reveal the archetypal fantasy of the theory we are in this manner justifying. The true origin is the archetypal fantasy itself, not the objective scene where the fantasy is "observed" as "fact." The origin of theory is in idea, in the human body as part of philosophy, and not in the human body as fact. The true origin is in the imaginal realm which appears when we regard the *tabula rasa,* the unknown dark field of primate, the primitive, the prehistoric, or the child.

On the Physiological Feeble-Mindedness of Woman

We are also obliged to consider Dr. Paul Julius Moebius of Leipzig, born in 1853, three years before Freud, who began his career in neurology, like Freud; who was interested in the brain and the eye, like Freud; and who also became fascinated with nervousness and sexuality, which at the turn of the century were *the* areas for the psychologically speculative mind.

Dr. Moebius wrote an influential book, published first in

1900 (the year of Freud's *Interpretation of Dreams*), which ran into its seventh edition by 1905 (Freud's *Three Essays on the Theory of Sexuality* appeared in that year). Dr. Moebius died in 1907 (afflicted by cancer of the jaw), but his works during those early years of this century had immediate success, adding to his professional renown a notoriety far beyond Freud's. Freud's *Interpretation of Dreams* did not sell; it took years to dispose of the small first edition. Moebius is known in the history of medicine for his early distinction between "exogenous" and "endogenous" classes of mental disease, for his work on migraine, thyroidism, and for other neurological research.[55] He is known in the history of culture for one book: *Über den physiologischen Schwachsinn des Weibes.* A word on the title: he calls woman "Weib," not "Frau," and justifies this appellation at length (pp. 11 and 44). The natural word is *Weib,* and if women do not like it, they are above their station. The natural equivalent of "Herr" is "Frau," of "Mann," "Weib." By "physiological feeble-mindedness" Moebius means principally the anatomy of the brain. Certain brain parts are congenitally inferior in women as compared to men.[56]

His work was buttressed by other research on sex differences, on castration, and by a monograph on *Sex and Head Dimensions,* the conclusion of which states:

> The differences in head between the sexes, just as those between the races, must be reduced to mental differences. It is clear enough that the relationship between brain and body is not the same in the two sexes. A normal man, even if he be small, needs a head circumference of at least 53 centimeters, whereas a woman gets along quite

55. G. Zilboorg, *A History of Medical Psychology* (New York: Norton, 1941), p. 442; F. H. Garrison, *An Introduction to the History of Medicine,* 4th ed. (Philadelphia: Saunders, 1967); but in *Der Grosse Brockhaus* only his work on women is mentioned by title. Freud respected Moebius' psychiatric and neurological writings. On their connection see Jones, *Sigmund Freud,* I, 323 n.

56. P. J. Moebius, *Über den physiologischen Schwachsinn des Weibes,* 7th ed. (Halle, 1905).

> well with 51 centimeters. Thus, for the tasks of a woman's life, a brain that has room within a head of 51 cm is sufficient. But for the tasks of a man's life it is not enough. With 51 cm one can be an intelligent woman, but not an intelligent man.[57]

By finding the basis for physiological inferiority in the brain, Moebius finds the area of inferiority no longer to be the sexual system or the "nerves." It has moved "up"; this corresponds to the area of the woman from which, according to Moebius, her greatest danger comes. For Moebius the danger was embodied in the modern suffragette, the headstrong woman who sought education, political rights, and social recognition for her mental capacities. He met this challenge directly. And he uses a medical, paternal tone—always a condescension of male superiority toward female inferiority

57. P. J. Moebius, "Geschlecht und Kopfgrösse," *Beiträge zur Lehre von den Geschlechts-Unterschieden*, No. 5 (Halle, 1903), p. 47 (my translation). After these findings were published, many women wrote Moebius letters, which he appended to the seventh edition of his *Über den physiologischen Schwachsinn des Weibes*. In these letters German women thanked him for relieving them of the burden of mental effort; they had been straining under the illusion of equality but now knew, owing to his physiological research, that this effort was against the primary givens of the female brain. Swedish women, however, protested vehemently in their letters. In *The Subjection of Women*, 2d ed. (London: Longmans, Green, 1869), John Stuart Mill anticipates Moebius' argument on brain size as demonstration for female inferiority: "Dismissing abstract difference of quality, a thing difficult to verify, the efficiency of an organ is known to depend not solely on its size but on its activity" (p. 121). Moebius was a late but adamant follower of Gall and belonged to the nineteenth century's "brain psychiatry" (see above, pp. 148 ff.) with its equation skull = brain = mind = psyche. Moebius' personal life, by the way, could be subject for a pathography, that form of psychiatric biography which he invented and applied to the genius of Rousseau, Goethe, Nietzsche, and Schopenhauer. Moebius' wife was ten years older than himself; the marriage was supposedly unhappy, and childless. He abstained from alcohol from his early thirties until his death. His last paper was titled, "On the Hopelessness of All Psychology." See L. Buchheim, "P. J. Moebius," *Neue Zeitschrift für ärztliche Fortbildung*, XLIX, No. 7 (1960); *Münchener Medizinischen Wochenschrift*, 5 March 1907, p. 447; E. Jentsch, *Zum Andenken an Paul Julius Moebius* (Halle: Marhold, 1907).

—saying that, since female feeblemindedness is a physiological necessity and postulate (p. 24), that since woman is a sort of "middle thing between child and man, mentally too in many aspects" (p. 14), she should be relieved of her suffragette illusions, which are too much for her capacity and only lead to degeneration of the species, the care of which, as wife and mother, is her first concern. Moebius' "middle thing" echoes Paracelsus' notion of women as *halbe Kreaturen.*

In addition to Moebius, we could dwell a while with that grand master of literary misogyny, Strindberg, and also with Otto Weininger, whose *Geschlecht und Charakter* (1903) appeared before Weininger was 23 (five months before his suicide in Beethoven's house). Arnold Schönberg pays tribute to both Strindberg and Weininger in his preface to his *Harmonielehre*, a suggestive fact considering, first, the "pathography" of a fictional composer infected through venereal disease, portrayed by Thomas Mann in *Doktor Faustus*, and which was cause for a Schönberg-Mann quarrel, and, second, the role of music in Apollonic consciousness. But these bypaths do not belong strictly within our theme. Moebius was a medical scientist, and it is female inferiority as presented through scientific evidence which mainly concerns us. Yet Weininger probably had the greater effect on the psychological state of Europe during the first two decades of this century. In him all the themes of our investigation coalesce. The female is soulless, sexually materialistic, and mentally inferior. Moreover, his work introduces themes we shall soon turn to: hysteria and parallels between hysteria, racial degeneration, and femininity.

First Conclusions

We have been examining the fantasies of female inferiority through the historical changes in consciousness. We have seen the inferiority, but where is the change in consciousness? The same view of female inferiority, based on one or another physiological argument, runs with undeviating fidelity from antiquity to psychoanalysis. History evidently has no effect on the permanent structure of an archetype. Changes have been in detail only; the substance of the arguments remains the same. Even when a token female superiority is asserted and given confirmation through physiological evidence—and here I am thinking of the ovists, who regarded all embryos as being produced from small embryos in the unfertilized eggs and who regarded the male role in procreation as subsidiary [58] —there is only an enantiodromia, an incredibly one-sided repetition of the same failure to envisage a *coniunctio* as necessary for procreating a new individual. As late as the nineteenth century, men could not accept the actual union of ovum and sperm as necessary for the embryo. Empiricists might say men could not accept this union because they could not see it; others might put the failure of sight secondary to the opacity of interior, archetypal vision, since in alchemical experimentations which ran parallel with those of science the *coniunctio* was presented as the fundamental prerequisite for conception of the homunculus and for the birth of the new being. Evidently alchemy was informed by another structure of consciousness. In alchemy, consciousness is *united* with matter from the start; they are involved with each other, so that the bisexuality of the *coniunctio* is implied throughout the process. In science, consciousness *cognizes* matter, placing a "cut," a boundary line, between itself and the material. In science, the femininity of matter can never be really known, so that the method defeats itself. Science could not see things

58. Needham, *Chemical Embryology,* I, 200. Some of these subsidiary roles of the male in procreation were described in these ways: the male merely opened the passage; the male acted as attracter of the eggs out of the female conservatory (Meyer, *The Rise of Embryology,* p. 163, reporting on a discussion in the Royal Society in 1672); the male provided the bathing fluid for the ovum (Spallanzani); male seed only prevented coagulation by its vital motion; male seed was useful only for fermentation; etc. The point in all is that controversy, originating in the disbalanced *coniunctio,* leads the investigators to come down *either* for the egg *or* for the sperm. The division in the consciousness of the observers becomes reflected in the division between theories and their adamant proponents.

that alchemy saw, despite the peculiarity of alchemical equipment, the confusion of its conceptual definitions, and the privacy of its results. It is as if science were inhibited from envisaging the equality of the sexes by the kind of consciousness required for scientific work, especially for observations upon the female and all that science holds to be feminine.

But it has not been my aim to point a finger at the past and scold it for errors. These have been accounted for by the historians: insufficiencies of theory, conceptual knowledge, technique, observational method. However, these errors have a nonhistorical source, too, which is that mixture of observation and fantasy in which the observer loses sight of the structure of his own consciousness and the fantasies it produces. Then the mistakes arise, not from inadequacies of science, but from inadequate psychology. So we are attempting here to bring psychological, or archetypal, understanding to these errors.

From this psychological point of view there have been two consistently recurrent errors: the first-Adam-then-Eve fantasy, which turns every investigation comparing the morphology of male and female bodies into the misogynist discovery of female inferiority; and the Apollonic fantasy, with its distance to materiality—a fantasy which denies a role to the female in the propagation of new life. The first can be condensed into the language of Oken (which could as well be Freud): "Ideally every child should be a boy." The second derives from Apollo's own statement: "There can be a father without any mother." Does not the first fantasy of female inferiority imply a disbalanced *coniunctio*, and does not the second fantasy, of Apollo, entail an inferiority of the feminine? Unless the opposites are conceived as a symmetry, as independent and distinct but necessary to each other, the *coniunctio* will be out of balance. Female inferiority maintains this imbalance. The imbalance resulted in that kind of *coniunctio* called by alchemy the *monstrum:* the disproportions of our modern consciousness, its view of femininity as inferior, whether this feminine component be the psyche or the body; it also resulted in the *need for psychotherapy to develop the inferior and feeble femininity.*

The image of female inferiority has not changed, because it remains the image in the masculine psyche. Theories of the female body are preponderantly based on the observations and fantasies of men. These theories are statements of masculine consciousness confronted with its sexual opposite. No wonder archetypal levels of unconsciousness intervene in theory-forming. We must bear in mind that the evidence in anatomy, as in all fields of science, is gathered mainly by men and is a part of their philosophy. We know next to nothing about how feminine consciousness or a consciousness which has an integrated feminine aspect regards the same data.[59]

59. In that branch of medical science we have been surveying, there are a few notable exceptions. At the end of the sixteenth century, a woman physician of Toledo, Louise Oliva Sabuco, used anatomy as a philosophical field upon which to combat the non-Christian views of Galen and the Arabs (K. F. Lander, "The Study of Anatomy by Women before the Nineteenth Century," *Proceedings of the Third International Congress for the History of Medicine* [London, 1922]). Another exemplary figure—a physician and "hysteric"—is Hildegard of Bingen. She reveals what a more developed female fantasy might do to our field, since her view of conception is that three forces take part: the female, the male, and the divinity (*Liber Scivias;* see C. Singer, "The Visions of Hildegard of Bingen," in *From Magic to Science* [New York: Dover, 1958]). Oddly, many of the writings that I have used for preparing this survey were written by women: Erna Lesky, Ilza Veith, Jane Oppenheimer, Vilma Fritsch, Liselotte Buchheim, K. F. Lander, and Esther Fischer-Homberger, who first pointed out to me that women do most of the historical investigations of hysteria. The work of Elizabeth Gasking, *Investigations into Generation, 1651–1828* (Baltimore, 1966), came to my attention too late for inclusion here. The real issue is not whether the research is done by a man or a woman but whether the consciousness of the investigator gives adequate place to those aspects called "feminine." An example where this is *not* the case is the work of Virginia Johnson, coauthor with W. Masters of *Human Sexual Response*. The emphasis upon female orgasm and upon the "freedom" of women through contraception and abortion are the ways in which the dogma of female inferiority is presenting itself at the moment: the prototype for free and healthy sexuality is male; by a technology of the orgasm, by legalizing abortion, and by perfecting the oral contraceptive women can more closely approximate male sexual patterns.

Even the determination of what constitutes appropriate data, the very questions asked, the way the eye perceives through the microscope are determined by the specific consciousness we call scientific, Western, modern, and which is the long-sharpened tool of the masculine mind that has discarded part of its own substance, calling it "Eve," "female," and "inferior." We have called this consciousness Apollonic, for, like its namesake, it belongs to youth, it kills from a distance (its distance kills), and, keeping the scientific cut of objectivity, it never merges with or "marries" its material. It is a structure of consciousness that has an estranged relation with the feminine, which we have taken to mean "the abysmal side of bodily man with his animal passions and instinctual nature, and 'matter' in general." The Apollonic fantasy, however, is not exclusively male, pertaining only to how men think and what they do. As an archetypal structure it is independent of the gender of the person through whom it works, so that the integration of the feminine is a concern pertaining not only to men but to women as well. Moreover, since the Apollonic structure is archetypal, the integration of femininity into this structure is an archetypal problem beyond the human level of personal needs and personal development. We are speaking about a kind of consciousness and the limitations imposed upon this consciousness by its archetypal structure. Our fantasies and the perceptions which they govern cannot change until this structure changes.

This structure produces these theories of the human body as part of a philosophy which guarantees the superiority of male consciousness and the inferiority of any opposite with which it will be conjoined. And there is no way out of the dilemma as long as this Jahwistic or Apollonic structure informs not only scientific thought but *the very notion of consciousness itself*. Consciousness of this sort, no matter how far it advances, no matter how much it believes in the Assumption of Maria, with all its androgynous implications, can hardly produce the uniform world-picture and a new reconciliation of the opposites, with which hopeful thought we began. For this kind of consciousness the elevation of the female principle and a new psychic recognition of female physicality seem structurally impossible; it is driven to repeat the same misogynist views, century after century, because of its archetypal base. There must be recurrent misogyny presented with scientific justification because the positivism of the scientific approach is informed by Apollo. Until the structure of the consciousness itself and *what we consider to be "conscious"* change into another archetypal vision or way of being-in-the-world, man's image of female inferiority and a disbalanced *coniunctio* in every sphere of action will continue. Until the male *Weltanschauung* moves; until Maria returns to Eve and Eve to Adam; until Maria assumes with her body and within man's body a place in consciousness itself, shedding the abysmal and the only passionate; until the *coniunctio* affects consciousness itself; until another archetypal structure or cosmos informs our view of things and our vision of what it is "to be conscious" with another spirit, we shall remain endlessly repeating and helplessly confirming with ever more subtle scientific observation our misogynist fantasies of the male-female union.

Hysteria

Before we can move further with the question of consciousness, we must first spend a few minutes with hysteria. It bears significantly upon our theme, as we shall soon see.

Freud and Breuer begin with hysteria. Psychoanalysis begins as treatment for hysteria. The discovery of the unconscious and the authentication of hysteria are theoretically and historically interdependent. Note how hysteria, so long considered exclusively a woman's disease, is the condition which gave rise to analysis, and note the peculiar intermixture of women, hysteria, sexual fantasy, and analysis still to this day: the preponderance of women in analysis; the woman as preponderant source of "case material"; the analyst and his "following" of women; the sexual fantasies as supposed root of hysteria[60] and the transference fantasies as supposed root of psychoanalysis. What archetype lies behind hysteria? What *Weltanschauung* of what superhuman power was there being manifested toward the end of the past century in those events called absence and trance, *arc de cercle*, religious eroticism, conversions of psyche into body—events that came with sudden onset and vanished just as suddenly? And why was woman particularly the one who fell into hysteria? (Even for the Egyptians hysteria was a female affliction.)[61] As Freud says, in his obituary on Charcot:

> This most enigmatic of all nervous diseases—no workable point of view having yet been found from which physicians could regard it—had just at this time come very much into discredit, and this ill-repute related not only to the patients but was extended to the physicians who treated this neurosis. The general opinion was that anything may happen in hysteria; hysterics found no credit

60. Pierre Janet throughout his writing opposed the idea of basing hysteria upon its sexual-erotic phenomena; in his view they were not etiological; see his *The Major Symptoms of Hysteria* (New York, 1929; reissued, 1965). Janet, along with Charcot and Freud, is a major writer on hysteria of the modern period. His attempt to free hysteria from misogyny was made by relegating the erotic component to a lesser and symptomatic role (whereas Freud put it in the foreground). However, since hysteria is considered by Janet to be an *abaissement du niveau mental* (lowering of the mental level), he continued to regard it as an inferiority of functioning, even if not an inferiority that is especially feminine. Jung derived ideas from Janet and refers especially and frequently to the idea of an *abaissement du niveau mental* and to the inferior part of a function. In these states of mind, called by some hysterical, there is a *participation mystique* with the surroundings and with a collective unconsciousness. Unfortunately, in Jungian analysis as now practiced in general, the *abaissement* and inferiority are associated with the red end of the archetypal spectrum—with emotion and with communal and physical life—and the inferior aspect of a function is considered inferior also in a value sense.

61. I. Veith, *Hysteria: The History of a Disease* (Chicago: University of Chicago Press, 1965), pp. 2–7. For a more profound discussion of theories of hysteria in the Enlightenment see M. Foucault, *Madness and Civilization*, trans. R. Howard (New York: Pantheon, 1965), pp. 136–58.

> whatsoever. First of all Charcot's work restored dignity to the subject; gradually the sneering attitude, which the hysteric could reckon on meeting when she told her story, was given up; she was no longer a malingerer.[62]

What was going on? "The painful affect, crying, screaming, raving," as Freud says.

The word "hysteria" appears first in the Hippocratic *On the Diseases of Women.* In a letter from Democritus to "Hippocrates," which was quoted as late as the seventeenth century by Sydenham in sympathetic support of similar annoyance, the uterus is declared to be "the cause of 600 evils and countless sufferings." [63] Sydenham stated that one of every six patients was hysterical.[64] As a disease of the womb (*hystera,* in Greek), hysteria could occur only in women. Plato explains this:

> What is called the matrix or womb, a living creature within them with a desire for child-bearing, if it be left

62. S. Freud, *Collected Papers* (London: Hogarth, 1953), I, 18–19. For a less favorable view of Charcot by another of his students see A. Munthe, *The Story of San Michele* (New York, 1929), pp. 302–13.

63. See E. Fischer-Homberger, "Hysterie und Misogynie—Ein Aspekt der Hysteriegeschichte," *Gesnerus,* XXVI (1969), 117 f. Contained within the root *hyster* we find a curious association of the feminine with the inferior. *Hystera* means "womb" in Greek, or refers to the ovaries (as in Aristotle's *History of Animals* and his *Generation of Animals*). *Hysteros* means "latter" and, in its many combinations, refers to the latter position in place (as behind), in time (as coming next or secondary), and in quality (as inferior). Liddell and Scott (*A Greek-English Lexicon,* 9th ed. [Oxford, 1968], pp. 1905b–1906a) give a long entry to *hysteros* in its variety of forms, which include the meanings: to come "too late," to lag "behind," to be "failing," to exhibit "shortcoming," "wanting," "need," "deficiency," "inferiority." According to them, Plato was aware of this double possibility when, in the passage on the womb in *Timaeus* 91C, he makes a play of meaning with "second woman." The *Lexicon* considers the common etymological root of both ideas (womb and inferiority) to reside in the Sanskrit *úd,* "up," together with its comparative forms "upper" or "higher" (meaning "latter"), which positions, if taken in a physiological sense, refer to womb, uterus, belly (also derivable from that Sanskrit root).

64. W. Szumowski, *Névroses et psychoses au Moyen Age . . .* (Paris, 1939), p. 9.

> long unfruitful beyond the due season, is vexed and aggrieved, and wandering throughout the body and blocking the channels of the breath, by forbidding respiration brings the sufferer to extreme distress and causes all manner of disorders.[65]

The womb is conceived to be self-moved, perhaps autonomous, and therefore a "living creature" (Cornford) or "animal" (Jowett and T. Taylor). Hysteria was the effect of the desirous animal in woman. It was a disease in which the autonomous animal dominates the human being, cutting her off from *pneuma*, respiration, spirit, and degrading her into the animality of her womb.

The first English work on hysteria was printed in 1603 by Edward Jorden, an expert on matters of witchery for James VI of Scotland. His book, *A Brief Discourse of a Disease Called the Suffocation of the Mother*, is a watershed, separating the ancient superstition called possession from the modern superstition called hysteria. He even lifted the area of affliction from uterus to brain. More: he moved the matter itself from an irrational religious problem to one of secular explanation. But the sinister misogynist implications remain. Here we must repeat a statement of the Zurich medical historian Dr. Esther Fischer-Homberger, upon whose paper "Hysterie und Misogynie" I rely in this section: "Where hysteria is diagnosed, misogyny is not far away." Female inferiority takes a new turn when hysteria becomes a secular, scientific matter. The witch is now a poor patient—not evil, but sick. The psychiatric protection from evil does not do away with the evil but merely shifts it into secular terms. The misogyny does not change; it appears in a new form. The nature of woman is still to blame—even more to blame. The etiology lies not in satanic forces but in her own womb, in the female structure itself. Her physiology is faulty.

The witch, after all, could be saved by God. Her femininity

65. Plato *Timaeus* 91C; see also F. M. Cornford, *Plato's Cosmology* (London, 1937).

could be restored by faith. In fact, in the medieval way of looking at hysteria, the disease was fundamentally religious, a crisis of faith. The *Malleus Maleficarum* (1494) derived the word *femina* from *fe* (faith) and *minus* (less): woman was of less faith than man—which recalls not only all we have heard about female inferiority but the recurrent question "Does woman have soul?"

The diagnosis of hysteria went through many vicissitudes, which we do not need to recount here, but "hysteric" and "witch" never lost their close association. For instance, in nineteenth-century French psychiatry, an old test for the witch—sticking her with pins and needles—was used in clinical demonstrations of hysteria.

Although the French recognized hysteria in men, it was mainly a malady of women. Even when Georget and Broussais considered it an affliction of the nervous system and not only of the uterus, it still belonged primarily to women. Again, physiological inferiority was blamed: ". . . only the immature, undeveloped nervous systems such as found in women, tended toward hysterical reactions."[66] By means of a circular argument, the frequency of hysteria among women was part of the evidence for the nineteenth century's conflation of evolutionary notions with the degeneration theory of feminine inferiority, culminating in Moebius. The weakness of faith of the *Malleus Maleficarum* now became a weakness of constitution, an inborn psychophysiological defect, a feeble-mindedness.

This defect of constitution was particularly associated with the sexuality of the female. Less than one hundred years ago, around the time that Freud studied with Charcot in Paris, Richer's treatment of hysteria at the Salpêtrière was focused upon the ovaries. Mechanical devices were invented for compressing them or for packing them in ice. In Germany,

66. Fischer-Homberger, "Hysterie und Misogynie," p. 122; cf. Altschule, "Venus Ascendant," in *Roots of Modern Psychiatry;* J.-M. Bruttin, "Différentes théories sur l'hystérie dans la première moitié du XIXe siècle" (dissertation, University of Zurich, 1969).

Hegar (1830–1914) and Friedrich (1825–82) were using even more radical methods, including ovarectomy and cauterization of the clitoris. The source of hysteria was still, as in Plato's time, sought in the matrix of the female body, upon which surgical attacks were unleashed.[67]

During this time before the First World War, there was a battle between French and German psychiatry based on statistical evidence on the frequency of hysteria.[68] German-language psychiatry generally resisted the idea that hysteria could be a disease of men, bringing as evidence the low frequency of hysterical incidents among males. If the French could show higher frequency among men, well, that was because Frenchmen were more hysterical, i.e., less fit for survival, more degenerate. Although Freud wrote as late as 1931 that hysteria is "characteristically feminine," [69] nevertheless to him goes the credit for carrying from Paris to Austria the notion of male hysteria. He brought Charcot and Bernheim into the German language, quite a threatening thing to do at a time when concerns with race, nervous degeneration,[70] and national character were much in the *Zeitgeist*. We shall return to this in a moment.

Although a disease, hysteria still seemed the work of evil, since the psychiatric descriptions of it point out the *moral* inferiority of the hysteric. J. Falret in 1866 considered hysteria as a moral insanity: "In one word, the life of the hysteric is nothing but one perpetual falsehood." [71] Griesinger writes of hysterics' "inclination to deceive and to lie, traits of decided envy, smaller or greater nastiness." [72] In 1893

67. "Die Hysterie," *Ciba Zeitschrift*, CXX (1950), 4418, 4423.

68. E. Fischer-Homberger, verbal communication of not-yet-published material.

69. S. Freud, "Female Sexuality," *Collected Papers*, V, 254.

70. A. Steiner, "Das nervöse Zeitalter" (dissertation, Zurich, 1964).

71. J. Falret, *Folie raisonnante ou folie morale*, cited in Veith, *Hysteria*, pp. 210–11.

72. W. Griesinger, *Pathologie und Therapie der psychischen Krankheiten* (Stuttgart, 1861); see also Fischer-Homberger, "Hysterie und Misogynie," p. 122.

Kraepelin called the hysteric a "virtuoso of egoism" and quite "ruthless." Kraepelin further said that hysteria was the disease form of the undeveloped, naïve soul, which for men was a psychopathic disorder, but "Hysteria of women corresponds rather with a natural developmental direction; in some circumstances it is a remaining upon a childish level." [73] We can see that Moebius was no oddity. Perhaps Kraepelin took more from him than the rubrics "exogenous" and "endogenous." (Moebius probably did influence Kraepelin's view of hysteria; in his textbook the first reference in his footnote on the literature of hysteria [p. 1547] is to Moebius.) Dubois says in his textbook of 1910 that a learned man, a man of reason, can never be a true hysteric; only men who show mental weakness, childish emotion, womanly emotion can be hysterical.

This excursus on hysteria has had two points. The first is a warning: *caveat emptor.* Beware when buying a psychiatric diagnosis: hysteria, like masochism above, is a case in point. Kraepelin's influence is not to be underestimated. His psychiatry belongs not only within a *Zeitgeist;* his diagnosis represents the great misogynist tradition we have been examining. In Kraepelin, the description of hysteria still echoes the description of the witch. Moreover, what Kraepelin published in the midst of the First World War, the four-volume eighth edition of his textbook—and his was the major textbook of psychiatry in the German language for thirty years, perhaps the major psychiatric text in the whole modern history of this field—shows traces of the psychiatric influence on the background of that war and points forward to ideas that entered the next period of history, our times and our wars. Kraepelin states in his chapter on hysteria:

> It is often maintained that the Latin and Slavic peoples show a stronger tendency for hysterical illnesses than do the German. Considering the greater excitability and pas-

73. E. Kraepelin, *Psychiatrie*, 8th ed. (Leipzig, 1915), p. 1647 (my translation).

> sion of the Latins and the definite emotional softness of the Slavs, in contrast with the calmer and more sober disposition of the Germans, this position would not be improbable. The Jews, too, burdened by long inbreeding, should be more easily hysterical.[74]

The second reason for my excursus into hysteria leads to the heart of our theme. I asked above, "What archetype lies within hysteria? What *Weltanschauung* of what superhuman power is there being manifested?" If we could find a key to hysteria, we could unlock not only the question of this syndrome but the deeper questions of why this syndrome is so closely tied to (*a*) male misogyny, (*b*) the repudiation of hysteria as necessary to Apollonic consciousness, (*c*) the discovery of the unconscious, and (*d*) the fundaments of psychoanalysis. Perhaps hysteria is the key itself, since it is so crucially related to each of these questions.

If hysteria is both puzzle and key, we might enter its puzzle by finding the key to it in its own kind of consciousness. An imaginative physician of the Renaissance, a physician with considerable literary talents too, has already opened the way. In his *Pantagruel*, Rabelais notes a striking similarity. He speaks of hysterical women as "Bacchic Thyades on the day of their Bacchanalia." He suggests a connection between hysterical woman and maenad. Dionysus has been evoked.

Dionysus and Bisexual Consciousness

We may recall that Dionysus is mainly a god of women. His cult was mainly a woman's preserve. Though he is male, and phallic,[75] there is no misogyny in this structure of consciousness because it is not divided from its own femininity. Dionysus "in one of his appellations, is 'man and woman' *in one person*. Dionysus was bisexual in the first place, not

74. *Ibid.*, p. 1657 (my translation). I am grateful to Dr. Fischer-Homberger for pointing out this passage.

75. W. F. Otto, *Dionysus: Myth and Cult*, trans. R. Palmer (Bloomington, Ind., 1965), pp. 164–65.

merely in the 'effeminate' later portrayals."[76] This figure and his spirit can inform consciousness so that it can at last move away from the line we have been following from Adam and Apollo. The recurring image can change. And the change that is indicated by Dionysus is one where female is not added to or integrated by male; rather, the image shows an androgynous consciousness, where male and female are primordially united. The *coniunctio* is not an attainment but a given. It is not a goal to be sought but an a priori possibility, always there for anyone. In fact the *seeking* of the *coniunctio*, as Apollo pursuing Daphne, is self-defeating because it hyperactivates the male, driving the psyche into vegetative regression, Daphne into laurel tree.

But let us recapitulate, for we are now moving toward the close. We have indicated that hysteria was essential to the discovery of the unconscious and to the origins of therapeutic psychology. We have taken the hint first from Rabelais that the misogyny with which hysterics were regarded indicated a Dionysian impulse within hysteria. We can elaborate upon the Dionysian impulse within hysteria in several ways: by referring to Dodds[77] and by following in detail

76. C. Kerényi, "The Primordial Child in Primordial Times" in *Introduction to a Science of Mythology* (with C. G. Jung) (London, 1951), p. 3. Some of his names were: Gynnis (the womanish), Arsenothelys (the man-womanly), Dyalos (the hybrid), Pseudanor (the man without true virility) (Kerényi, *The Gods of the Greeks* [London: Thames & Hudson, 1951], p. 73).

77. E. R. Dodds, "Maenadism," in *The Greeks and the Irrational* (Boston: Beacon Paperbacks, 1957); Dodds, Introduction to the *Bacchae*, 2d ed. (Oxford, 1960), p. xvi, n. 2, and pp. xxxiii ff.; M. Bourneville and P. Regnard, "Iconographie photographique de la Salpêtrière," *Progrès médical* (Paris) (1877–80); H. Meige, "Les possédés des dieux dans l'art antique," *Nouvelle iconographie de la Salpêtrière* (Paris, 1894). See also H. Jeanmaire, *Dionysos* (Paris: Payot, 1951), pp. 9 f. and 489–91, for iconographical comparison, and the bibliography in E. L. Blackman, *Religious Dances*, trans. from the Swedish by E. Classen (London: Allen & Unwin, 1952). Besides the para- and pathopsychological exaggerations usually stressed (e.g., by T. K. Oesterreich, *Possession*, trans. D. Ibberson [London: Kegan Paul, 1930]), there are other "Dionysian signs" in hysteria. For ex-

his indications for comparing the Dionysian scenes in antique evidence with the collection of pictures of hysterics assembled by nineteenth-century French psychiatry; by studying the curious statistics of Kraepelin, where the overwhelm-

---

ample: (1) *Onset and termination are abrupt:* ". . . the active manifestations come on suddenly, and after lasting a short time, usually disappear" (differential diagnosis from T. D. Savill, *Lectures on Hysteria* [1909], cited in Veith, *Hysteria*, p. 243). Dionysus is the especially epiphanic god, suddenly coming and just as suddenly vanishing, says Otto (*Dionysus*, pp. 79 f.). (2) *Suggestibility* belongs to that form of mania called "telestic," ruled by Dionysus. Dionysian "madness" is shared communal experience. Dionysus frees one from the confines of one's adapted individuality. As Dodds puts it, he "enables you for a short time to *stop being yourself*" (*The Greeks and the Irrational*, p. 76). Cf. Janet, *Major Symptoms of Hysteria*, p. 322, where he defines hysteria as a "malady of the *personal synthesis*" and characterizes it as "*a tendency to the dissociation and emancipation of the systems of ideas and functions that constitute personality*" (italics in original). One of Dionysus' names was the "Loosener." He was an enemy of tyrants, and his cult brought social change (see W. Jaeger, *The Theology of the Early Greek Philosophers*, Gifford Lectures of 1936 [New York: Oxford Paperbacks, 1967], pp. 57–58), which on a psychological level can be understood as the emancipation from the tyranny of the usual personality, dominated by its usual ego. (3) Hysteria *imitates* other disorders and diseases, notoriously appearing in manifold guises, its diagnosis difficult owing to its ungraspable mimicry, its definition impossible (Lasègue). Dionysus, according to Plutarch (*De E* 388F), "undergoes transformations of his person, and at one time kindles his nature into fire and makes it altogether like all else, and at another time he undergoes all sorts of changes in his form, his emotions, and his powers." (4) The *theatricality* of hysteria is characteristic and is described in various ways: *attitudes passionnelles;* the mimicry, or ability of hysteria to imitate many forms of psychic disorder; *Clownismus;* the "*belle indifférence*" of Janet, indicating neither lying nor moral insincerity, as the ego would see it, but rather that what is transpiring is an act, a scene being played, in which the feelings are disinvolved and shallow, partly for protective reasons. Theater, a province of Dionysus, plays an unusual part in the scientific research on hysteria. Munthe (*The Story of San Michele*, p. 302) describes Charcot's Tuesday lessons as "stage performances of the Salpêtrière before the public of Tout Paris." They were held in an amphitheater, the classical place for medical demonstrations but also the classic scene of Greek theater. The young patients "were always ready to 'piquer une attaque' of Charcot's classical grande hystérie, arc-en-ciel and all, or to exhibit his famous three stages of hypnotism: lethargy, catalepsy, somnambulism,

ing preponderance of hysterics were unmarried country girls aged 15 to 23, working in city households as serving maids and cooks (remember the women of Thebes, called away by Dionysus from their household duties);[78] by paying careful attention to an insight of Freud's in 1908 in a short paper called "Hysterical Phantasies and Their Relation to Bisexuality." There Freud makes the astonishing statement: "An hysterical symptom is the expression of both a masculine and a feminine unconscious sexual phantasy."[79] (Curiously, "At Argos the chief festival of Aphrodite was called Hysteria," and "Connected with the same form of the cultus was the strange hermaphroditic festival . . . which bore the special name of the Feast of Wantonness, at which

---

all invented by the Master and hardly ever observed outside. . . . Some of them smelt with delight a bottle of ammonia when told it was rose water, others would eat a piece of charcoal when presented to them as chocolate. Another would crawl on all fours on the floor, barking furiously, when told she was a dog." (One might compare the mother of Pentheus, in the *Bacchae*, holding the bloodied head of her son in her lap, believing him a lion.) The major young psychiatrists (Freud, Janet) of the period went to these weekly performances and learned about hysteria from Charcot and his female performers.

78. Kraepelin, *Psychiatrie*, pp. 1648–49. According to Otto (*Dionysus*, pp. 134–35), other women besides those of Thebes were called out by Dionysus. "Thus the daughters of Minyas, who wished to remain faithful to their household duties and attend their husbands, were driven out by Dionysus. . . . The Argive women, too, are said to have been seized with Dionysiac madness and to have left their homes. In Nonnus we find again and again the picture of the woman who runs away from domestic life and the handiwork of Athena, to rush with hair dishevelled to the choral dances of Dionysus." (Further examples in W. K. C. Guthrie, *The Greeks and Their Gods* [London, 1968], pp. 166 ff.) The vision given by Dionysus to the women who leave their tasks of Athena, their marriages of Hera, is a "madness," i.e., it enables them to see the madness in the tasks of the sane world of everyday. The feminine conflict between the call of Dionysus and the duties of Hera and Athena is reflected again in the figures of Mary and Martha. There is a conflict of service between the domesticating and civilizing institutions of society (Hera and Athena) and the Dionysian consciousness of "nature," that is, the spontaneous comings and goings of the libido and their psychic reflection in fantasy.

79. S. Freud, *Collected Papers,* II, 57.

women dressed as men, and men as women, the men even wearing veils [Plutarch *De virt. mul.* 245E].")[80]

Freud hinted that the hysterical symptom is an expression of a message from a bisexual archetype. Might we say that every such symptom can be taken as a preformation of the hermaphrodite—not merely on the level of Freud, where masculine means "active" and feminine "passive," but by understanding that even in the symptom there is a preformation of the *coniunctio.* If taken on this level, placed within this cosmos, the symptom becomes a votive offering, a thing through which one pays one's debts to the bisexual dominant, the God of one's bisexuality. The things we have to bring to the Gods today are our symptoms, in the sense that what we dedicate to the Gods becomes thereby sacred. By conceiving symptoms as sacrifice, they take on new meanings and receive soul. Our afflictions and psychopathologies evoke the feminine side as carrier, sufferer, as nurse to that sufferer and to the child. The feminine side also holds out joyful abandon-

80. J. Hastings, ed., *Encyclopaedia of Religion and Ethics,* I, 605b, "Aphrodisia." Liddell and Scott, *Greek-English Lexicon,* p. 1906, regard the so-called "Hysteria" suspiciously like a pun on *mysteria,* hinting that it not be given much value. But the juxtaposition of two events through punning means psychologically more than the mere linguistic accident. Nonetheless, there are puzzles in this reference from Hastings. Argos is sacred mainly to Hera, yet this festival to Aphrodite took place there. Swine were sacrificed, yet swine were not as a rule sacred to Aphrodite but rather to Demeter and Hecate. (See also Pauly-Wissowa, *Real-Encyclopädie der classischen Altertumswissenschaft* [Stuttgart, 1894——], I, 2738–39, "Aphrodite.") Although this festival has yet to be described more precisely, it does remind us of the sympathetic mythological relationship between Dionysus and Aphrodite. She was his "Mother" in some tales, as well as his "Wife"; together they generated Priapus, which, we may recall, was once considered the specific cure for hysteria by Charcot and by Freud (cf. Part Two, note 21). On the Dionysus-Aphrodite connection see C. Kerényi, *The Gods of the Greeks,* pp. 176, 270–72. As Dionysus was bisexual, so too Aphrodite: see the "bearded" Aphrodite in the Pauly-Wissowa reference above. For sculptural imagery associating Aphrodite, Eros, and the Dionysian cf. C. C. Vermeule, "Aphrodisiaca: Satyr, Maenad, and Eros," in *Essays in Memory of Karl Lehmann,* ed. L. F. Sandler (Locust Valley, N.Y., 1964).

ment to them and so a release through them. Dedication of the afflictions returns them to a connection with the archetype which is reaching us through these symptoms and psychopathologies. And finally, the Dionysian approach, if I may call it such for a moment, would not separate the bisexuality in the symptom, not attempt to get consciousness out of the suffering, extract the active male light from the passive suffering, since this would be to divide the bisexual totality and to favor the male knower at the expense of the female known. Thus this approach will be able to forego an *analytical* therapy that aims at transforming the existent bisexuality of a symptom or fantasy. It will not analyze the internal ambivalence of a complex which paradoxically cries for interpretation and just as strongly resists it. In other words, by this one example, consciousness informed by the Dionysian approach brings quite a different point of view, not only to hysteria, but to the theory and practice of therapeutic psychology which has arisen from hysteria.

The analytical viewpoint tends toward divisions: conscious from unconscious, cure from neurosis, individuation from collectivity, even eros from psyche. The aim may be a synthesis, but the means and method are division. Dionysian consciousness proceeds otherwise. One of the names for Dionysus was "The Undivided," and one of his main representations was as child. The child refers to a view of reality which is not divided. Plato (*Sophist* 249D) says: "Like a child begging for 'both,' he must declare that Reality or the sum of all things is both at once." A Dionysian perspective toward therapy would not exclude the child for the sake of maturity, since the child is the synthesis itself. The childish may not be put away, but shall be retained within consciousness for the sake of "both." Moreover, a psychic affliction would not be divided into a healthy and a sick aspect, requiring, thus, a healer and a patient. The affliction would not be divided from its own potential of nursing, which is constellated by the suffering and the childishness. The torn and rendered suffering, rather than cured by the medicine of Apollo, becomes an initiation into the cosmos of Dionysus.

But another God is not merely another point of view. The Gods are not persons who each rule over a different area of human activity. As W. F. Otto says, they are ways the world reveals itself.[81] Each archetype informs consciousness so that another kind of world shines through. Does the unified world-picture, that theme with which we began this essay, therefore require one cosmos of one God? I do not think it does.

Each cosmos which each God brings does not exclude another; neither the archetypal structures of consciousness nor their ways of being in the world are mutually exclusive. Rather, they require one another, as the Gods call upon one another for help. They supplement and complement. Moreover, their interdependence is given with their nature. Jung said at Eranos in 1934: "The fact is that the single archetypes are not isolated . . . but are in a state of contamination, of the most complete, mutual interpenetration and interfusion." [82] In this statement Jung voices the Neoplatonic tradition. As Wind says, "The mutual entailment of the gods was a genuine platonic lesson." For Ficino, "it is a mistake to worship one god alone." For Schiller in the German revival, "Nimmer, das glaubt mir, erscheinen de Götter, / Nimmer allein" (*Dithyrambe*).[83] Belonging to one God only, any single cosmos, any single way of being in the world, is itself a kind of hybris when it refuses the requirements of the dominants for each other.

But monotheistic consciousness entails this hybris. Although it is immensely supportive to an egocentric psyche, monotheistic psychology is also immensely damaging to our aim of shifting perspectives away from the ego as sole cen-

81. W. F. Otto, *Theophania* (Hamburg, 1956), pp. 76–79.
82. C. G. Jung, "Archetypes of the Collective Unconscious," in *Integration of the Personality* (London, 1940), p. 91; cf. *CW*, IX, i, par. 80.
83. E. Wind, *Pagan Mysteries in the Renaissance* (Harmondsworth: Peregrine, 1967), p. 198.

ter of consciousness. An archetypal psychology that would give proper due to many dominants, that would recognize the interpenetrating psychological reality of many Gods—and not merely the highest: Yahweh, Zeus, ego, or self—and the psychological legitimacy of each cosmos, is forced to question, even abandon, psychological monotheism and its emphasis, for instance, upon the ego-self axis, which is, after all, only the usual Judeo-Protestant monotheism in psychological language. This language usually presents the ego in a direct line of confrontation and covenant with a single self, represented by images of unity (mandalas, crystals, balls, wise men, and other patterns of order). But according to Jung the self has many archetypal instances. The puzzling relation between self and the archetypes reproduces the ancient enigma of the many-in-the-one and the one-in-the-many. In order to give full value to the differentiated manyness of both the archetypal world of divine figures, *daimones*, and mythic creatures, as well as to the phenomenal world of our experiences, where psychological actuality is vastly complicated and manifold, we shall focus intensively upon the *plurality* of the self, upon the many Gods and the many existential modes of their effects. We shall leave to one side theological fantasies of wholeness, oneness, and other abstract images of a goal called self.

The abandonment of psychological monotheism is radical indeed. It not only collapses the rule of the old ego; it is a reflection in the *psyche* that in a certain sense God is dead—but not the Gods. When psychology takes the archetypes seriously, it is led necessarily to freeing consciousness from its bonds to one dominant mainly, and to reflecting in theory the empirical fact that consciousness moves like Hermes, the guide of souls, through a multiplicity of perspectives and ways of being. If the psyche is, as Jung described it, a structure of multiple scintillae, will it not reflect many Gods? A psychology adequate to his archetypal view of psychic structure must reflect this multiplicity of centers and affirm a psychological polytheism. This statement of psychological polytheism is the necessary preamble to an evocation of Dionysus. To evoke him alone and to stand solely in that consciousness which he permeates would be to commit the error of Nietzsche, who took one God and laid all at his feet, thus perpetuating, despite his intention, the tradition he tried to leave.

The Mistaken Dionysus

To evoke Dionysus scares up a flight of shadows. These shadows arouse anxiety; anxieties become soothed by rationalizations into prejudices. So we are inhibited from discussing this dominant by a psychological block. Our anxiety and our prejudices show how strongly the ego resists and is bound to its Apollonic structure. After all, Nietzsche proclaimed Dionysus against Christ, at the same time announcing the death of our God. (Swinburne, however, now largely forgotten, saw it differently. He put Apollo against Christ.) Of all these shadows, not the least is the academic pall. Often enough it has been charged that anyone contrasting the Apollonic with the Dionysian is amateur in things mythological and Greek. But we are not talking of the Greeks, or their religion, or even of scholarly fantasies about the Greeks and their religion. We are talking of the psyche of contemporaries, of ourselves, and of the Dionysian possibilities for therapeutic psychology. After all, Dionysus was *the* God of madness, even the mad God. Then would not this Dionysus structure offer insight into the cosmos of madness from within its own consciousness? This archetypal dominant is surely the *sine qua non* for any depth psychology that would be therapeutic. And since to this mad Dionysus is attributed the origin of tragedy, will not this dominant be indispensable for any depth psychology that would be a cultural humanism? We can let the academic inhibition pass because our contrast of Apollonic and Dionysian comes not from an unscholarly misreading of Greek evidence. Our approach is psychological. One is led to use mythical names for structures of the psyche by its affinity for mythical expression for archetypal realities. If "Apollo" *versus* "Dionysus" is merely a Romantic fantasy in the eyes of academic scholarship, the validity for psychology of these terms lies just in the fantasy. Nietzsche by the age of 28 had already elaborated these appellations for kinds of consciousness in what Cornford called "a work of profound imaginative insight, which left the scholarship of a generation toiling in the rear." [84] Since then the psychological rightness of his insight is attested to by its recurrence, although its implications have still to be realized by psychology.

The mythical is the speculum of the psychological, its reflection beyond the personal. Myth provides the objective aspect for the subjective meanings in psychic events. Without myth it would all be me, personally, narrowed to the history of a case. Myth stands back of psyche, acting as a foil for objective reflection. Thus mythology cannot help becoming metapsychology, indispensable to any ontological description of psychology. The deeper psychology thinks into its own being, the more mythical it becomes, the more it relies upon mythical substructures to give account—all of which Freud indicated very early on and then elaborated throughout his life.[85] Thus, when we speak of a mythical image like Dionysus, we are not bringing something in, an import from classical scholarship and the history of religions, an extraneous referent as example or metaphor. We are but acting in the tradition of depth psychology, which knows itself through myth, whose objective basis outside itself is neither biological nor empirical nor in any of the positivist sciences, but which takes its anthropolgy, its study of man,

84. F. M. Cornford, *From Religion to Philosophy* (New York: Harper Torchbooks, 1957), p. 111 n. An early contrast between Apollo and Dionysus can be found in Plutarch *De E* 389.

85. *CW*, IX, i, pars. 7 f. and 261 f.; VIII, pars. 325 ff. See also G. Tourney, "Freud and the Greeks: A Study of the Influence of Classical Greek Mythology and Philosophy upon the Development of Freudian Thought," *Journal of the History of the Behavioral Sciences*, I, No. 1 (1965).

from his existence as a mythical being whose life is the demonstration of his fantasy, his fantasy a product of the imaginal realm.

The second shadow evoked by Dionysus is a darker one. When he is named, there is summoned up in the modern northern European mind, in which we each have our share, a specter of Wotan, and with him the devils, pagan distractions, and destruction of culture. Our notions of Dionysus come principally from nineteenth- and twentieth-century scholars working in the German language (with some notable exceptions from Great Britain and Scandinavia), that is, from people in whose backgrounds Wotan once loomed. Dionysus is conflated with Wotan, and the fear of Dionysus is confounded with the justifiable dread of that primordial Germanic shadow, Wotan. The description of things Dionysian and of the Dionysian kind of consciousness is distorted by the Wotanic perspective. As Kerényi says: ". . . in that which concerns the image of Dionysus, researchers and scholars have submitted to the influence of German philosophy to a much higher degree than they themselves realize." [86] Jung, taking Nietzsche as example, points again and again to the Germanic blending of Dionysus with Wotan. Jung writes: "In Nietzsche's biography you will find irrefutable proof that the god he originally meant was really Wotan, but, being a philologist and living in the seventies and eighties of the nineteenth century, he called him Dionysus." But then in the next sentence, which concludes the paragraph, Jung himself falls prey to the same notion: "Looked at from a comparative point of view, the two gods have much in common." [87] Elsewhere he even calls the maenads "a species of female storm-troopers." [88] Of course, from the cosmos of

86. C. Kerényi, "Dionysos le Crétois," *Diogène,* XX (Paris, 1957), 4 (my translation).

87. *CW*, XI, par. 44.

88. *CW*, X, par. 386. Jung may have been referring to the legendary invasion of India by the "army of Dionysus" in which the maenads formed a contingent. But this legend also reflects psychic events in

modern northern European consciousness the two Gods have an unconsciousness in common—they share "the unconscious," so to speak, as its lords. As Jung says: ". . . the Christian *Weltanschauung*, when reflected in the ocean of the (Germanic) unconscious, logically takes on the features of Wotan."[89] These two figures stand indistinguishable in the shadow of our tradition, one transalpine, the other cisalpine. But between them, between Dionysus and Wotan, the cult and consciousness of one and the cult and consciousness of the other, between the complex holiness of Ariadne and the simplist fertility of Frigg-Jord, between the wine madness of the one, the satyrs and the women, and the wild-hunt madness of the other and the heroic warriors, there stand differences no smaller than the Alps. How can we put these figures together, except where they have merged by our shadow and joined into the single devil of our projections? Even where they have specific traits or emblems in common, this does not make them kin. All Gods share attributes, for the archetypes are "in a state of . . . mutual interpenetration." Wotan also has traits in common with Apollo (the wolf and the blackbird of prophecy), with Hermes-Mercurius, and with Ares. It is not the traits but the structure of consciousness to which these traits belong—their function within the myth as a whole, the way in which they perform —that reveals the kind of consciousness. From this perspective, Wotan and Dionysus share the shadow of "madness" cast by our Adamic-Apollonic consciousness; but in themselves they differ, and their consciousnesses and their "madnesses" need to be kept distinct.

Besides supposed academic amateurism and the Wotanic projection, there is a third shadow that is raised by the evocation of Dionysus. His cult belongs mainly to women. Women, we *know* from our unchanging image of female inferiority, are unstable, feeble-minded, and of lesser substance.

---

which all the components—"India," "army," "invasion," etc.—have a symbolic rather than a historical meaning.

89. *CW*, IX, i, par. 442.

Their God, too, must be inferior. W. F. Otto shows that the views of Dionysus of late nineteenth-century classical scholarship, which runs parallel with the late nineteenth-century classical psychiatry of Kraepelin, like that psychiatry exhibit overt misogyny. Both humanisms (psychiatry and classical studies) were at that time pretending to positivism and objective science and were affected by the rigorous detachment and formalism of excessive Apollonic consciousness. Describing this anti-Dionysian school in classical scholarship, Otto writes:

> Now the fact that the women play a dominant role in the cult of Dionysus is precisely what Rohde and his followers have seized upon as best authenticating their opinions. Everyone knows how excitable women are, how easily frightened their imagination is, and how inclined they are to follow without question. These frailties in the character of women supposedly explain the unexplainable: that a people like the Greeks could fall victim to a religious frenzy.[90]

Otto goes on to quote both Rohde and Wilamowitz, furthering his point that the low view of the Dionysian is tied to a low view of the feminine. In other words, the low value given to the Dionysian affects our view of hysteria. Psychiatry and classical scholarship rely upon each other's misogyny.[91]

90. Otto, *Dionysus*, p. 126.

91. Moebius presents a good example of psychiatry referring to classical scholarship. In his study *Über das Pathologische bei Nietzsche* (Wiesbaden, 1902), p. 50, he writes: "Dionysus is really the God of Hysteria. . . . This is already shown by the fact that [in his cult] women [*Weiber*] are in the foreground, altogether contrary to the usual Greek custom. Thus Nietzsche, without noticing it, chose the patron of hysteria for his saint" (my translation). Here Moebius refers to Rohde for the classical evidence, thus completing the circle, since Rohde refers to psychiatry, e.g., J. F. K. Hecker, *Die Tanzwuth* (1832; English translation by B. G. Babbington, *The Epidemics of the Middle Ages* [London, 1846 and 1888]).

Dionysus Reimagined

We too begin with the interrelation between psychopathology and mythology, with their dependence upon each other. If we are to shift our consciousness in regard to the feminine, we shall have to shift our view about hysteria and the Dionysian, rewriting its description.

Nilsson writes:

> It has been said that history must be rewritten in every generation to be made understandable to the people of that generation. The like is true of the history of religions. Every synthesis, all views depend on the spiritual horizons of the writers and the readers and is conceived and elaborated accordingly.

Guthrie confirms this, particularly in writing about Dionysus: ". . . the personal outlook of the writer or the spirit of his age will affect his exposition of the cult, if it be only in the choice of a starting-point, which must inevitably give prominence to some features and relegate others to subordinate places."[92] Even the conservative Nilsson would understand the need for rewriting the description of Dionysus and elaborating it according to the spiritual horizons of today. Scholarly evidence no longer exclusively delimits this horizon; the psyche and its fantasy of Dionysus also bring a perspective. He will appear differently after the dogma of the Assumption and the idea of the *coniunctio*. The conception and elaboration will reflect the psyche in which the events formulated by these concepts are operative.

Kerényi, Dodds, Linforth, and especially W. F. Otto have begun to rewrite this description. Dionysian consciousness is being removed from the psychiatric distortion that begins with Rohde and continues, for example, in the major French

92. M. P. Nilsson, "Second Letter to Professor Nock on the Positive Gains in the Science of Greek Religion," *Harvard Theological Review*, XLIV (1951), 151; W. K. C. Guthrie, "Dionysos," in *The Greeks and Their Gods*, p. 145.

work by Jeanmaire.[93] He leans heavily on the Charcot school of hysteria (just as Rohde was influenced by J. F. K. Hecker's medical interpretation of popular epidemics), so that the Dionysian cult becomes just one more example of frenzied possession, its specificity lost in comparisons with the ravings of a Stone Age primitive, an Abyssinian in trance (*zar*), a shaman, a Rhineland peasant with Saint Vitus' dance, a Hasid, a medieval cloistered nun with erotic delusions, a Sicilian hearing the tarantella, or a case in a Parisian hospital. The specific quality of the Dionysian is lost in Jeanmaire's erosion of categories. Hecker, the father of modern historicism as an approach to disease, invented the discipline of historical pathology.[94] He approached the religious and the psychiatric with the methods of nineteenth-century comparative sociology. So he saw hysteria in the cult of Dionysus, while we are trying to see the cult of Dionysus in hysteria. The sociopsychiatric distortion best explains the God and his worshipers by hysteria; in our view, hysteria is best explained by the cult of the God as an archetype that has become repressed and dissociated so that its way of informing consciousness shows certain distortions. In hysteria we witness a classical instance of the "return of the repressed" (Freud).

If the God returned in this manner, then hysteria shows a latent consciousness insisting upon entering awareness. The women who pestered Mesmer, fainted for Charcot, fright-

93. H. Jeanmaire, *Dionysos*, pp. 106 ff.

94. Hecker, *Die Tanzwuth* (1832). The first volume of Hecker's path-breaking major work, *Geschichte der Heilkunde*, appeared in 1822, when he was 27. He, together with those who have followed in this line of comparative sociological or anthropological descriptions, has seen the archetypal background to these dancing/raving phenomena in the sense that they are exceptionally affective states, numinous to observer and participant, and ubiquitous in many ages and cultures. But what they have *not* seen is that the archetypal is something more than a "category" for grouping similar phenomena. They miss the feeling of and belief in a *spiritus rector*, a transpersonal dominant, the reality of the God. And this God is experienced as causal and real; categories are neither causes nor reals.

ened Breuer, and exasperated Freud, these desperately driven "cases," forced recognition of another structure of consciousness (called the unconscious). They are the true originators of depth psychotherapy. Because the return of the repressed God brought a kind of consciousness, there now was light in this formerly impenetrable shadow of madness. From this light, too, Dionysian madness needs rewriting. Linforth makes several separations which Rohde did not. Not all of the Dionysian is mad, and not all of what is called mad is insane. The madness of ritualistic enthusiasm is clearly to be separated from disease and insanity. This madness, according to Plato, is beneficial and even admirable. Linforth, echoing Plato, speaks of "the benign figure of Madness herself, who still as in the past accords her blessings to man." [95]

"Dionysus has still his votaries or victims," says Dodds, "though we call them by other names." [96] "Hysterics" is a name for the victims; yet they are victims less of Dionysus than of secular psychiatry, which also is responsible for "wrong" or "black" maenadism.[97] The white kind of votary refers to "hysteria subdued in the service of religion." [98] But we cannot subdue hysteria in this manner unless we first recognize the God in the syndrome and see hysteria as a manifestation of his imagination. We no longer have the right maenadism, the right telestic or ritual madness,[99] because

95. I. M. Linforth, "Telestic Madness in Plato, *Phaedrus* 244DE," *University of California Publications in Classical Philology* No. 13 (1946), p. 172; "The Corybantic Rites in Plato," *ibid.* See also F. Matz, "Dionysos als Mysteriengott," section II of "Dionysiaki-Teleti," *Akademie der Wissenschaften und der Literatur, Abhandlungen der geistes- und sozialwissenschaftlichen Klasse* (Wiesbaden), XIV (1963).

96. Dodds, "Maenadism," in *The Greeks and the Irrational*, p. 278.

97. "Failure to distinguish the 'black' maenadism described by the Messengers from the 'white' maenadism described by the Chorus has been responsible for much misunderstanding of the *Bacchae*" (*ibid.*, p. 279, n. 18).

98. *Ibid.*, p. 272.

99. On telestic madness see Dodds, *The Greeks and the Irrational*, pp. 75 ff., with notes and references; G. Rosen, *Madness in Society* (London, 1968), pp. 78 ff., 135–36; Linforth, "Telestic Madness in Plato."

we do not have the God. Our misogynist and Apollonic consciousness has exchanged him for a diagnosis. So without initiation into Dionysian consciousness, we have only that Dionysus that reaches us through the shadow, through Wotan and the Devil of Christianity. Without the awareness of the archetypal in the behavior which gives meaning to the madness, there is nothing left but the secular *nomina* of psychiatry and comparative sociology.

Dodds says, when approaching the Dionysian, ". . . our first step must be to *unthink all this:* to forget the pictures of Titian and Rubens, to forget Keats . . . to remember that *orgia* are not orgies but acts of devotion, and that *bacheuein* is not to 'revel' but to have a particular kind of religious experience." [100] We may carry our "unthinking" even further, through an aspect of Dodds himself, who, with his amazing range of mind and interest in the exceptional, sometimes "gives prominence to some features," the exaggerated irrationality of this religious experience, the patho- and parapsychological possession, "and relegates others to subordinate places": stillness, the soul and death, wine, marriage, theater, music and dance, vegetative nature and animal instinct, with its conservative laws of self-regulation, and the flow of life into communal events. Especially we must not forget that Dionysus is Zeus-Son, the renewal of the High God through his most physical and yet psychological son, at the center of whose cult from the earliest times is the *child*, the mystery of nursing and of psychological rebirth through underworld depths.

If, as Guthrie says, one must make a starting point somewhere when encountering the Dionysian, then why not the God's own starting point, childhood? "The childhood of Dionysus is very prominent in his myths, and no other god is comparable with him in this respect, not even Zeus." [101]

100. Dodds, Introduction to the *Bacchae,* p. xii (italics mine).

101. M. P. Nilsson, "The Dionysiac Mysteries of the Hellenistic and Roman Age," *Skrifter Utgivna Svenska Institutet i Athen,* VIII (Lund, 1957), 111.

Nilsson further shows that in the Dionysiac mysteries of the later period in Italy "the child holds a principal place in the representations of the Bacchic cult, mysteries, and myths in this age." [102] Small children, even babies, were "initiated." And to go back to the earliest Dionysus, in Crete, Kerényi finds him there as the divine force of living nature (*zōē*) and the taming of that nature.[103] Compulsion and inhibition belong together, as we said earlier, in our discussion of Eros. Animal life, Dodds reminds us, is not unrestricted potency but self-regulation. It has its borders both territorially and in behavior. In Dionysus, borders *join* that which we usually believe to be separated by borders. The philosopher is also a lover; Socrates is a drinking Silenus; the riotous Dionysus has but one wife, Ariadne. Dionysus presents us with borderline phenomena, so that we cannot tell whether he is mad or sane, wild or somber, sexual or psychic, male or female, conscious or unconscious. Kerényi says that, wherever Dionysus appears, the "border" also is manifested. He rules the borderlands of our psychic geography.[104] There the Dionysian dance takes place: neither this nor that, an ambivalence—which also suggests that, wherever ambivalence appears, there is a possibility for Dionysian consciousness.

Zōē is another way of speaking of this ambivalence. Or it can be called the *durée*, which was Harrison's [105] fantasy of

102. *Ibid.*, p. 106.

103. Kerényi, *Der frühe Dionysos* (Oslo and Bergen: Eitrem-Vorlesungen, 1961).

104. In yet one more important way Kerényi ("Die Herkunft der Dionysosreligion . . . ," *Arbeitsgemeinschaft für Forschung des Landes Nordrhein-Westfalen*, LVIII [Cologne, 1956]) attempts to rescue the cult from its savage interpretation by insisting that it originates in Crete, proceeding from the cultured south into Greece; whereas the standard view has been that Dionysus descends from the barbaric north of Thrace or the orgiastic, excessive east of Asia Minor. The locus of origin depends largely upon how we "place" this structure of consciousness, since historical evidence meets with mutual refutations and dissolves in conjecture.

105. J. E. Harrison, "Introduction," *Themis* (Cambridge, Eng., 1927), p. xiii: "I saw why Dionysos, the mystery-god, who is the expression and representation of *durée*, is, alone among Greek divini-

Dionysus in terms of Bergson's stream of life. *Zōē*, like the child, is still without specific characteristics given by biography and the identification with a male or female structure.

The force of life, like the child, needs nursing. The Dionysian experience transforms women not into raving hysterics and rebels but into *nurses*.[106] They become nurse of the natural, giving suck to all life, its indiscriminate *zōē*, both keeping alive the animal and the child by feeding "animal" and "child" through the ritual of eating flesh and by letting flow their compassionate milk. The obsession with the horrible aspects of the cult has turned our eyes away from seeing its full reaches and as an *entirety;* furthermore, even the horrible aspects can be doubted. Nilsson questions whether "the *omophagia* was ever, even in exceptional cases, a cannibalistic meal." [107] In reflecting on these matters, we must

---

ties, constantly attended by a thiasos, a matter cardinal for the understanding of his nature. The mystery-god arises out of those instincts, emotions, desires which attend and express life; but these emotions, desires, instincts, in so far as they are religious, are at the outset rather of a group than of individual consciousness." She then proceeds to place Dionysus with the Mother and make a polarity between "life" (Dionysus) and "conscious intelligence" (the Olympians). The typical division in the psyche of our Western scholarship appears as a statement about the Gods. Again it is assumed that Dionysus—like the "unconscious"—has no intelligence and that the mysteries of this God are rather like mob phenomena.

106. Kerényi, "Dionysos le Crétois," p. 27.

107. Nilsson, *The Minoan-Mycenaean Religion and Its Survival in Greek Religion*, 2d rev. ed. (Lund: Gleerup, 1968), p. 580. On the fantasy of child-eating as part of ritual in secret cults see J. M. Robertson, *Christianity and Mythology* (London: Watts, 1910), pp. 208 ff., with notes and references; see also E. R. Dodds, *Pagan and Christian in an Age of Anxiety* (Cambridge, Eng., 1965), p. 112. The Jews, too, were long accused of ritual child-killing "in order to eat the blood in their unleavened bread"; see the "evidence" and the refutations in H. L. Strack, *The Jew and Human Sacrifice* (London: Cope & Fenwick, 1909), pp. 169–235. The psychological point in these discussions is not the "fact" (whether or not babies were actually eaten, and the anthropological "evidence"), but that gruesome and horrible images, that is, spontaneous psychopathological fantasies, play a central role in the transformation mystery of the psyche. Because of the archetypal necessity for this fantasy, the motifs of child-killing and child-eating will reappear in connection with mystery cults re-

remember not to take *literally* statements within myth or about ritual. Do we really believe the Greeks tore apart and ate babies? Translating the fantasy to our times would imply that the wafer of communion is a residual substitute for a historically actual cannibalism.

Such statements have a meaning, not on the positivistic level of historical fact, but on the imaginal level. They are symbolic expressions. Dionysian events, like all mythical statements, make sense through a psychological hermeneutic, as reflections of psychic events, which is the way Jung has taught us to regard myth. We should not attempt separated interpretations of this or that aspect of the Dionysian or be thwarted in getting at its central meaning by those pathopsychological aspects which make sense only in terms of the unity given by the central meaning. To place the horror in the center would be to follow the psychiatric distortion, reducing Dionysus to hysteria.

According to Rohde, the central meaning of Dionysus is his relationship to the underworld of the soul: Dionysus, Lord of Souls. Nilsson writes: "The characteristic peculiarity of this movement is its mysticism."[108] Accordingly, it will be

---

gardless of the historical evidence *pro* or *contra*. (Human sacrifice did take place in connection with the Saturn cult of North Africa, which was not Greek but Roman and African, not Dionysian but Saturnian.) For the arguments that claim human sacrifice in the Dionysus (*omadios* = "raw-eater") cult see F. Schwenn, *Die Menschenopfer bei den Griechen und Römern* (Giessen, 1915). In this connection A. Brelich's sophisticated "Symbol of a Symbol" should be read (in J. M. Kitagawa *et al*., eds., *Myths and Symbols: Studies in Honor of Mircea Eliade* [Chicago, 1969]). Brelich discusses the questionable historical evidence and then regards killing rites in Greek antiquity as symbolic as such rather than as residual relics of actual practices. The truth and ubiquity of the archetypal theme of "human sacrifice" does not necessitate historical enactment. See, further, F. Saxl, "Revived Belief in Human Sacrifice," in "Pagan Sacrifice in the Italian Renaissance," *Journal of the Warburg Institute*, II (London, 1938–39), 364 ff.

108. E. Rohde, *Psyche*, trans. W. B. Hillis, 8th ed. (London: Routledge & Kegan Paul, 1925), pp. 168, 271; Nilsson, *The Minoan-Mycenaean Religion*, p. 576.

in terms of psychic consciousness or mystery consciousness that the horrible phenomena are to be comprehended. They play a special role in the process of the soul. The horrible in the cult can be compared with the role of the grotesque, obscene, and horrible in the art of memory. These patho-psychological aspects are specially effective means for connecting with the archetype. They evoke the emotional, instinctual level of the psyche. They are not to be taken literally in terms of themselves but as "horror stories" within the entirety of the psychic process. Heraclitus pointed to this (Frag. 15, Diels-Freeman): the obscenity and madness in the cult of Dionysus are accounted for, even morally justified, by the identification of Dionysus with Hades, the invisible principle of psychic existence that "underlies" the visible world. Thus the "horror" is for the sake of the soul, whose subconscious dominants (underworld lords) are Hades and Dionysus and Persephone.

All the aspects that so frighten us need to be viewed against their appropriate psychic background, not to make them less fearful or mad but to place the fear and the madness within the right context. Of course we cannot wholly regain this context of the ancient *orgia* and *entheos*. But through the process of unthinking the misogynist and psychiatric bias we may at least save ourselves from an identification with Pentheus, high in his tree, looking down and seeing from the outside what the initiated see from within quite differently. (After all, even in the horrible presentation of the *Bacchae*, it is the rational consciousness of Pentheus that constellates the black maenadism of Dionysian suffering; the Stranger [Dionysus] is "serene and dignified.") [109]

Because it is of Dionysus, Euripides' *Bacchae* perforce involves us in the nature of madness, raising the shattering insight that perhaps the antagonists of the God and his consciousness are more mad than his followers. Brown suggests that the only "way out" from the madness of black maenad-

109. Dodds, Introduction to the *Bacchae*, pp. xxviii, xliii f.

ism is by means of "constructing a Dionysian ego";[110] but since he too takes his starting point for this ego from his own background in classical studies, he too stresses the orgiastic (in the violent modern sense), leading to the "Freudian left" and the foolishness of Marcuse. Brown either relegates to a lesser place, or omits entirely, the inevitable conclusion that any ego informed by this structure will reflect the psychic interiority of this figure, as Lord of Souls, not only as "Resurrection of the Body." But anima is wanting in Brown's books. Yet, the new ego he calls for must reflect the femininity of Dionysus, the psychic qualities described above in Part One and the interiority of imagination described in Part Two. A Dionysian ego must express bisexuality.

A bisexual image of ideal consciousness appears in many guises. We find it in mystical concepts of an androgynous man and an androgynous Adam. We find it in Jung's alchemical *coniunctio*. We find it, too, in Portmann's biological descriptions of the organism in its germinal state as hermaphroditic and undifferentiated into sexes.[111] Do these not echo Kerényi's description of *zōē* and Dionysus and of the child as "origin" and as renewal of consciousness? In another work Portmann offers Sancho Panza as exemplar of an ideal human type.[112] The feminine component is best embodied in the pyknic, as a roundly physical and cyclically psychic constitution. He suggests in his way what we have been proposing from another perspective as Dionysian consciousness.

The interiority of animal life described by Portmann takes us further than the *zōē* of Kerényi. *Zōē* might then be conceived not only as the force that drives the green blood of nature, the *élan vital* of vegetative life, but also as the interior-

110. N. O. Brown, *Life against Death* (London, 1959), pp. 174 ff., 308 ff. Since that book, Brown's position has psychologically advanced, leaving Marcuse behind in political literalism; see their discussion in H. Marcuse, *Negations* (London, 1968), pp. 227–47.

111. A. Portmann, "Dualität der Geschlechter: Einheit und Vielfalt," *Eranos Jahrbuch*, XXXVI (Zurich, 1968).

112. A. Portmann, *Don Quixote und Sancho Panza* (Basel, 1964).

ity of that force, personified as Dionysus. If Dionysus is the Lord of Souls, he is the soul of nature, its psychic interiority. His "dismemberment" is the fragments of consciousness strewn through all of life, through every erogenous zone and plexus of our physical bodies. In him the bisexual pair are united. Like eros, *zōē* is the universal libido, and, like psyche, it is the reflection within the libido.

Zōē as bisexual libido radically changes Freud's view as given by Jones. Freud considered the libido to be masculine and active, a function of Eros, a movement of life. The female principle was passive and masochistic, so that woman was not only an *opus contra naturam*, but her principle was rooted, not in Eros, but in death. Brown has revised this view of the libido presented by Freud and Jones: the libido is double in nature (as Dionysus), with a passive constituent as well as an active one. Bisexuality combines not only male and female, active and passive. It also brings together life and death. Dionysus is again destroyed and again reborn; moreover, this is not merely a successional process. One aspect of life is riven so that another aspect—the psychic and called "death"—can reach awareness.

There was a Greek figure who did combine life and death as a form of consciousness: Tiresias. He alone "kept his wits in the House of Hades." [113] He plays an extraordinary role in many myths—those of Oedipus, Pentheus, Narcissus, Ulysses—representing a function that can see through life into death.[114] Tiresias was of both sexes, implying that only his kind of consciousness can penetrate into the invisible world of Thanatos and all those psychic components of human nature that derive from death and can only be understood in terms of the soul's one certainty: death. To put it more clearly and more enigmatically: approximation to the her-

113. H. J. Rose, *A Handbook of Greek Mythology*, 6th ed. (London, 1958), p. 195.

114. W. H. Roscher, *Ausführliches Lexikon der greichischen und römischen Mythologie* (Leipzig: Teubner, 1924–37; reissued, Hildesheim: G. Olms, 1965), *s.v.* "Tiresias."

maphrodite is a death experience; the movement into death proceeds through bisexuality. Death and bisexual consciousness are what Dionysus involves.

In order to reimagine Dionysus, we have first needed to unbind the *myth* of Dionysus so that it may move from the fixed and frightening interpretations by which the last century confined it. The image of freeing the God has been used by Plutarch (*De E* 389C; *De Iside* 378F); it is a rite of spring.

Reentering Dionysian Consciousness

Again let us recapitulate: Dionysus represents a radical shift of consciousness where bisexuality is given, a priori, with this archetypal dominant. This structure offers an end to misogyny. We have rediscovered Dionysus' relevance in the historical development of our field from hysteria. We have exposed prejudices regarding him. These prejudices have kept us from entering this other kind of consciousness, and so we have stood outside, misapprehending what takes place not only in the Dionysian materials which scholarship examines but in the Dionysian materials of the unconscious which therapy examines. To "enter" means "to be initiated," and the Dionysian cult required initiation. Yet we cannot approximate the old *orgia,* nor do we wish to be driven there by the return of the repressed as black maenadism.

Perhaps there is another way. Can we reenter Dionysian consciousness through our theme of female inferiority? Perhaps consciousness can be transformed through the feminine, which is close to that archetypal dominant. This is the perspective that psychology can bring to Nilsson's idea of rewriting our conceptions of Dionysus in terms of contemporary experiences. The shift of consciousness from Apollonic to Dionysian would then be not an act of will, a conversion, an initiatory plunge into "the other side"; rather, another consciousness would enter into us as we approximate our own bisexuality.

Earlier in this essay we said that psychological questions of the most profound sort lie waiting to be released from centuries of concretization in the alchemical sludge of female inferiority. Bodily woman has received the projection of the abysmal side of bodily man. To alter this and to restore the feminine, we need first realize and then *release the psychic aspect* in these concretizations.

The way to another consciousness thus begins by taking back those feminine aspects of the primal union, by returning to our own primary bisexuality. It means a reinvestiture in the feminine aspects of which we have been divested and which we have called female. Our consciousness would then begin to unthink its long identification with only male qualities and to unthink that line of thought from "Apollo," through Aristotle and Galen, to Freud and Moebius. The *physiological* qualities which have been declared inferior and to belong to the female would now become *psychological* qualities appropriate to man or woman. Inferiority would no longer be only feminine, because we now see it as part of a conjoined human consciousness; and the feminine would no longer be inferior, because it belongs to this structure of generally human consciousness. This conjoined structure is what the archetypal dominant of Dionysus means for a unified consciousness and a unified world-picture. This is what the Assumption of Maria means in actual living: to take back into the psyche what has been put upon the body, to take back centuries of misogyny, to take back into consciousness the physical, the feminine, and the inferior. This is the redemption of what Jung called "the earth, darkness, the abysmal side of bodily man with his animal passions and instinctual nature, and . . . 'matter' in general."

What were those physiological qualities that now become psychological, those qualities supposedly inherent in female nature that would now become part of general human consciousness for man or woman? Let us rehearse them again.

One major theme of female inferiority was incompleteness and imperfection. The experience of this consciousness remains partially unfulfilled, not able to rise into perfection.

We would have the experience of passivity and an inability to proceed very far against nature. We would be aware of a fundamental defect and lacuna in our consciousness and of a dependency upon something else, out of which it comes. This lacuna of the feminine void is not to be overcome, fulfilled, completed. Or, rather, the emptiness is the completion, so that this lacuna becomes the place of reflection, the place of psychic awareness, and offers the space of carrying and containing; it is psyche itself.

Remembering the Scholastics, our consciousness would provide the blood of nourishment and be able to feed itself from what processes it generates within its own imaginal matrix. Consciousness would no longer be only a male *aura seminalis,* instigator and propagator. The reddening spoken of in alchemy, and the self-feeding by means of the pelican, would thus be indicated.

Another major theme was the introvertedness of the female (remember Galen's reasons for the inferiority of the female reproductive system). This consciousness would give the experience of infoldedness or interiority, things not coming to final fruition in exteriorized forms. Its movement is slower, sadder, cooler, "heavier in the legs," taking longer "perfection time," and it would also incorporate left-handedness in its symbolic senses. These aspects were all attributed to the female body.

From Moebius we might take back "small-headedness," the long identification of the male with the mental. Consciousness would no longer be identified solely with primary and manifest traits, with what is big, visible, and forward, but, remembering Genesis, we might also take back from Eve her "secondary" nature: less the will to win than to survive, less the sense of creativity than of having been created, of creatureliness.

From Freud come two other major themes: castration and passivity. We would be aware that something driving is missing, a basic inoperancy of phallic compulsion. With the return of passivity to consciousness, the inertia of depression and the helplessness of suffering would take on another quality. Depression and suffering would belong to consciousness, be part of its composition, not afflictions coming to it unconsciously, making it unconscious, dragging it away and down, lowering its level. Depression would then no longer be a sign of inferiority or be felt as defeat.

Depression on a Dionysian model differs from our usual notions of it. As Otto points out, Dionysus is the God par excellence of comings and goings.[115] The movement of the libido represented by Dionysus comes and goes. The ego cannot control these movements. The heroic consciousness of the ego has an upward path. It may digress, meet obstacles, even descend to the underworld, but its course of upward progress places a negative sign upon digressions and descents. For example, submersion under the sea in the heroic view is a "night sea journey" through a mother-monster, out of which one emerges having gained an insight, an integration, or a virtue. The immersion is to be endured for the sake of later advantage on the path of linear development. One keeps the fire going and a knife at hand so as to come out well. Christian depression is also heroic: the night of despair is necessary for the reward of resurrection and the ascent from darkness, after a three-day weekend. Suffering is a way of getting. But Dionysus has a "home" in the sea. The libido descends for refuge when driven by the excessive demands of Lycurgus, the blind tyranny of the ruling will which that mythic king in the *Iliad* exemplifies. Dionysus is a god of moisture,[116] and the descent is for the sake of moistening. Depression into these depths is experienced not as defeat (since Dionysus is not a hero), but as downwardness, darkening, and becoming water. (A major caution in alchemy was: Begin no operation until all has become water.) The movements of the libido are mythical events in which we participate, and as such they are objective. When the ego forgets this and takes the vanishing per-

115. W. F. Otto, *Dionysus*, pp. 73 f.
116. *Ibid.*, pp. 160 f.

sonally, it makes depression by identifying with the God. When Dionysus appears, there is revel and celebration; his disappearance is a winter of discontent. To believe *we* make these movements, can control them, or are to blame for inflation or depression is hybris. The God comes and goes; we cannot manipulate him. By taking these movements into the ego as a responsibility, we verge onto *la folie circulaire*, the manic-depressive cycle. Connecting the flux of libido to an archetypal dominant gives to depression a religious aspect. Depression may be a crisis of both mood and energy; also it is a crisis of belief. By believing in the God and believing that, as he always goes away, so will he always return, the movements can be respected as natural and necessary to the libido itself.

Because the qualities we are speaking of have been attributed to the female as *body*, this consciousness would affect the body itself. It would be a body-consciousness, giving the experience of a somatized awareness of self in concrete, actual behavior. This would in turn transform that old frustration of reflection divided from action, where consciousness is conceived mainly in terms of speech and mind, giving over the unconscious to the body and its "actings-out." The body might no longer be the realm only of abyss and passion; it might now fill up with slowness and interiority. We may recall those early images of Dionysus, somber, still, long-robed, unheroic, soft: a figure of vegetation and the vegetative reactions of the psyche.

We can also learn something from hysteria. Hysteria somatizes consciousness. A classical conversion hysteria converts psychic meanings into somatic demonstrations: the central idea is acted, the intelligible account of things converts back into the ritual *drōmenon;* psychic events become body events; meanings enter behavior. If our aim is to free psychic events from body, whenever to "make conscious" means mainly to express in intelligible order, of course hysteria will be judged regressive, and hysterical symptoms will refer to an *abaissement du niveau mental.* But if our aim has changed because our consciousness has changed, then the lowering of the mental level becomes a gain in value. Then hysterical reactions are also attempts to refind nature. Then hysterical reactions may be seen as desperate attempts to re-find body, to incarnate, to find initiation into life. The frigid, silly, light, excited young creatures of Paris and Vienna in whom nineteenth-century psychiatry discovered hysteria did not invent their performances. Nor were they Charcot's and Freud's private fantasies. The "hysterics" were acting, yes—but in the sense of *mimēsis*, an enactment of the dominants that were ruling their psyches. Their emptiness referred to the empty places left by the God and awaiting his return. In the end their raving histrionics did bring recognition of Eros and Dionysus—not directly to the girls themselves, for they were experimental subjects, but indirectly, through the psychoanalytic theory of neurosis. This theory gave conceptual formulation to the Eros-Dionysos-Aphrodite-Priapus constellation. Would we not have had another archetypal constellation, and thus another theory altogether of neurosis and the unconscious, had Freud's point of departure been depression and melancholia instead of hysteria? Jung began with schizophrenia; his work shows the impress of the Mercurius-Hermes-Trickster constellation, with its emphasis upon dualities, in both his psychological theory and his psychological style.

If, as Freud suggested, hysterical reactions are a prodromal bisexuality, they may be comprehended today as indications of the feminine need for initiation into body, life, and love in terms of the dominants that govern hysteria. Here "feminine" does not mean only the girls between 15 and 23, or the women in the kitchens, or the households of Thebes, but the young, "hysterical," flightly anima discussed above in Part One. What place has this component in Apollonic consciousness? What chance for entry into life, for initiation, for body and love? Remember the chases of Apollo and the fleeing maidens. Is not their flight continuing in the anima reactions of Apollonic consciousness? In contrast to Apollo's failures with conjunction, Dionysus attracts the feminine, drawing it forth like the sap in plants, the wine, and the milk that flows at his birth.

Finally, these transformations of masculine consciousness through a group of qualities formerly called feminine and inferior should now permit us to insight inferiority itself from within this new structure of consciousness. Hitherto we have always spoken of inferiority from a masculine, scientific, Apollonic view. The inferior was part of a polarity in which the male had the superior place. But how might it look from within itself? Perhaps this structure of conjoined consciousness is less hierarchical and without self-divisive polarities. Perhaps it may be conceived not mainly in terms of spatial levels and *Schichtentheorie* (this model of the psyche—usually in three layers—occurs repeatedly in this same line of thought from Plato and Aristotle, continuing without break to Freud and his id, ego, and superego). Hierarchical models require the inferiority of lower positions. But we can experience and conceive consciousness by means of other images. For example, rather than superimposed levels, we might speak of polycentricity, of circulation and rotation, of the comings and goings of flow. In this structure all positions are occasionally inferior, and no positions are ever finally inferior. In this kind of structure, inferiority in its old sense would come to an end. The only possible inferiority for an archetypal psychology would be the concentration upon one center alone—ego or self or one God—which must by definition fail to represent the entire range of archetypal forms.

Conclusion: The End of Analysis

I SHALL NOW REVIEW MY THESIS and present one additional conclusion. The relatively simple theme of female inferiority has brought us to touch upon many questions, and deep ones indeed. We have reviewed a historically long line of thinking. We have seen that the beginnings of therapeutic psychology in hysteria and the consequent "discovery of the unconscious" lie also along this line. Maybe this same line will lead us as well to the end of therapeutic psychology, where "end" means its *telos* or *causa finalis*, its purpose fulfilled or goal, "that for the sake of which" it comes into being. I mean also by the "end of analysis" its termination in time: therapeutic psychology as over and done with.

Because psychoanalysis found the feminine faulty, it shares in that structure of consciousness we have traced to mythemes of Adam and Apollo. That psychoanalysis rests on this same archetypal basis is demonstrated by its fantasies: confrontation with the female body produces fantasies of its inferiority, which are then elaborated by scientific observations into misogynist theory. The Apollonic structure of its *Anschauung* has determined therapeutic psychology from its beginnings in the direction of science. Because this urge toward science is governed by the same archetypal background as the tradition of misogyny, we are obliged to consider very carefully every attempt to resurrect science in our psychology. Any movement returning our psychology to science would go back on the steps Freud and Jung made toward leading consciousness into bisexuality through involvement with the Dionysian. Any scientific direction of our psychology will have negative implications, not only for the feminine aspect of psychological depth therapy and psychosomatics. More: the scientific direction precludes the *coniunctio* by its archetypal misogyny. Matter, body, and female —and psyche too—in the hands of science tend more and more to be left out, placed "out there" for objective methods of Apollonic cognition. The Apollonic, as Otto points out, "desires not soul but spirit." "Apollo . . . is oblivious to the eternal worth of the human individual and the single soul." [117] Yet, the single soul is the ground, and its individuation the goal, of our psychological occupation. "Soul-making," as we have described it in Part One, and "making-conscious,"

117. W. F. Otto, *The Homeric Gods*, trans. M. Hadas (New York: Pantheon, 1964), p. 78.

in the Apollonic sense of "more light," seem incommensurables.

We may remember that depth psychology rises out of hysteria. The original substance of our field consists of the problem of the feminine and of an unconscious whose description points to its mainly Dionysian potential. Yet depth psychology describes consciousness in a highly Apollonic manner. Even Jung, who was most open to a new view of consciousness, describes it as follows: "A high degree of consciousness . . . is characterized by a heightened awareness, a preponderance of will, directed, rational behaviour, and an almost total absence of instinctual determinants." Of course, as he says, "The unconscious is then found to be at a definitely animal level. . . . An extreme state of unconsciousness is characterized by the predominance of compulsive instinctual processes." [118] An Apollonic definition of consciousness occasions an unconscious that is Nietzschean or, to say the least, a province of the Great Mother. The identification of consciousness with the heroic-Apollonic mode forces one into the absurdities of Neumann, who writes: "But one thing, paradoxical though it may seem, can be established as a basic law: even in woman, consciousness has a masculine character. The correlation 'consciousness-light-day' and 'unconsciousness-darkness-night' holds true regardless of sex. . . . Consciousness, as such, is masculine even in woman." [119] Thus Neumann was compelled to work out the nature of feminine consciousness in the rest of his works in terms of the Great Mother (the counterpole to the hero and the hero's Apollonic definition of consciousness). But what of the Goddesses—Athene, Demeter, Aphrodite, Artemis, and Psyche? Are these not modes of consciousness reflected in the existence of women?

It seems unjustifiable to give the name "consciousness" to

118. *CW*, VIII, par. 249.
119. E. Neumann, *The Origins and History of Consciousness*, trans. R. F. C. Hull (New York and London, 1954), p. 42.

that dried and sunlit condition of the psyche in which there is an "almost total absence of instinctual determinants." Do we not speak more precisely if we follow the suggestions of the second essay and abandon the terms "conscious" and "unconscious" for evaluating kinds of behavior? Let us rather speak, then, of archetypal structures of behavior and fantasy, each of which has degrees of awareness and not any single one of which is "better" (more "conscious") than another since each is determined by its own God or Goddess. What we have been calling "consciousness" all these years is really the Apollonic mode as hardened by the hero into a "strong ego" and which has predetermined the nature of the Dionysian in terms of its own bias.

Thus therapeutic psychology has an inherent contradiction: its method is Apollonic, its substance Dionysian. It attempts to analyze the collectivity, the downwardness, the moisture of libidinal fantasies, the child, the theatricality, the vegetative and animal levels—the "madness," in short—of the Dionysian by means of the distance, cognition, and objective clarity of the other structure. Its method and goal accord essentially with the dictum of Augustine for the soul's itinerary: "ab exterioribus ad interiora, ab inferioribus ad superiora" (from outer to inner, from below to above).[120] A therapeutic psychology which would transform the unconscious (Dionysian) into consciousness (Apollonic), no matter how imaginatively sophisticated its method, continues in the main line of our tradition. Even where it may encourage Dionysian experience, the experience is for the sake of consciousness. Emotion is for the sake of reflection in tranquility. Experience (mystical, erotic, depressive) remains something one "has," alien from usual life, like a dance at the borderlands from which one returns to the normal consciousness of sunlight. Despite programmatic intentions about

120. Augustine *Enarratio in Ps.* 145. 5. Cf. Jung's *Psychological Types* (*CW*, VI), par. 566, on hysteria and extraversion: "Hysteria is, in my view, by far the most frequent neurosis of the extraverted type."

"integrating the shadow" and "joining the opposites," analysis must unavoidably continue to cast shadow yet further upon matter, body, and female, for these are the areas of the exterior and inferior (the so-called unconscious projected into so-called life). Hysteria will tend always to be the paradigm of an exteriorized inferior psyche.

This same inherent contradiction of opposing the Dionysian with the Apollonic also determines our notion of cure. By attempting to integrate the feminine by the masculine, we perpetuate the malady we are attempting to treat. The treatment thus is really part of the malady itself and continues to contribute to it. So it does seem that analysis as an *analytical* method is unable, because of its archetypal idea of consciousness, to achieve its aim, to come to its end of uniting consciousness with the physical, the feminine, and the natural in a *unus mundus*. The *coniunctio* is thus put off into a goal in time. What is not possible now becomes possible in the future, through process. The *coniunctio* is carried by a utopian *telos* that can never be realized, because this process has no end term unless it abandons the past analytical method. Analysis can go on expanding consciousness in a special form of ego development, a process which occurs at the cost of female inferiority and thus cannot end. All of this means that analysis as we have known it is interminable.

Freud saw this dilemma better than anyone. In his old age, and in a last, strictly psychoanalytic paper, Freud reflected with characteristic pessimism upon the phenomenon he had brought into the world. He called this paper, published during his last year in Vienna, "Die endliche und unendliche Analyse" (Analysis Terminable and Interminable). He raises the question: "Is there such a thing as a natural end to an analysis—is there any possibility at all of bringing an analysis to such an end?" [121] More than thirty pages later he concludes that one reaches the "bedrock," the place where analysis could be said to end, when the "repudiation of

121. Freud, *SE*, XXIII, 219.

femininity" in both man and woman has been successfully met. In a woman the repudiation of femininity is manifested in her intractable penis envy; in a man this repudiation will not allow him to submit and be passive to other men. Freud says the repudiation of femininity is a "remarkable feature in the psychical life of human beings"; he believes it biologically given and thus "bedrock" to the psychical field.[122]

If this repudiation is the bedrock of analysis, then it is the root of repression and neurosis as well. Feminine inferiority now becomes the fundamental affliction of consciousness, the etiological specific that brings about both our psychic disorders and the method of analysis aimed at these disorders. But this method is unable to fulfill its goal, come to its end, since it suffers from the same repudiation of femininity. We are cured when we are no longer only masculine in psyche, no matter whether we are male or female in biology. Analysis cannot constellate this cure until it, too, is no longer masculine in psychology. *The end of analysis coincides with the acceptance of femininity*. Our theme has thus led us to the crucial question of therapeutic psychology: its ultimate purpose.

The burden of my brief has been to show that female inferiority is not biological and that misogyny has not a biological source but a psychological one. Misogyny seems to arise through viewing the biological aspect of the female, as if the Apollonic constellates consciousness with particular power when consciousness is confronted with the abysmal side of bodily man, with man's corruptible nature. The bedrock structure of misogyny is psychological; it rests upon an archetypal form of consciousness that is transpersonal. Thus therapeutic psychology is faced with a predicament which Freud saw better than anyone. The bedrock structure of therapeutic psychology, i.e., the Apollonic archetype, justifies both his complaint that "psychology cannot solve the

122. *Ibid.*, pp. 250, 252.

riddle of femininity"[123] and his pessimism about termination of analysis. Analysis cannot terminate unless it abandons its own archetypal basis, the first-Adam-then-Eve view of things, which requires an analytical Apollonism of interpretation, *sinngebend und formgebend,* an objective and detached selfhood, a heroic course of development, of quest and search, and, above all, consciousness as light, the ego-Self as its carrier, and analysis as its instrument. If our aim is "more light," can we ever reach the end implied by the Assumption of Maria, the union with dark materiality and the abyss?

In Jung's language, psychotherapy achieves its ultimate goal in the wholeness of the conjunction, in the bisexuality of consciousness, which means, as well, conscious bisexuality, that incarnation of durable weakness and unheroic strength that we find in the image of Dionysus. Bisexual consciousness here means also the experience of psyche in all matter, the fantasy in everything literal, and the literal, too, as fantasy; it means a world undivided into spirit and matter, imaginal and real, body and consciousness, mad and sane. As Jung pointed out, the dogma of the Assumption of Maria ends the repudiation of femininity. It signifies consciousness of bisexuality in the God-image. There can no longer be separations into components, into positive and negative and a polarity of opposites. So, it also signifies the end of analysis. For the termination of analysis in both Freud and Jung coincides with the termination of misogyny, when we take Eve back into Adam's body, when we are no longer decided about what is masculine and what feminine; what inferior, what superior, what exterior, what interior; when we have taken on and taken in all those qualities not per se female but hitherto projected, declared inferior, and fallen from us into the physical body of woman, there concretized, ob-

123. Freud, *New Introductory Lectures on Psycho-Analysis,* trans. W. J. H. Sprott (London: Hogarth, 1957), p. 149.

served by the scientific fantasy to be biophysical "facts," and thus lost to psychological realization. To take back this "inferiority" frees the feminine and her body, and matter itself, from its Apollonic contempt and compulsive fascination. To take back this "inferiority" has been the reason why we have gone to those bodily regions held in contempt and disdain yet so compelling to philosophers: we have been in search of essential psychological qualities needed for bisexual consciousness.

We cannot escape the conclusion that analysis as a therapeutic psychology may well be self-defeating. Its inherent contradiction prevents realizing its end. We may then differentiate analysis as we have known it from therapeutic psychology in general, and we may begin to search for other therapeutic procedures adequate to the kind of consciousness we have been describing. The experiences of many persons already point in another direction. Although analysis has been Apollonic in theory, technique, and interpretation in terms of the ego and its life, again and again for many persons it was Dionysian in experience: a prolonged moistening, a life in the child, hysterical attempts at incarnation through symptoms, an erotic compulsion toward soul-making.

The end of the former analysis as a therapeutic psychology for the individual leads to the end of analysis as a collective phenomenon. We are left at the termination of this essay with pointers toward a postanalytic age. Are the pointers not already indicated by what has been said? A consciousness that requires no psychotherapy in the old sense would have its bedrock in bisexuality, where those realities of the psyche called "feminine" and "body" are integral with consciousness. This means a submission of the spirit to its own inferiority, a spirit limited by the femininity of its psychic reality. The notion of the collective would also be revisited, and perhaps new meanings will appear, meanings not possible without the perspectives for soul-making encouraged by Dionysus, Lord of Souls.

Of these meanings, the therapeutic goal of the *coniunctio* would now be experienced as a weakening of consciousness, in the former sense of that notion, rather than an increase of consciousness through "integrating" the anima. The *coniunctio* now would be weird and frightening, a horror and a death, inclusive of psychopathology. Then we would be taking back our sickness, no longer certain what is sick and what healthy, no longer in the Apollonic manner of medicine dividing psychopathology from psychology, no longer needing soul patients and soul doctors. Yes, this means Tiresias and the sacrifice of the mind's bright eye so that one can see the images in the cavern of *memoria*. But more, too; for it means an effeminization in the sense of a loosening and forgetting, a permanent regression to the childlike half-creature of Moebius and Paracelsus, a permanent "softening of the brain," a true loss of what we have long considered to be our most precious human holding: Apollonic consciousness.

A therapy that would move toward this *coniunctio* would be obliged to stay always within the mess of ambivalence, the comings and goings of the libido, letting interior movement replace clarity, interior closeness replace objectivity, the child of psychic spontaneity replace literal right action.

Another vision might be given, too, to the old conundrum of individuation on the one hand, collectivity on the other. If Dionysus means the undivided, then his mode of consciousness returns to an early meaning of that word: "knowing with." "Conscious" once meant in English "a knowing together," or a together-knowing, shared like a secret between those let in on it.[124] As we cannot go it alone, so we cannot know it alone. Our consciousness cannot be divided from the other. An other is implied, not only because the soul cannot exist without its "other" side, but also because consciousness itself has an erotic, Dionysian component that points

124. C. S. Lewis, "Conscience and Conscious," *Studies in Words* (Cambridge, Eng., 1967).

to participation. Pressed far enough, this line of thought means that we are conscious only in some form of related sharing and that man, when he is alone, reflecting or becoming conscious or individuating, may in fact be unconscious. Although Dionysus may be a solitary stranger, even somber, depressed, and of the forests and mountain tops, his entourage indicates a style in which awareness is at one with life as it is lived with others.

Analysis has long recognized pressures within the psyche which urge it to flow into collective life. As an analysis intensifies, there is movement toward others: Freudians have called it acting out; Jungians, a leakage of the hermetic vessel. Dionysus is the God of acting as he is the God of moisture. It is his nature to leak and flow into communion. Telestic *mania* belonged to Dionysus; it referred to the commingling of souls, leveling and democratic, as in the wine and the dance. Analytical consciousness has required an inhibition of the psyche's urge for sharing, just as it has favored the elite individual alone and disfavored his collective tendencies—again, Dionysus in the service of Apollo.[125]

The need for participation may be satisfied by mobs and crowds, which, though dangerous, should not be confused with the worthiness of the need itself. We have prejudicially turned against all collective consciousness, that is, "together-knowing," because many of its forms are indeed threateningly Wotanic. But Dionysian consciousness requires a *thiasos*, a community; and this community is not only exterior, in other people, but is a communal flow with the complexes, a commingling of consciousness with the "other" souls and their Gods, a consciousness that is always infiltrated with its complexes, flowing together with them.

When we look back upon the past seventy years, or back yet further to the women in the hospitals of Paris and Nancy,

125. Dodds, *The Greeks and the Irrational*, p. 76: "Apollo moved only in the best society, from the days when he was Hector's patron to the days when he canonized aristocratic athletes; but Dionysus was at all periods *demotikos*, a god of the people."

we can see the psyche going to therapy in search of eros. We have been looking for love for the soul. That is the myth of analysis. We have been going to analysis during this past century for soul-making. Where else was one to find the psyche taken seriously? Unfortunately, the events that transpired between eros and psyche were not taken seriously enough. The eros that constellated necessarily in the consulting room did not accord with the model of consciousness that informed analysis. Consciousness had been supplied inadequately with myth. Psychology's metaphors had lost their memory and their imagination. So this eros was named transference, and the psychic reactions to the eros were called transference neurosis, requiring analysis. We went for soul-making only to have the actual erotic process which makes soul negated by psychological language. Freud insisted that the analysis of the transference was crucial to the outcome of the treatment, as well it was. Analysis of the transference meant the submission of Eros to the Apollonic structure of consciousness, with its end aim of distance to emotion, of psyche = consciousness. In addition, the imaginal process of the *memoria* was also brought into service of the Apollonic aim. The erotic and Dionysian imagination, now named the id or the unconscious, was to be worked on and worked through. By means of active imagination, the freedom of the imaginal was connected with the ego, disciplined for the sake of "becoming conscious." The results are at hand: trained analysts of greater "consciousness" who are also imaginal duds.

In Part One we considered the end of transference—where end also means purpose—to be soul-making through the eros-psyche relationship. In Part Two we exposed the end of the unconscious, again in the sense of its purposeful function, to be a progress toward an imaginal consciousness. The purpose of "the unconscious" has been to make possible the rediscovery of the imaginal. Now, in Part Three, we find the purpose of neurosis, that "bedrock" upon which analysis has been built, to be the integration of female inferiority. Transference, unconscious, neurosis—in each case that which was previously regarded literally as a problem with conceptual solidity has partly dissolved into its background fantasy through the metaphorical perspective of archetypal myth. Here, at the conclusion of the book, the archetypal perspective continues to inform our view. The destructive assault on the old analysis and the constructive indications for another therapy reflect Eros and his burning.

The creative force of Eros and the impulse of Dionysus cannot let Psyche alone. They are its dominants in the therapeutic sense of its development, and so they press the soul toward a psychology in which they have full place and which brings an archetypal perspective toward its problems. The effect of the Gods on the psyche is *the re-vision of psychology in terms of the Gods.* Under the compulsion of the unrecognized dominants, the psyche creates those impossible human problems like transference, neurosis, and hysteria and the syndromes named in Part Two which are insoluble on the human level alone. The psyche is thus forced by the Gods to evolve an archetypal psychology to meet its needs, a psychology based not on the "human" but within the "divine." Archetypal psychology, in short, regards all fantasy, all suffering, and all behavior as having archetypal significance, providing opportunity for discovering the Gods which shelter and provoke every event of the human soul.

We have begun to move toward the end of analysis by "unthinking," first, what was taken for granted about eros in analysis, then the language that has hurt the imagination, and finally that which has hitherto (and for reasons we have presented) been considered—wrongly, irreverently, blasphemously—to be Dionysian. It is so difficult to imagine, to conceive, to experience consciousness apart from its old identifications, its structural bedrock of misogyny, that we can hardly even intuit what this bisexual God might hold in store for the regeneration of psychic life.

SUBJECT INDEX

INDEX OF PROPER AND MYTHOLOGICAL NAMES